ELECTRONIC
music

ELECTRONIC
music

SYSTEMS, TECHNIQUES, and CONTROLS

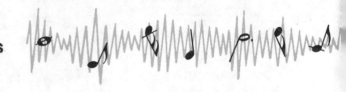

ALLEN STRANGE

WM. C. BROWN COMPANY PUBLISHERS

Consulting Editor
Frederick W. Westphal
Sacramento State College

To Frank and Pauline

*The availability of a particular patchcord
is inversely proportional to its need.*

Anonymous

contents

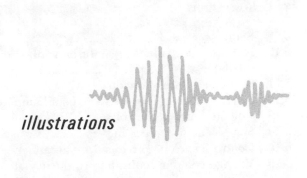

illustrations

preface

A quarter century has passed since Pierre Schaeffer and Pierre Henry began their Paris investigations into the art of sound manipulation. Since these initial experiments at the research center of the Radio-Diffusion Française, electronic music has evolved through many different phases of technological and aesthetic development. An art that is so closely related to a technology is in a very vulnerable position, because its development is dependent, in part, upon the development of the technology. To say this does not imply, of course, that such an art form cannot reach a high point in its aesthetic development until the technology has reached a comparable position. Schaeffer, Henry, Philippot and other composers of the Groupe de Recherche de Musique Concrete have produced some very wonderful music. But a dependence on technology does mean that radical changes in the aesthetics can and usually will be brought about by development and changes in the associated technology. (Witness the presence of stereophony and holography, each a development of photographic technique, which itself is an extension of the aesthetic of painting.) Kinetic art, environmental structures, mixed media, computer-generated films—these are all examples of developments of art forms that are very dependent upon the existing and future technology. And each of these disciplines has an aesthetic quite different from its "parent" discipline. A person viewing a computer-generated film by the two sons of filmmaker John Whitney must be prepared for an experience quite different from the experience he receives from viewing a film by Federico Fellini. And as the technology of computer graphics evolves, so will the visual parameters employed by the Whitney brothers.

Due to advances in sound-recording and reproduction equipment, the use of information theory, the development of transistorized and integrated circuitry, and to in-depth studies into the nature of sound and the corporeal influences of other disciplines, electronic music has gone through various changes with respect to its orientation to the art of sound. Beginning with musique concrete, the art went through these stages: elektronische musik, classic studio technique (see Lowell Cross, "Electronic Music, 1948-1953" in *Perspectives of New Music*, vol. 7, no. 1 [Fall-Winter, 1968], pp. 32-65), punched tape computer synthesis, and live electronic sound manipulation. ("Synthesis" is an unfortunate choice of terms that has led to electronic music systems being referred to as "Synthesizers." As most of the music produced on these systems is by no means synthetic, the author will avoid the use of this term whenever possible.) In the early 1960s the development of integrated electronic music systems and voltage-controlled modules began a new era of electronic music. The concept of voltage control had done away with many of the tedious "classic" techniques required of the electronic music composer prior to this time, and the relative ease of the newer techniques involved, along with the publicity which accompanied the commercial aspirations of the manufacturers of electronic music systems, brought about a sudden audience/composer appeal to electronic music.

The nature or kinds of sounds produced by the various systems are bound to influence the aesthetic boundaries of the art. At the same time, each electronic music system has its own favorable and unfavorable sonic characteristics. In the past, a composer active in the field found it very easy to identify the sound of the various studios. The Columbia-Princeton Studio, for example, has its own characteristic sound as compared to that of the Tape Music Center at Mills College in California. By the same token, the different makes of electronic music systems have their own particular sound; after a minimum of listening, it is quite possible to identify a composition produced with the aid of a Buchla system as compared to a composition produced on a Putney, Moog, Synket, or ARP system. What these devices have in common, which is a subject of major interest to the composer today, is the concept of voltage control.

What are the processes the "electronic composer" follows, then, to make a composition? What are the parameters involved in the production of electronic music? What are the available techniques and how do they work? "Conventional music" composers have a number of devices such as homophony, polyphony, inversion, retrograde, dodecophonic systems, tonality, aleatory processes, etc., that they may or may not use in the creation of their art form. In the same way, electronic music composers utilize various techniques and methods, sometimes in combination with "conventional" techniques and sometimes completely apart from those aspects of structuring sound. This book will describe and explain these electronic music techniques for the composer/musician/listener who is not familiar with them. It will not attempt an aesthetic appreciation of electronic music, but rather will discuss, in layman's terms, the techniques available to the electronic music composer of this decade.

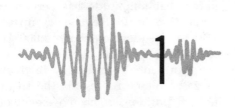

parameters of sound in terms of AC voltage

When working in the electronic medium, a basic reorientation to sound must take place. The two basic properties of sound, pitch and loudness, must be conceived of as frequency and amplitude. In turn, frequency and amplitude must be thought of as results of an alternating current (AC) voltage. This can best be exemplified by examining the physical movements of a high-fidelity speaker. If a speaker cone is connected to an alternating current, certain physical changes take place. When no voltage is applied to the speaker, the speaker cone is in a neutral position (fig. 1.1A). When a "positive" voltage is applied to the speaker, the cone is pushed outward (fig. 1.1B) and then, when the positive voltage decreases, returns toward its original position. As a "negative" voltage is applied to the speaker, the cone is pulled back to a point opposite the positive voltage position of the speaker (fig. 1.1C).

Every time the speaker cone is moved by the alternating current (positive, returning to a neutral position, negative, and again returning to a neutral position) masses of air or pressure waves are moved past our ear, producing the sensation of pitch. If the speaker cone is moved back and forth 440 times in one second, for example, we hear a sound which is referred to as "tuning A." If the cone moves back and forth at a rate of 256 times a second, we perceive a pitch of "middle C." Each back-and-forth movement caused by the application of a positive voltage followed by a negative voltage is referred to as a "cycle." Therefore, 440 CPS (cycles per second) produce "tuning A." Recently the term "cycles per second" has been replaced by the term "Hertz" or in its abbreviated form "Hz," with 440 Hz being the same as 440 cycles per second.

The volume, loudness, or amplitude of a sound is determined basically by how far the speaker cone is moved back and forth. If an alternating current displaces a speaker cone 1/4 inch in each direction from its neutral position 256 times a second, the ear will perceive "middle C" at a certain loudness level. If the speaker is displaced 1/2 inch from its neutral position at the same rate of frequency, the ear will perceive the *same* pitch but at a louder volume or, in audio terms, at a greater amplitude (see fig. 1.2). It should be

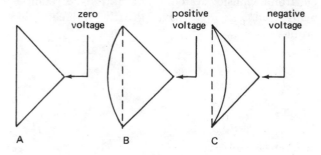

zero voltage   positive voltage   negative voltage

A   B   C

Fig. 1.1.   Speaker cone movement

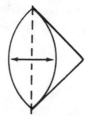

1/4-inch cone displacement equals amplitude X

1/2-inch cone displacement equals amplitude 2X

Fig. 1.2.   Amplitude of sound

noted that amplitude has certain effects on pitch perception in all frequencies up to 1,000 Hz and also for frequencies above 4,000 Hz.

Characteristics of frequency and amplitude are represented graphically in figure 1.3. The line of zero voltage represents the speaker cone in the neutral position, or no movement of air. The horizontal direction of the line represents the passage of time. The plotted curve on either side of the zero-voltage line represents the back-and-forth movement of the speaker cone, or positive and negative voltage, which in relation to the time each cycle takes represents frequency or pitch. The height of each cycle gives an indication of amplitude or volume. Figure 1.3A in comparison with figure 1.3B represents a lower frequency with a higher amplitude.

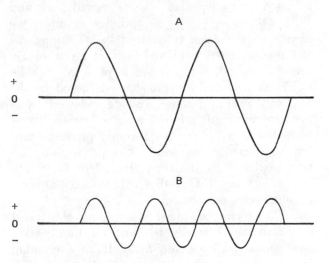

Fig. 1.3. Sine waves with differing amplitude and frequency.

When the electronic music composer wishes to produce a specified pitch he sets an "oscillator" to generate an AC current of the frequency desired. Oscillators are calibrated with a dial that corresponds to the desired frequency. The dial is usually referred to as a "pot," which is an abbreviation for "potentiometer," a resistance device that in this instance controls the frequency of the oscillator. There will usually be a second pot to control the amplitude of the frequency, but in many cases such an amplitude control is external to the oscillator. This will be discussed later. At this point, it will suffice to know that an oscillator is a frequency-producing device that has the capability of producing any desired *single* frequency.

Our range of hearing perceives only those frequencies between 18 Hz and 22k Hz. (The letter *k* represents a multiple of 1,000; therefore, 2.2k Hz represents 2,200 Hz. There are many differing opinions about the actual audio range. These different statements of audio perception range from a low of 16 to 30 Hz and a high of 18k Hz to 30k Hz.) As we shall see later, however, frequencies far below and above the audio range are necessary to the production of many types of sound. Oscillators that specialize in frequencies below our hearing range are known as "subaudio oscillators" and generate frequencies as low as one cycle every minute and lower. Oscillators specializing in frequencies immediately above the audio range are referred to as "ultrasonic oscillators." The three types of oscillators overlap in respect to the frequency range covered. The ideal oscillator for use in electronic music is one that will cover all three frequency ranges with the same degree of accuracy. Unfortunately, in most commercial systems being produced today, the manufacturer must make a choice between the sweep range (the range of frequencies which may be produced by a single sweep of the dial without switching to a different multiple—see chap. 4, p. 17) and stability. Over varying periods of time, an oscillator with a very wide sweep range may have a tendency to drift away from the preset frequency. A more stable oscillator usually will involve switching to various multiples of a limited sweep range, or the total range of the oscillator may be more limited. Frequency drift at one time was a very critical and annoying trait of earlier electronic music systems but improved components and circuitry have greatly reduced this problem.

basic waveshapes and their characteristics

If we think of "waveshape" as the graphic representation of the rise and fall of voltage from zero to maximum positive and/or negative and back again, it is possible to identify various types of sounds graphically. While transients, phase, amplitude, attack, and decay all contribute to the character of a sound, one chief reason we are able to aurally discriminate between various types of sounds is due to their harmonic content. That is, an oboe sounds different from a clarinet partially because of the different overtone contents of the sound produced by each instrument. ("Overtone" is a generic term that includes both "harmonics" and "partials." For precise musical definitions of these terms refer to J. J. Josephs, *The Physics of Musical Sound* [New Jersey: D. Van Nostrand, 1967], pp. 67-68.)

The most noncomplex type of sound is the sine wave. This particular waveshape ideally contains no overtones (see fig. 2.1). The closest sound to a pure sine wave in a symphony orchestra is that of a flute. As is shown in figure 2.1, sine-wave voltage is in a particular state of motion. Starting at zero, it gradually increases to maximum positive, then decays to maximum negative, then returns to the original starting place.

A sine wave exhibits this same basic pattern no matter what frequency or amplitude is required. Figure 2.1B shows the same frequency as figure 2.1A but with an increased amplitude. The device that electronically produces sine waves is referred to as a sine-wave oscillator. Sine waves, as with any other waveshapes, can exist in any frequency range. Due to distortions caused by various components of the oscillator and/or distortions in the reproduction equipment, however, a good

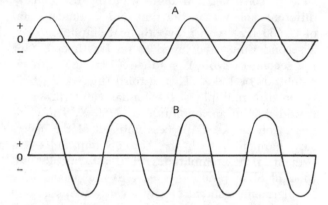

Fig. 2.1. Sine waves

sine wave is very difficult to produce and the composer usually has to settle for something less.

Figure 2.2 is an oscilloscopic (graphic) representation of a "sawtooth" or "ramp" wave. In contrast to the pure sine wave, a sawtooth wave contains all harmonic overtones of the fundamental frequency. These harmonic overtones have relative amplitudes that decrease exponentially as they exist higher up in the harmonic series. A sawtooth oscillator will produce this basic waveshape in

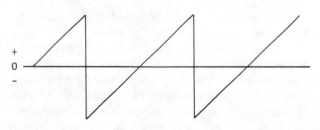

Fig. 2.2. Sawtooth or ramp wave

any frequency range. Some oscillators serve a dual function and can generate both sine and/or saw-tooth waves. One of the available systems provides a sine-sawtooth oscillator that utilizes a pot to produce any number of consecutive harmonics beginning with a quasi-sine wave (about 2 percent harmonic content) and gradually adds harmonics until a sawtooth (about 60 percent harmonics) is produced. The sound of a sawtooth wave is very bright and piercing, somewhat like the sound of an oboe.

A third basic waveshape is the "triangle" or "delta" wave (fig. 2.3). This waveshape consists of a fundamental frequency and all of the odd-number harmonics, with amplitudes falling off in ratios of 1/9, 1/25, 1/49, etc. By using a classic studio technique of "additive synthesis," it is possible to construct a triangle wave by using many different sine waves. Starting with a fundamental of C (65 Hz) with a hypothetical amplitude of x, a second sine wave tuned to 65 Hz times 3 (for the second overtone) is added (195 Hz) with an amplitude of 1/9 X. Then a third sine wave which is the fifth multiple of the fundamental (325 Hz) is added with an amplitude of 1/25 X. The composer continues this process until all of the necessary harmonics with the correct amplitudes are present. If the amplitudes of the harmonics are thought of in ratios, it is easy to understand how the harmonic content of any given wave is largely dependent on the amplitude of the fundamental.

Fig. 2.3. Harmonic content of a triangle wave up to the 9th multiple.

Perhaps the waveshape that is the most useful to the composer is the "pulse" or "rectangular" wave. As shown in figure 2.4, the positive and negative voltages of a pulse wave are never in a transient state. They are instantaneously positive, then instantaneously negative, whereas the sine, sawtooth and triangle waves all exhibit various types of gradual rise and fall between positive

and/or negative states. If a pulse generator is programmed to oscillate anywhere below 7 to 10 Hz, the speaker cone can be heard snapping back and forth, as it is shown doing in figure 1.1 in the previous chapter.

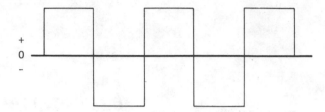

Fig. 2.4.   Pulse or rectangular (square) wave

Figure 2.4 shows a particular type of pulse wave known as a "square" wave. A square wave is related to a triangle wave in that it also contains odd-numbered harmonics, but with quite different amplitude relationships. The amplitude relationships of the harmonics of a square wave are 1/3, 1/5, 1/7, 1/9, etc. A clarinet in the chalumeau register produces a sound that is very close to that of a square wave. Figure 2.5 illustrates in standard musical notation the harmonic content of the four basic waveshapes. The relative amplitudes are indicated by the size of the note. Note that there are no even harmonics in any of the symmetrical waveforms.

No mention has been made concerning the phase relationships of the various harmonics. Although phase is very important to the construction and to the sonic characteristic of these waves, contemporary electronic music systems make all of these waveshapes available and the composer is usually not concerned with their construction. (A complete Fourier analysis of the waveshapes is beyond the scope of this book.)

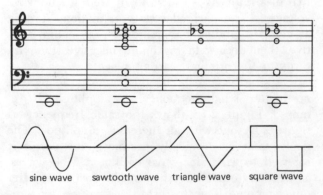

Fig. 2.5.   The four basic waveshapes and their harmonic content (up to the 9th multiple).

Due to the many uses of the square wave, it is thought of as a basic waveshape, even though it is a variety of a pulse wave. There are many other types of pulse waves, and they are defined by what is known as their "duty cycle." The duty cycle of a pulse wave is the positive or "on" portion of the entire cycle. Figure 2.6 shows the duty cycle of two different pulse waves.

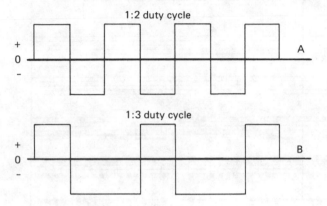

Fig. 2.6. Pulse-wave duty cycles

The ratio of the duty cycle to the rest of the wave gives an indication of the harmonic content of the waveshape. In the case of the square wave (fig. 2.4), the duty cycle is one-half of the total wave, or a ratio of 1:2 (as in fig. 2.6A). Expressed as a fraction, the duty cycle of a square wave is one-half of the total wave, and it is the denominator of this fraction that tells us its harmonic content. The denominator "2" indicates that every second harmonic is absent from its harmonic overtone series, confirming the earlier statement that the square wave consists only of a fundamental and the odd-numbered harmonics. A pulse wave with a duty cycle of 1:3 (as in fig. 2.6B) contains the fundamental and the first, second, fourth, fifth, seventh, eighth, tenth, etc., harmonics.

By controlling the width of the duty cycle, it is possible to generate many different types of harmonic series, and thus a pulse generator with a variable duty cycle can be a very useful tool in the construction and control of timbres.

A variation of a square wave (pulse wave with a 1:2 duty cycle) is the "staircase" wave, figure 2.7, which may be produced by combining the outputs of several square-wave oscillators. The staircase wave is used in many inexpensive electronic organ circuits and produces a sound somewhat like that of a triangle wave, but having a

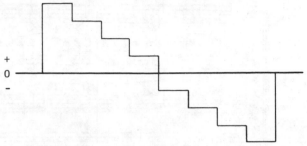

Fig. 2.7. Staircase wave

slightly brighter timbre. The harmonic content of the staircase wave is 1, 2, 3, 5, 6, 7, 9, 10, 11, 13, etc. A pulse wave with a 1:4 duty cycle would produce the same series, since it also would have every fourth harmonic absent.

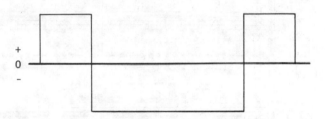

Fig. 2.8. Pulse wave with 1:4 duty cycle

Composers such as Ravel and Hindemith, and more contemporary composers such as Ligeti and Kagel, have been very concerned with the mixing of various instruments to produce new orchestral timbres. One of the classic examples of this additive approach to orchestration is in Ravel's *Bolero*. Beginning in measure 149, Ravel combines a horn, celeste, and two piccolos to produce a sound unlike any of the individual instruments used. Examination of the score discloses that Ravel's apparent tri-tonality is actually a reinforcement of the harmonic series of each pitch in the melody. The horn plays the fundamental while the celeste plays the first and third harmonics and the piccolos provide the second and fourth harmonics. A more recent approach to this type of composition is Maricio Kagel's *Music for Renaissance Instruments* (Deutsche Grammophone Records, no. 137 006), in which the composer is concerned with constructing various types of non-harmonic sounds.

This same basic method is applied to electronic music in classical techniques of timbre construction. Suppose, for example, that a composer wished to create the sound of a tubular bell or

Fig. 2.9. From the score of *Bolero* by Maurice Ravel. (Reproduced with the authorization of Durand & Cie, Editeurs-proprietaires, Paris.)

chime. The overtones present in this timbre are non-harmonic; that is, they do not exist in a consistent mathematical ratio to each other. In beginning to construct this timbre, six sine-wave oscillators would be tuned to the pitches shown in figure 2.10 (a musical notation of the non-harmonic partials found in the sound of a tubular

Fig. 2.10. Non-harmonic partials of a tubular bell.

bell), and then various amplitude relationships, transient factors, and attack and decay characteristics would be experimented with. Unless a composer is very familiar with all of these parameters, additive synthesis is usually a matter of trial and error until the right combination is eventually discovered. The *Gravesaner Blatter/Gravesono Review,* published in Switzerland since 1955, has made available various studies in timbre construction and analysis.

Another way to additive synthesis is through the "waveform generator." This type of generator is essentially several single sine-wave oscillators housed within a single chassis operating in a consistent relationship to each other. If each single oscillator has its own frequency and amplitude pot, many types of overtone relationships are made possible. Many other types of "clangorous" and "non-harmonic" timbres are available through the use of modulation and filtering techniques, and these will be discussed later.

Many of the electronic music systems available incorporate multi-function oscillators which provide several different waveshape outputs all exhibiting the same frequency. Some oscillator designs provide independent outputs for each waveshape, while others have just one output with provisions for switching from one type of waveshape to another. Another multi-function oscillator format provides a mixing function within the oscillator chassis that allows the composer to mix several varying waveshapes of the same frequency to produce unusual composite waveshape outputs.

The last electronic sound (as differentiated from many other sounds available through trans-

ducers such as microphones, pressure-to-frequency converters, prerecorded tapes and discs, etc.) to be considered is white sound, or white noise (also sometimes referred to as Gaussian or thermal noise). Perhaps the most descriptive term is "white sound." Analogous to a color wheel that produces the color white as the wheel is rapidly rotated, white sound is a mixture of all the audible frequencies at random amplitudes. Therefore, the term "white" is preferred over "Gaussian"—and the present writer prefers the use of "sound" because of the negative implications of the term "noise." White sound is audible as a hiss or as the sound of a jet engine.

If white sound is defined as all of the audible frequencies between 18 Hz and 22k Hz, then a mixture of all the frequencies between 18 Hz and about 1k Hz could be called "pink" or "red" sound. Inversely, the band of frequencies at the other end of the spectrum may be referred to as "azure" or "blue" sound. There are no defined frequency boundaries for these color analogies; they are defined only as to their audible character. Colored sound is very useful for mixing with other waveshapes to produce "colored" or "weighted" pitches. White sound is also used in the production of various types of attacks and to cover or "mask" certain unwanted sounds.

Thus far, only the basic types of sound *sources* have been discussed. It is essential that the reader understand how sound can be thought of as AC voltage, and that these voltages can be shown graphically on an oscilloscope (as they are represented in the various figures used in this book). Since the scope of this writing does not permit the discussion of *every* type of sound available to the composer, we have given the four basic waveshapes—sine, sawtooth, triangle, and pulse—and the concept of white sound. An understanding of these is all that is needed for a basic understanding of electronic music system operation and voltage control.

In the early days of electronic music, composers were limited to very basic classical techniques that were quite time-consuming, and often the end results did not justify the means involved. Because of limited techniques, and in part due to interest in serial and pointillistic techniques, the composer was still quite concerned with conventional composition processes, and the nature of the sounds were many times of a secondary concern. With the development and incorporation of refined and programmable equipment, however, composers have become more and more interested in strictly timbral composition. Just as certain composers of the past were known for their genius of melodic development, certain composers of today have become concerned with a music in which preconceived pitch and rhythms are of only a resultant concern. If these composers working in the electronic medium were strictly limited to the four basic electronically generated waveshapes, their output would probably be very limited. I do not mean to imply that limiting one's self to certain materials will affect the aesthetic value of a composition (*I of IV*, by Pauline Oliveros [Odyssey Records no. 3216 0160], for example, is a very good example of a successful electronic composition that utilizes *only* sine and square waves), but that the situation would be analogous to one in which a composer limited himself only to the use of "canon" in all of his works.

3

amplitude modulation

Many early composers of electronic music approached a sound as only one of the contributing parameters to a musical composition. Today, composers are interested in the parameters that contributed to that sound. In the past, the control of these parameters was a very involved and tedious technique dependent, in large part, on the composer's skill with a splicing block. Today, the problem of producing precise changes in amplitude, frequency, location of sound, timbre, etc., has been reduced to the simpler task of producing voltages.

The first type of voltage control to be discussed pertains to amplitude. The amplitude of a sound can easily be controlled through an amplifier in the same manner that you control the volume of a radio with its volume control, and this type of control is sufficient if very rapid and/ or extreme changes in amplitude are not required. But if an amplitude change of 30 dbs* 500 times every second is required, say, manual control becomes impossible. In the electronic music systems of today, however, it is possible to produce such a rapid and extreme amplitude change by using a varying voltage. By generating a frequency of 500 Hz, for instance, and applying it to the gain (volume) control of an amplifier, it is possible to achieve such a rapid amplitude change. This would be "amplitude modulation," which is shown graphically in figure 3.1. The steady amplitude output of the amplifier—the "carrier" signal (fig. 3.1A)—is a constant waveshape. "Pushing" a second waveshape—the "program" signal (fig. 3.1B)— against this constant amplitude, forces it to change, but while it changes in direct relationship to its own amplitude and the amplitude of the program signal, it retains its original frequency, giving the

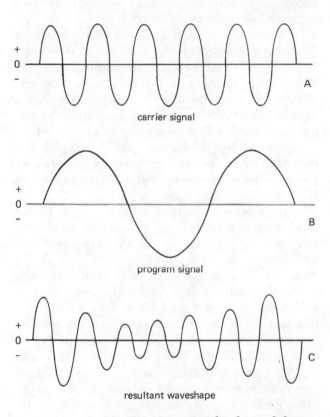

carrier signal

program signal

resultant waveshape

Fig. 3.1. Amplitude modulation

amplitude-modulated output shown in figure 3.1C, an output varying in amplitude in direct relationship to the frequency and amplitude of the modulating waveshape, or program. The terms "carrier" and "program" are jargon used in communications as "amplitude modulation" (AM) is used in radio

*Db is an abbreviation for "decibel," a unit for the ratios of loudness. Refer to chap. 7 for a more detailed explanation of decibel rating.

broadcasting. The frequency of the program will define the speed or rate of amplitude modulation and the amplitude of the program will define the amount or peak of modulation. If a program frequency has a very low amplitude, the amplitude of the carrier will not be displaced very far; the greater the amplitude of the program, the greater the amplitude variation of the carrier signal. The actual device that makes this type of signal modification possible may be incorporated into the carrier generator (oscillator, filter, amplifier), or it may exist as a separate module having two inputs, one for a program and one for the carrier and at least one output for the modulated product.

By using a very low-frequency carrier (.01-7 Hz), it is possible to actually hear the program waveshape. For example, using a 2 Hz sine wave to modulate a constant carrier signal, one will hear a steady rise and fall in the amplitude of the carrier. If a triangle wave is used as the modulating signal (program), the amplitude of the carrier will rise gradually, then instantaneously change direction. By using a square wave as the program signal, the carrier will be instantaneously loud and soft, with no audible rise or decay time in the amplitude. Amplitude modulation with a 5 to 9 Hz sine or triangle wave will produce a very pleasing tremolo (as opposed to "vibrato," which is "frequency modulation").

Amplitude modulation is not limited to the production of various rates of tremolo. As the frequency of the program signal approaches the audio range, it is more and more difficult for the human ear to detect each individual amplitude fluctuation in the carrier, and "sidebands" are produced. An analogy would be to spin a coin on a flat surface. If the coin is spun rapidly, the eye cannot perceive the sequence of heads-tails-heads-tails, etc. What the eye does perceive is a blur that is almost a sum of the two images. This is the principle of sideband generation. In amplitude modulation, if the program signal is approaching the audio range, at least three signals are produced. The most evident signal is the actual modulated carrier. In addition to this carrier, the modulation process produces two entirely new frequencies known as "sideband" frequencies. One of these new frequencies is the *sum*, in Hz, of the carrier and program frequencies; it is called the "upper sideband." The second new signal is the *difference* between the program and the carrier, or the "lower sideband." These sidebands are softer than the carrier signal and tend to sound like nonharmonic overtones and subtones; therefore, they

are useful in timbre constructions. When a program signal consists of more than one frequency, two sidebands are produced for every frequency contained in the program. Such a complex program may be the result of very high harmonic content or a result of the mixing of two or more signals. In either case, the more components present in the program, the more sidebands produced by the process of amplitude modulation. The frequencies of the sidebands are always equal to the sums and differences of the carrier and the program components.

As an example of amplitude modulation and sideband production, consider modulating a 1,000 Hz sine wave (carrier) with a 200 Hz sine wave (program). The result would be the original 1,000 Hz signal plus 1,200 Hz and 800 Hz signals. If the program consisted of a 200 Hz and a 300 Hz signal, the result would then be frequencies of 1,000 Hz, 1,200 Hz, 1,300 Hz, 800 Hz, and 700 Hz. Similarly, if the program consisted of 5 frequencies, 10 sidebands would be produced, 5 on each side of the carrier. A very good example of composing with amplitude-modulation techniques is Karlheinz Stockhausen's *Hymnen* (Deutsche Grammophone Records no. 139421/22).

Another amplitude-oriented method of sideband production is a process called "heterodyning," which is sometimes referred to as "non-linear" mixing. If two signals of near equal frequency are superimposed on each other, they will mix into a single tone with amplitude variations equal in frequency to the difference between the two original frequencies. For example, if a 500 Hz signal and a 504 Hz signal are heterodyned, the result is an amplitude variation at a rate of four times per second. Such amplitude modulations are often called "beats" or "beat frequencies." If the beats are fast enough to be perceived as audio frequencies, then sidebands are produced, again the result of sum and difference frequencies. (For an example of this technique at work, listen to *I of IV* by Pauline Oliveros. The entire composition is basically a result of heterodyning effects between eleven ultrasonic oscillators and one subaudio oscillator.)

While heterodyning is very similar to amplitude modulation in its production of sidebands, the basic difference is that amplitude modulation also results in a change in the carrier, or modulated signal, while heterodyning produces no direct change in either of the signals. If the different frequencies are slow enough to be perceived as "beats," the sideband is usually below the audio range. In this case, heterodyning could be considered a type of amplitude modulation.

A third type of amplitude-oriented signal modification is "balanced" or "ring" modulation. A ring modulator has two inputs—one program, and one carrier with one output. The modulated product of the two input signals are sidebands made up of the sum and difference frequencies, just as in amplitude modulation. The difference with ring modulation is that neither of the input signals, carrier or program, appear at the output. Therefore, ring modulation of two sine waves having frequencies of 1,500 Hz and 400 Hz, would produce two signals: one at 1,900 Hz, and one at 1,100 Hz. If one of the original signals, for example the 400 Hz, was a square wave, however, the output would be quite different. Since a square wave consists of an infinite number of odd harmonics, each harmonic will have the potential of generating its own set of sidebands. For a more detailed and technical description of ring modulation and its applications, see "The Multiplier-Type Ring Modulator" by Harold Bode (*Electronic Music Review* no. 1, Jan. 1967).

A refinement of ring modulation techniques, and a very useful tool to the composer of electronic music, is the "klangumwandler" or the "frequency shifter," sometimes referred to as a "single sideband generator." In normal musical transposition of a chord, one is actually performing an act of multiplication. For example, if a C-major triad is transposed up a perfect 4th to an F-major triad, all that has taken place is a multiplication of each tone in the chord by approximately 1.335, thus, 261.6 (C) × 1.335 = 349.2 (F); 329.6 (E) × 1.335 = 440 (A); and 391.9 × 1.335 = 523.2 (C). Similarly, each overtone of a single pitch undergoes the same process when the pitch is transposed; hence, the overtone structure of the pitch remains in a constant ratio and the character of the pitch does not change. Suppose now that the transposition is achieved by addition. Using the C-triad transposed to F-triad example, we would add 87.6 Hz to the E (329.6), resulting in 417.2 Hz, a pitch only 2.1 Hz above A♭. In the same manner, an addition of 87.6 Hz to the G (391.9) results in 479.5, a pitch almost exactly between A♯ and B. Applying this addition process to a single pitch with any type of harmonic overtone structure would result in a restructuring of the overtones so that they would no longer exist in a harmonic relationship to each other.

This entire process is known as frequency shifting or spectrum shifting and is done with a

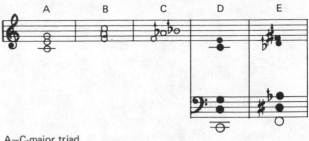

A—C-major triad
B—transposed up a perfect 4th
C—shifted by an index of 87.6
D—65.4 Hz "C" with the first 4 harmonic overtones
E—shifted by an index of 21.9 (also an interval of a perfect 4th)

Fig. 3.2. C-major triad transposition and shifts

klangumwandler or frequency shifter. The amount of shift expressed in Hz is often referred to as the "index." The actual unit consists of two inputs and one output. One input is for the signal that is to be shifted and the other input is for a signal that will actually cause the shift or "program." If one wished to shift a 600 Hz sine wave by an index of 327 Hz, one input would receive the 600 Hz sine wave and the other input would receive a signal (usually a sine wave) of 327 Hz. It is possible to shift the spectrum up at an interval defined by the program frequency (as described above) or down by the same index. The direction of the shift is selected either by a "dc-tuning" switch, or the frequency shifter may have two separate outputs, one for the upward shift or upper sideband and one for the downward shift or lower sideband. This is possible because frequency shifting is actually the isolation of the upper or lower sideband of a ring-modulated product (often referred to as "single sideband" generation). The klangumwandler has been used extensively for many years in the creation of electronic music and still remains a very valuable tool in the composition of new timbres.

For the sake of clarity, this discussion of modulation techniques has only been concerned with sine waves, because of the limited number of sidebands produced. It is possible to amplitude-modulate, heterodyne, ring-modulate or frequency-shift any sounds that can be transmitted as an electrical signal—which means practically any sound that exists. Of course the more components that exist in either the program or the carrier, the more sidebands produced, resulting in a more complex waveshape.

Chapter 6, "Gating," will deal with further implications of amplitude-variation techniques.

4

frequency modulation

While amplitude modulation, because of its many associated methods, is a very important technique to the composer, the control of another parameter—frequency—is perhaps of even greater importance to him. Throughout musical history, until today, the composer has been *primarily* concerned with pitch change or, in electronic terms, frequency modulation. As the term implies, frequency modulation is the control of the frequency of a sound. When a singer or instrumentalist utilizes vibrato he is actually changing the frequency of the sound at a rate of about 6 or 7 times each second or, in other terms, frequency modulating at 6 or 7 Hz. If the musician increases the modulation rate to about 13 or 14 Hz, he will begin to produce a trill. By definition, frequency modulation could be applied to any type of frequency change. Even methods as conventional as playing a scale or arpeggio could be considered a manner of frequency modulation. But in electronic music applications, the term usually refers to a special type of interaction of waveshapes to produce various changes in timbre.

Just as in amplitude modulation, frequency modulation (FM) is achieved by controlling a parameter, in this case frequency, of a carrier signal with the frequency and amplitude of a program signal (fig. 4.1). As the frequency of the program signal approaches the audio range, the modulated product, as with amplitude modulation, begins to exhibit characteristic sidebands. But this is where the similarity between AM and FM ends. The frequency spectrum* of a frequency-modulated signal usually has many more sidebands than an amplitude-modulated signal, these sidebands produced on either side of the carrier at intervals

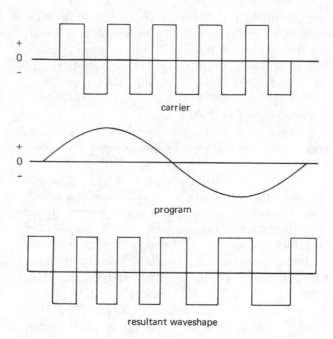

Fig. 4.1. Carrier and program waves with frequency-modulated waveshape.

equal to the frequency of the program signal. To illustrate, suppose that a 1k carrier is to be frequency modulated by a 50 Hz program. The modulated product will have the potential of having sidebands at 1,050 Hz and 950 Hz, 1,100 Hz and 900 Hz, 1,150 Hz and 850 Hz, continuing ad infinitum. The number of sidebands, however, is dependent on what is known as the "modulation index."

*A frequency spectrum refers to any vertical sequencing of the components of a wave, with the highest frequency at the top. A frequency envelope is a graphic representation of the frequency components and their relative amplitudes aligned along a horizontal axis.

Let us assume that the carrier and program frequencies are sine waves. (More complex waveshapes, in relation to frequency modulation, will be covered after a basic understanding of this technique is complete.) In frequency modulation (in contrast to amplitude modulation), the various sidebands have different amplitudes. Another potentially useful phenomenon is that the amplitude of the carrier signal decreases as the amount of modulation increases. This is very important to FM broadcasting, because if the carrier is distributed over the entire frequency spectrum of the modulated product, it is less vulnerable to unwanted distortions and interference. All of these characteristics of frequency modulation are also largely dependent on the "modulation index."

In order to clearly define this term, one must first understand what is known by "peak frequency deviation." Expressed in Hz, the maximum amount that a modulated product varies from the original unmodulated carrier is called the peak frequency deviation. If a carrier frequency of 500 Hz is modulated up to a high of 700 Hz and down to a low of 300 Hz, the peak frequency deviation is 200 Hz (700-500=200; 500-300=200). By referring to figure 4.1, one can see that the peak frequency deviation is dependent on the amplitude of the program signal. Peak frequency deviation divided by the frequency of the program is the modulation index. In the above example, if the frequency of the program was 50 Hz, the modulation index would be 4.

$$\text{modulation index} = \frac{\text{peak frequency deviation}}{\text{program frequency}}$$

$$\text{modulation index} = \frac{200}{50} = 4$$

The significance of this index is that it indicates the number of significant sidebands on each side of the carrier (a total of 8 in the example given, 4 above and 4 below the carrier). Since the program frequency also determines the intervalic relationship of the sidebands, it is possible to precisely predict the frequency spectrum of any FM signal.

For a second example, suppose that a 1,500 Hz carrier is to be frequency modulated by a 60 Hz program. If the amplitude, which can be con-

trolled by the composer, results in a peak frequency deviation of 360 Hz, then the modulation index will be 6.

$$\text{modulation index} = \frac{360}{60} = 6$$

In turn, this indicates that 12 significant sidebands, 6 above and 6 below the carrier, will exist at the exact frequencies of:

1,860 Hz
1,800 Hz
1,740 Hz
1,680 Hz
1,620 Hz
1,560 Hz
(1,500 Hz carrier)
1,440 Hz
1,380 Hz
1,320 Hz
1,260 Hz
1,200 Hz
1,140 Hz

Figure 4.2 is an approximate musical notation of this spectrum.

With amplitude modulation, the amplitude of the sidebands is dependent on the amplitude of the carrier frequency. With frequency modulation, the relative amplitudes of the individual sidebands are very irregular. The most important fact for the composer to know is that the amplitude of the modulated carrier is dependent on the modulation index. It is possible, and sometimes very desirable, to have the total amplitude of the carrier signal distributed throughout the various sidebands. When it is, the original carrier frequency is not audible and we hear only the sideband frequencies. There is no constant ratio of an amplitude increase or decrease as the sidebands go further from the center frequency (carrier), but in all cases any sidebands existing beyond the point of the modulation index are so weak in amplitude that they are insignificant. Beyond this point the sidebands are less than 1 percent of the original carrier amplitude.

All types of sideband-generating techniques are useful in producing percussive effects, clan-

Fig. 4.2. Notated spectrum of a frequency-modulated sine wave.

gorous sounds,* and various other non-harmonic spectrums, but since frequency modulation often results in the carrier frequency being absorbed by the sidebands, the modulated product will not have a well-defined pitch. A strong sense of pitch motion can be accomplished if the sidebands are shifted constantly so that the ratios between them remain the same. To illustrate this technique, suppose that the intervalic pattern in figure 4.3 is to be simulated using a clangorous spectrum generated by frequency modulation. The same pitches

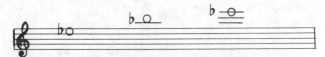

Fig. 4.3. Interval pattern to be simulated with frequency modulation.

are represented by 622, 932, and 1,244 Hz respectively. Beginning with the E♭ (622 Hz), and frequency modulating with an arbitrary program of 40 Hz that has an amplitude which will produce a peak frequency deviation of 80 Hz, this will produce two sidebands on each side of the carrier,

$$\frac{80}{40} = \text{a modulation index of 2}$$

spaced 40 Hz apart (fig. 4.4). If the second pitch in the sequence, B♭ (932 Hz), is frequency modu-

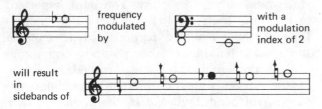

Fig. 4.4. Frequency modulation of E♭

lated by the same 40 Hz program, with the same frequency deviation, the sidebands shown in figure 4.5 will be produced.

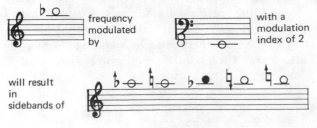

Fig. 4.5. Frequency modulation of B♭

In terms of conceived pitches, the sidebands produced by the E♭ carrier are slightly farther apart than the sidebands produced by the B♭ carrier, and this will result in a slightly different timbre. If the composer wishes to have a certain pitch sequence and, at the same time, keep the timbre constant, he must change the program frequency in accordance with the carrier, keeping both frequencies apart at a constant ratio. The original timbre (fig. 4.4) was based on a

40 [clef] to 622 [clef] ratio

which is rounded to a simpler fraction of 1:15. To keep this ratio constant with the next pitch, 932 Hz [clef], a program of 62 Hz [clef] must be used (62:932 = 1:15). By changing both frequencies in this manner, the sideband ratio will remain constant, therefore keeping the timbre constant. The third pitch in the series 1244 Hz [clef] would require a program of 82.7 Hz

$\left(\text{[clef]} \quad \text{approx.} \right).$

The immediate problem is to have two oscillators generate frequencies at a constant ratio apart. As demonstrated in the preceding paragraph, the mathematical computation of the program frequencies can be a very complex task. Even after the exact frequencies are known, the problem remains of how to ensure that the oscillators will consistently produce them. This seemingly difficult task is readily accomplished with voltage control. If a carrier oscillator is set to produce frequency "f_c" when controlled by voltage V, and the program oscillator is set to produce frequency "f_p" when controlled by the same voltage V, the ratio between f_c and f_p will remain the same because the voltage V will always cause an exponential change (see fig. 4.12) in the frequencies, always keeping their interval ratios the same and resulting in a constant timbre.

Figure 4.6A shows the frequency modulator as a module separate from the carrier and program oscillators. Certain types of oscillators can

*Clangorous sound or a "klang" is any individual characeristic timbre, usually constructed of non-harmonic overtones.

produce internal frequency modulation; instead of a single voltage control input, an oscillator of this type would have a multiple of control inputs. If the carrier frequency was being determined by voltage V, and a program frequency was also used as a control voltage, this would be another method of frequency modulation (fig. 4.6B). The program frequency could still be controlled by voltage V, as in figure 4.6C, or may be controlled by another voltage source. However, as soon as a different

source of voltage is used it becomes more of a problem to maintain constant ratios.

Still another method of frequency modulation is illustrated in figure 4.7. In this case a frequency/voltage loop is created as oscillator A is generating a frequency that is used to voltage control the frequency of oscillator B. In turn, the frequency of oscillator B is used as the voltage control for oscillator A. When two oscillators control each other, as in this example, which is the carrier and which is the program? The only usable answer would be to consider that the oscillator being monitored* is generating the carrier signal. In communications the program, or original message, is what is finally monitored, but the electronic music composer is usually more interested in making a message out of the modulated carrier.

There are endless variations of these frequency/voltage patterns which may be utilized by the composer, depending on the ingenuity of the individual. The type of thinking necessary is very similar to that needed in creating a good canon; both techniques involve the creative use of limited relationships of frequencies.

*To monitor a signal is to perceive it in some manner. This may be done aurally, or visually through an oscilloscope or VU meter.

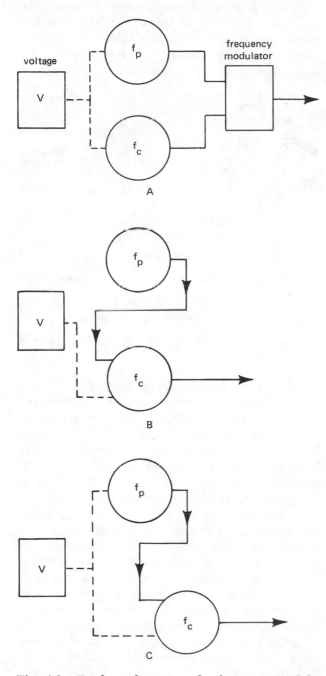

Fig. 4.6. Patch configurations for frequency modulation.

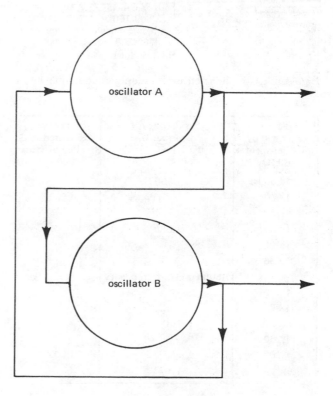

Fig 4.7. Frequency-voltage loop

For the sake of clarity, all of the examples used so far in this discussion of frequency modulation have utilized sine waves as the carriers and program signals. It is possible to frequency modulate any two signals, but it must be remembered that for every frequency component, or overtone, in either the program or the carrier, there will be a separate modulation index and an extra set of sidebands. Referring back to figure 4.2, the sine-wave program and sine-wave carrier produced 6 sidebands on each side of the carrier. By using the same frequency and peak frequency deviation (360 Hz) and changing the program signal to a square wave, a much more complex product is generated. In consideration of only the first two overtones of a 60 Hz square wave, which are 180 Hz and 300 Hz (fig. 4.8), this adds two more modulation indices and produces an extra 6 sidebands. The first overtone will add sidebands of 1,869 Hz, 1,680 Hz, 1,320 Hz, and 1,140 Hz. The second overtone will add sidebands of 1,800 Hz and 1,200 Hz. All of these sideband frequencies except 1,140 Hz were present in the original example (fig. 4.2). The reason for this is that the

overtones added by changing from sine to square wave were harmonic, or whole-number multiples of the fundamental. Therefore the additional sidebands will bear the same relationships to each other. The only new sideband that was added was the 1,140 Hz frequency, which was due to a large modulation index (fig. 4.9).

When overtones exist in a non-harmonic relationship to each other, an even more complex spectrum is produced. If the spectrum in figure 4.10 was a program signal used to frequency modulate a 1,568 Hz sine wave, and the peak frequency deviation was 50 Hz, a total of 70 sidebands ranging from 13,008 Hz to far below 1 Hz would be produced. So complex a spectrum would

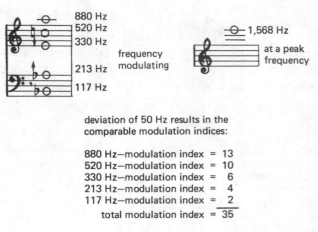

deviation of 50 Hz results in the comparable modulation indices:

880 Hz—modulation index = 13
520 Hz—modulation index = 10
330 Hz—modulation index = 6
213 Hz—modulation index = 4
117 Hz—modulation index = 2
total modulation index = 35

Fig. 4.10.   FM spectrum

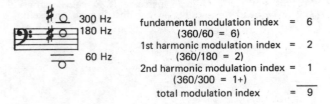

fundamental modulation index = 6
(360/60 = 6)
1st harmonic modulation index = 2
(360/180 = 2)
2nd harmonic modulation index = 1
(360/300 = 1+)
total modulation index = 9

Fig. 4.8.   Computation of frequency-modulation index

sidebands generated by the fundamental (60 Hz)	sidebands generated by the 1st overtone (180 Hz)	sidebands generated by the 2nd overtone (300 Hz)
1,860 Hz	1,860 Hz	
1,800		1,800 Hz
1,740		
1,680	1,680	
1,620		
1,560		
	1,500 Hz carrier frequency	
1,440		
1,380		
1,320	1,320	
1,260		
1,200		1,200
	1,140	

Fig. 4.9.   Spectrum of FM sidebands

sound very thick and, due to inner heterodyning of the sideband frequencies, would approach being a sound much like weighted or colored sound (a frequency or group of frequencies which are mixed with a small portion of the white sound spectrum to "weight" the frequencies in that direction).

In the production of any type of sound it is best to let your ear be the prime and final judge. The theory and technical aspects behind any kind of sound treatment should only serve as a guide in choosing what techniques will be the most successful in creating the desired sound. With a basic knowledge of modulation theory, it is usually more expedient to let the ear decide which timbre is best suited for the specific event. During the exploratory process, one will almost always discover many new sounds that normally would not be realized if the aesthetic expeditions were limited to mathematical processes.

Since methods of frequency modulation are dependent on applications of frequency control, it will be of benefit to introduce voltage controlled oscillators, or VCOs, at this time. VCOs are available in many different types and designs and each has its own manner of operation. Although they share the same concept of voltage control, the actual design formats and operational modes may differ according to the individual manufacturers. The basic VCO has a signal output and a control input. Refined VCOs may have any number of inputs and outputs with various types of control pots for fine tuning and controlling the response characteristics of the oscillators. All of these devices will be described individually in terms of their relationship to VCO applications.

In communication applications, the VCO usually has one output for the generated frequency. In electronic music applications, because of the possibility of the various interrelated control functions, the ideal oscillator will have a multiple of outputs for any single frequency. The outputs may be paralleled, meaning that any one of the output signals will exhibit the exact same characteristics as any other output signal, or they may be 180° out of phase with each other. The "phase" of any given signal is the relative starting point measured in degrees. One complete cycle of any wave is said to have 360°. If the positive portion of a waveshape begins at the same time the negative portion of another waveshape begins, the two waves are 180° out of phase with each other. In figure 4.11, signals A, B, and C all have the same frequency and amplitude but begin, in reference to a zero voltage point, at different times. If A is

used as the reference signal, then B is 90° out of phase with A and C is 180° out of phase with A. The phase relationships of waveshapes are very important to the electronic music composer and will be discussed with respect to location modulation techniques.

Most VCOs have some type of control pot that allows for manual control of the frequency. Some oscillators utilize one control that covers the entire frequency range, while others utilize a frequency-range switch that will produce multiples of a more limited frequency-control pot. For example, if the frequency-range switch was set at X1 and the frequency-control pot was set at 20, the frequency produced would be 20 Hz or 20 times 1. Without disturbing the frequency pot, but changing the range switch to X10, the frequency would change to 200 Hz. By setting the range switch to X100, the frequency would be 2,000 Hz. Some oscillators have range switches calibrated in terms of "feet," like an organ or harpsichord stop. This type of calibration is the same as exponents of 2 (octaves) and the calibration notation is simply a matter of convenience for the composer who finds it difficult to think in terms of Hz. A refinement of the frequency pot is a "vernier" pot that allows for very minute and critical tuning of individual frequencies. When working with very high frequencies, the relationships are very small and the vernier is useful for making fine frequency distinctions. The main frequency-control pot may sometimes be called a vernier, but this term is usually reserved for a control limited to a very small range.

The amplitude produced by the VCO may be controlled in various ways. Oscillators usually have a fixed amplitude output that is referred to as "line level" or 600 ohms (Ω). The amplitude may be internally variable with the use of an "attenuator" or "volume control." An attenuator is also referred to as a "gain control," while the amplitude level is called "gain level." Usually the composer will choose to control the gain through the use of an external amplifier (these methods will be covered in chap. 6).

VCOs may employ two types of control voltages. The AC control input is usually used for frequency modulation purposes. This input will usually be labeled "AC control" or "frequency modulation input." Any AC voltage applied to this input will cause a modulation above and below a center or "fixed" frequency. Another type of voltage control is DC (direct current). Unlike AC, DC is a constant-magnitude, non-fluctuating volt-

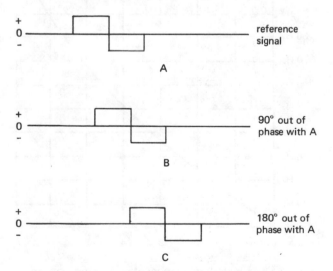

Fig. 4.11. Phase relationships of a pulse wave

age that maintains a fixed level. Due to this non-fluctuating characteristic, DC voltage will hold the oscillator at a fixed frequency, just as the frequency control pot does. In terms of application, DC voltage control can be an electronic substitution for the frequency control pot and is usually used to program constant frequencies. In modern electronic music systems, DC control voltages may range from zero to 15 volts or higher. If a DC voltage of .5 is applied to the control input of a VCO, it may produce a hypothetical frequency of 90 Hz. If the DC voltage is increased to 2 volts, the frequency may increase to 180 Hz. If a composer wished to produce a pitch sequence as in figure 4.12, a classic studio technique would require him to record the first frequency, stop the recorder, change the oscillator to the next pitch and then record it, and continue this process for the remaining pitches. After all the pitches are taped, the composer would then splice out the unwanted silences and clicks produced by stopping and starting the recorder. At the same time he would cut each piece of tape in accordance with the desired length of the note. This could not be achieved manually, because the turning of the frequency pot would result in unwanted glissandi between the desired frequencies. The entire procedure would be further complicated by the probability that the composer could not accurately turn to the exact desired frequency, especially if the passage was at a very rapid tempo.

Fig. 4.12. Notated passage to be produced with voltage-controlled frequency.

By using DC voltage control, however, the passage would be very simple to produce. By using a device that would produce a sequence of instantaneous DC voltages,* and applying them to the DC input of a VCO, the changes in DC voltage would result in an instantaneous change in frequency. Tempo and rhythm would then be a function of the speed of the instantaneous voltage changes.

Direct current voltage may affect the oscillator (or any other voltage-controlled device) in one of two ways: linearly or exponentially. With linear control, the frequency changes in direct relationship to the change in voltage. That is, if a 1 volt increase in voltage causes the frequency to increase by 10 Hz, a 2 volt increase will cause a 20 Hz increase. With exponential control, however, the frequency will bear an increasing relationship to the applied voltage; the greater the voltage increase, the greater the *rate* of change of the frequency. That is, 1 volt may cause a 10 Hz increase, 2 volts a 25 Hz increase. Figure 4.13 is a graphic

*Voltage sequencers and keyboards are discussed in chap. 5.

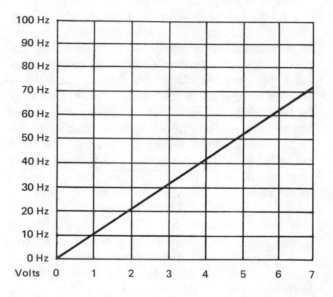

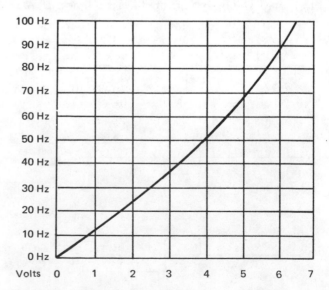

Fig. 4.13. Linear and exponential voltage control of frequency.

representation of linear and exponential voltage control of frequency. The exponential mode allows for a larger frequency range to be controlled by a smaller amount of voltage, while linear operation allows for finer gradual frequency changes with the same amount of voltage. (See also on this subject chap. 6.)

Other VCOs, usually manufactured for industrial applications, are of slightly different design. These usually do not have a fixed frequency control and the output is dependent only on one voltage application. The frequency output of these oscillators is usually limited to a very specific range as compared to the very wide range of the VCOs used in electronic music.

Another type of frequency modulation that should be mentioned is the "sync" inputs found on many industrial and communications oscillators. With the use of a sync input, the oscillator can be made to generate a frequency comparable to the frequency of an external pulse oscillator. If oscillator A, with a sync input, is generating a frequency of 900 Hz, and pulse oscillator B is generating a frequency of 1k Hz (1,000 Hz) the pulse waveform of oscillator B may be applied to the sync input of oscillator A to cause it to shift its frequency to 1k. Oscillator A will tend to generate the same frequency as the frequency of the pulses applied to its sync input. In other words, the frequency of oscillator A will sync with oscillator B. Even though the sync input receives a pulse waveshape (in this case, any waveshape that exhibits a steep amplitude characteristic), its own waveshape is not affected. But there are two chief reasons why this type of frequency control is not satisfactory for most electronic music applications. The first is that the time it takes for the oscillator to respond and stabilize to a new pulse frequency is not fast enough for many electronic music uses; the second is that if the controlled frequency is not reasonably close to the pulse frequency, it will have a tendency to sync with one of the harmonics of the pulse frequency. For example, suppose that oscillator A is generating a frequency of 200 Hz and a 60 Hz pulse wave, in this case a square waveshape, is applied to the sync input. Since the square wave exhibits odd harmonic overtones of the fundamental (180 Hz, 300 Hz, 420 Hz, etc.) oscillator A may sync with the 180 Hz harmonic because it is so close to its own original frequency of 200 Hz—and even if a 60 Hz sync is achieved, it may be unstable. This does not mean that the technique cannot be used. There is a certain amount of instability in any oscillator, but the

composer learns to work around and take advantage of this drawback and if one is familiar with the various characteristics of sync control, the apparent drawbacks may be used to the advantage of the composer. Just as Mahler realized that he had to re-program his dynamic notations to compensate for the individual amplitude characteristics of the various instruments, the electronic music composer learns how to program out the various inadequacies of his equipment.

Sync control is not to be confused with pulse modulation. Pulse modulation refers to changing some characteristic of the pulse and is often used as a voltage control in itself. Pulse modulation is discussed in relationship to Schmitt triggers and timing pulse generators in chapter 5.

All of the above frequency control methods result in "frequency translation." Frequency translation is any technique which will produce a second frequency bearing *any* relationship to the original signal. This includes FM sideband generation and the amplitude-modulation techniques which result in the production of new frequencies. A more specified type of frequency change is frequency division and multiplication, which involve only whole-number multiples or divisions of the original frequency. Musically speaking this is the same as transposition.

Frequency multiplication occurs in the following manner: a frequency is applied to a device that will block out the fundamental and any unwanted harmonics. If the original waveshape contains all of the harmonics, then it is possible to have any whole-number multiple of the fundamental, because harmonics are defined as whole-number multiples of the fundamental. For example, consider that an original sawtooth wave of 140 Hz, which by definition contains all of the harmonic overtones, is applied to a selective filter or wave trap* and only one of the whole-number multiples (280 Hz, 420 Hz, 560 Hz, etc.) is allowed to pass through. If the 280 Hz is passed through the filter, the original frequency will be multiplied by 2; if the filter passed 420 Hz, a third multiple of the fundamental, the transposition would be a perfect 12th. Figure 4.14 is a diagrammatic representation of this method. If the original frequency is a sine or pulse wave that does not contain the 3rd harmonic, a distortion device of some sort will have to be placed in the system so that the desired har-

---

*Frequency selective circuits as applied to frequency changers are discussed in detail in I. M. Gottlieb, *Frequency Changers* (New York: Howard W. Sams, 1965).

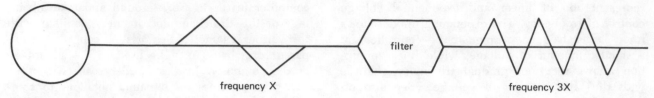

Fig. 4.14. Frequency multiplication via a filter

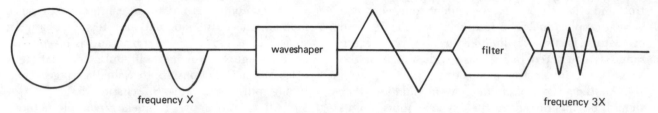

Fig. 4.15. Frequency multiplication via a filter and waveshaper

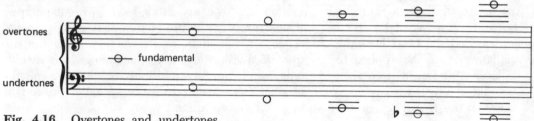

Fig. 4.16. Overtones and undertones

monic will be generated (fig. 4.15). These harmonic-generating devices—any device that will change the overtone content of a wave—are usually referred to as waveshapers. Because harmonics are of lower amplitude than the fundamental, and due to a certain amount of loss (referred to as "insertion loss") in the filter and shaping device, an amplifier is usually needed to bring the multiplied product back up to its original level.

There are many methods of frequency division, such as neon-bulb dividers, thyratron dividers, synchronized relaxation oscillators, multivibrators and univibrators. All work on the same operational principle of subharmonic relationships. Subharmonics are whole-number divisions of a fundamental frequency.

Frequency division does not actually produce these undertones; rather, it produces pulses to sync the oscillator at the correct ratio. If a fundamental C (261.6 Hz) produces pulses at a rate of 261.6 times per second, and if every other pulse is used to trigger an oscillator, a frequency of 130.8 Hz,

or lower octave C, will be produced. If every third pulse is used, a frequency of 87.2 Hz, or low F, will result.

In electronic music applications, frequency multiplication and division are used for pitch transposition and for the production of related control trigger pulses. It must be remembered that due to the process involved, frequency multiplication and division also produce a certain amount of waveshaping, especially if the original signal is a sine wave. This can be compensated for by the use of filters to eliminate the unwanted harmonics. Another type of frequency changer, the "zeitdehner" or "timestretcher," may be used to transpose frequencies: this device is discussed in chapter 12. Frequency division can also be accomplished by using "flip-flops," a special type of computer memory circuit that has the ability to store and release information according to external cue signals. In essence, the flip-flop achieves frequency variation by turning the signal on and off at various rates.

control-voltage sources

In most instances of recorded electronic music, the composer fills a dual role of creator and performer. In the older studios of Europe, it was a common practice for the composer to realize his work through the aid of an engineer; he would seldom come in direct contact with the equipment. But due to simplified methods and design, along with the contemporary composer's increasing knowledge of electronic methods and an instinctive curiosity about the internal workings of his art, the electronic music composer today has a tighter reign over the compositional processes. One of the major appeals of electronic music is that it offers the composer an opportunity to come into direct physical contact with the various parameters in which he is interested. This is appreciated by some composers because of the unrestricted control it affords; it is appreciated by others because of the actual kinesthetic sensations involved, much as in the act of painting or sculpting. Just as a horn player controls the various aspects of the produced sound by his breath, keys, and hands, the electronic music composer may control the parameters of the sound he produces through the use of control voltages. An entire composition may be the function of voltage application; consequently, the composer is often more concerned with methods of voltage production than the manner of application. (Certain groups of composers are now experimenting with "electric music" in which amplifiers and oscillators are done away with and the basic sound source is the acoustical result of high voltage.)

There are an endless number of kinds of voltage sources the composer may use, and every studio may have its own particular version of a basic type that has been built or modified to meet a specific need. This chapter will discuss the basic designs of control sources and some of the more common refinements and modifications found on much of the commercially available equipment. There will be no attempt to describe any particular design and, in fact, all of the discussed refinements and modifications are usually not found on any one system. There are so many individual variations in design that complete coverage would amount to a detailed description of every electronic studio in the world.

Control voltages are electronic substitutes for what is usually a manually operated pot. Conceptually, the simplest control voltage is a DC battery like the type used to power a transistor radio. Applied to any voltage controlled device, the steady DC output would sustain the controlled parameter at a constant level until the battery began to lose its energy. A further refinement would be a constant voltage supply whose level would be manually variable. With such a supply one would not have to be concerned with de-energized batteries and would have a certain degree of control of the parameter involved. This, of course, would provide no more of an advantage than the manually controlled pot on the particular module. Control-voltage processors have a function similar to a manually controlled battery, but with many more advantages (see page 35).

The most popular, but not necessarily most useful, source of control voltage is the voltage keyboard or keyboard controller. This is essentially a multiple voltage source that will produce a separate instantaneous DC voltage for each separate key. The keyboard may be visually similar to an

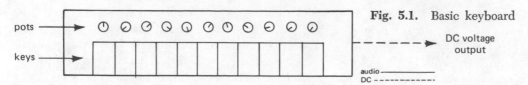

Fig. 5.1. Basic keyboard

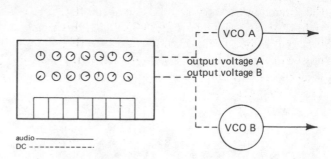

Fig. 5.2. Voltage control of two VCOs with separate voltage banks of a keyboard.

organ keyboard or it may be a series of metal plates (commonly known as capacitance plates or a "touch keyboard") which are touched by the performer. The similarity to an organ or piano keyboard is often confusing because the voltage keyboard does not necessarily change pitch. It produces voltages which may be used to control pitch as well as amplitude, timbre, or any other desired parameter. Ideally, each individual key would have the capability of producing its own voltage independent of the other keys. This may be achieved by each key having its own voltage pot which could be manually set. By having individual controls, the keyboard is not limited to having any particular voltage sequence—going from left to right would not necessarily mean higher voltages. By depressing the individual keys, there would be a change to the preset voltage of that particular key.

Note that in figure 5.1 there is only one main output for the voltage. The basic voltage keyboards are "monophonic," since they will produce only one voltage at a time; that is, if controlling an oscillator with them, only one pitch at a time can be produced. The output may be divided to control any number of modules, but each module would receive the same voltage. Some keyboards will produce the preset voltage for only the time that the particular key is depressed. Other keyboards will continue to generate the voltage until the next key is depressed. This is often referred to as a "hold-no hold" function and certain designs of keyboards will function in either mode, selected by a "hold-no hold" switch.

Figure 5.2 is a type of "homophonic" keyboard. With this particular design, each key is able to produce two independent preset voltages. The top row of pots are preset and that voltage is taken from output A. The lower row of pots are also preset and that output voltage is taken from output B. It is thus possible to have any single key produce two independent voltages which may be used to control two independent modules.

In certain instances it may be very useful to have a third independent output with its own set of control pots. Each output would also have a set of corresponding pots for the presetting of each

key, and each separate voltage output could then be used to control any voltage-controlled module in the system.

Another keyboard design achieves voltage regulation by using only two pots: "range" and "scale." The range pot determines the total amount of voltage the keyboard will produce. If the keyboard is being used to control the frequency of an oscillator, and the range pot is at a maximum, the pitch difference between the two extreme ends of the keyboard may be as much as 15 octaves, depending on the particular design. If the range pot is at a minimum setting, the total range of the keyboard could be as small as one-half step. If the keyboard had 40 keys, then there would be a possibility of having 40 different pitches between any two adjacent half-steps. The relationship between the individual voltages is controlled by the scale pot. This control allows for fine tuning of the voltages so that it is possible to achieve various types of scalar relationships of the controlled parameter. Certain keyboard designs make use of a keyboard programmer. This is a memory circuit which can be instantaneously switched in to provide various pre-programmed tunings. It must be remembered that very fine and subtle control of all of the parameters is just as important as the fine control of pitch, and that the keyboard should not be approached as strictly a frequency controlling device.

Another operating characteristic of many voltage keyboards is that the output voltage may be a function of the manual force or velocity applied to any individual key. Keyboards consisting of capacitance plates will produce voltages proportional to the applied finger pressure. This would be very useful if the keyboard has a separate output for the preset voltages and for voltages produced by finger pressure, since it would be possible to create various phrasings and accents by using the preset voltage to control frequency and using the finger-pressure voltage to control the amplitude of each frequency (fig. 5.3). With this patching, the individual amplitudes, along with possible crescendi and diminuendi, would be a function of finger pressure and pitch would be a function of preset voltages.

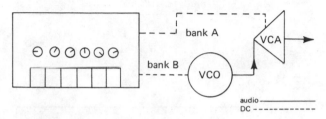

Fig. 5.3. Amplitude and frequency control from a keyboard.

The major disadvantage of capacitance plates is that each person has an individual skin resistance that may also affect the produced voltage. Person A, in using a capacitance keyboard, may produce 7 volts when a hypothetical pressure is applied. Person B, applying the same amount of pressure, may produce a higher or lower voltage, depending on the amount of electrical resistance in his body. The answer to this problem might be a keyboard with organ keys that will produce a voltage proportional to the depth the individual key is depressed. By depressing the key one-eighth of an inch, a certain voltage would be produced; depressing the same key one-quarter of an inch would produce a proportionally higher voltage. This type of keyboard requires the performer/composer to acquire a very specialized keyboard technique in order to accurately control the depression of the keys.

The major advantage of the keyboard is that the instantaneous change of voltage creates an instant change in the output of the controlled module. For instance, any sustained sound would undergo a great many amplitude changes if the keyboard were controlling the gain of an amplifier. Any sequence of frequencies could be produced, at any performable tempo, in any rhythmic pattern by using the keyboard to control an oscillator. In the same manner the keyboard could be used to simultaneously change frequency and amplitude to achieve endless pointillistic variations.

At times it may be desirable to have a gradual voltage change, as in figure 5.4. (These DC voltages in fig. 5.4 were taken from a prototype system designed by Donald Buchla and may not be the same for other systems.)

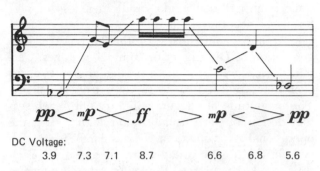

Fig. 5.4. Frequency/amplitude/voltage relationships

This gradual voltage change may be achieved on certain keyboards by using a "portamento" control. The word "portamento" must be understood in its literal sense (Italian—"to carry"), since the gradual change of voltage need not be applied to frequency. The portamento control setting will determine the time it takes for the voltage to change from one level to another. This rate may be a few milliseconds or sometimes as long as 10 seconds. If two adjacent keys produced the voltages of 3 and 4 volts respectively, and the portamento control was set at 1 second, the utilization of the keys would produce a 1-second rate change from one voltage to the other. If the voltages were controlling an amplifier, the effect would be a 1 second crescendo or diminuendo. The next logical step in design would be a voltage control of the portamento rate.

A device usually associated with the keyboard is the "ribbon controller" or the "linear controller." This is a tight band about 2 feet long that will produce a voltage proportional to where it is touched by the performer. The linear controller is usually equipped with a pot which will determine the total output voltage, similar to the range control on the keyboard. If the total output is 5 volts, and it is controlling an oscillator, it would be possible to produce a 5 octave glissando by sliding one's finger from one end of the ribbon to the other. An ascending glissando would be achieved by sliding from left to right and the opposite action would produce a descending glissando. If the total output of the ribbon was set at 1 volt, the same physical action would produce only a 1 octave glissando. This device will produce the same effects as the portamento control on the keyboard. The basic differences are that the ribbon has a smaller range but the individual characteristics of the voltage sweeps can be more immediately controlled by the performer. An extended voltage range with the same length ribbon could result in a loss of performance accuracy.

A final characteristic of the keyboard is the generation of DC trigger or "timing" voltages. Certain devices will produce a particular event whenever they are cued to do so by a trigger voltage. The magnitude of triggers will vary with each system design but are usually a bit higher than the operational AC voltage of the system. Within each system, the trigger voltages are all the same. Each time any key is pressed the keyboard will generate a trigger voltage of a constant magnitude. This particular voltage is taken from a special trigger output on various modules designed for that purpose.

One of the more cybernetic means of voltage production is the "joystick." A joystick is two or more potential voltage sources which are simultaneously controlled by a vertically-positioned lever. The two voltages are physically controlled at an angle of 90° to each other on an X-Y axis. Movements of the joystick from right to left would produce a relative change in voltage X, while movements of the stick toward and away from the body would produce relative changes in voltage Y. The advantage of the joystick is that it provides simultaneous but independent control of any two voltage-controllable parameters. If voltage X is being used to control amplitude and voltage Y is being used to control frequency, an endless number of amplitude-frequency relationships can be realized. Movement of the stick at a 90° angle in relation to the body would vary the frequency independent of amplitude, and a right-left movement of the stick would vary the amplitude independent of frequency. Moving the stick at an ascending angle would result in an abrupt change in frequency with a relatively slow change in amplitude. (fig. 5.5A). The opposite effect (abrupt change in amplitude with a relatively slow change in frequency) could be produced by moving the stick at a right angle (fig. 5.5B). A circular rotation of the joystick would produce a continually varying change in the two parameters in constant opposite relationships (fig. 5.5C). A more complex joystick could provide for simultaneous control

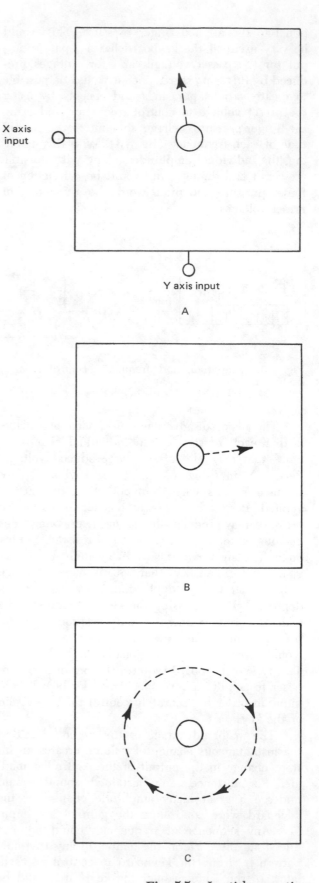

Fig. 5.5.   Joystick   operation

of a third parameter by making a control voltage a function of the vertical or up-down movement of the stick. With this X-Y-Z axis, the composer would simultaneously control amplitude, frequency, and timbre or any other combinations of three selected parameters.

Many other types of control voltage sources react in response to an applied trigger voltage. Before discussing these devices and their applications it is necessary to understand how the trigger voltages are achieved. The simplest source of a trigger voltage is the trigger output of the manually operated keyboard, as explained earlier. Every time a key is depressed a trigger pulse appears at the trigger output of the keyboard. A more complex source is the "Schmitt trigger," which is used in several electronic control modules. Essentially a Schmitt trigger is a voltage-controlled source of trigger pulses. The speed and amount of trigger pulses are dependent on some external AC or DC voltage. Every time the Schmitt trigger receives an AC or DC voltage of a preset magnitude, it will fire a trigger voltage. The Schmitt trigger is usually equipped with a "threshold" pot that will determine what amplitude or magnitude the input signal must be in order for a pulse to be generated (see fig. 5.6). If the input voltage (either AC or

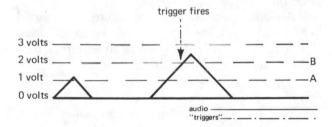

Fig. 5.6. Triangle waves used to fire a Schmitt trigger.

DC), in this case a triangle wave, has an amplitude of 1 (5.6A), and the threshold setting on the Schmitt trigger is 2 (fig. 5.6B), a trigger pulse will not be produced. Raising the amplitude of the wave to 2, and leaving the threshold setting the same, fires the trigger, because the input amplitude is equal to or above the threshold setting. Such a threshold control is very useful in programming the trigger to fire at a given instant. If the trigger is to fire at the peak of a crescendo or on a very accented event, it would be a very simple matter to set the threshold level at the peak of the amplitude level of the monitored signal. By applying this signal to the Schmitt trigger input, the

trigger would be fired when the amplitude of the input reached the threshold level.

The basic Schmitt trigger consists of an input, output, and a threshold level control. Because of its many applications in electronic music production, several variations of this basic design are available. One very useful refinement of the trigger is the "pulse length" pot. If a trigger is firing pulses at a rate of 60 per minute, each individual pulse has the capability of lasting almost one full second. Under certain circumstances it is desirable to control the length of the individual pulses; this is referred to as a percentage of the pulse period. At the rate of 60 per minute, a 100 percent pulse length indicates that the pulse is present for the entire period. A 50 percent pulse length indicates that each pulse will last for 1/2 of a second. Pulse length in no way affects the rate at which the pulses are being produced. Various pulse lengths with the same rate are shown in figure 5.7.

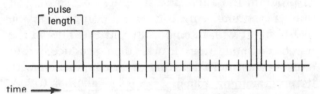

Fig. 5.7. Varying pulse lengths

Pulse length is controlled either by a pot calibrated in terms of percentages of the pulse rate, or it may be voltage controlled by means of an external DC voltage. The applications of different pulse lengths are usually made in association with various transient producing devices discussed later in this chapter.

The maximum reaction time, or possible number of pulses per second, is largely dependent on the frequency response of one of the trigger's electronic components, the transistor. Response time may be as rapid as 1 megacycle (1,000,000 Hz). Since the firing time, or frequency of pulse outputs, is dependent on a signal input, this can also be considered as voltage control of the firing time.

Trigger voltages are also referred to as "timing pulses." A timing pulse generator, however, is a trigger generating device with more refinements than the typical Schmitt trigger. The timing pulse generator (TPG) has three possible modes of operation. The first mode is a constant pulse output, or "repetitive" mode. In this mode, the TPG will produce trigger pulses at a rate proportional to

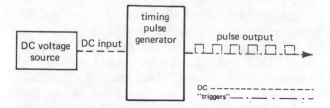

Fig. 5.8.   DC control of a timing pulse generator

the magnitude of the input DC voltage (fig. 5.8). In the repetitive mode, the TPG may also be controlled by an internal "pulse rate" pot. With this control, the firing rate may be manually adjusted to slower than once every 10 seconds. The second operational mode of the TPG is "single pulse," which allows the performer to manually fire individual pulses by pressing a button. This mode is very useful in performing difficult-to-program rhythmic patterns and achieving simple synchronizations with other events. The third, and perhaps most useful mode of operation is "start-stop." By using other trigger pulses, it is possible to program the automatic stopping and starting of pulse repetitions. Any trigger pulse applied to the "start" input will automatically put the TPG in the repetitive mode, and it will then produce pulses equal to its internal setting or in conjunction with its programming signal. As soon as another trigger is applied to the "stop" input, the TPG will stop. By using the start-stop mode, it is possible to program the TPG to perform unlimited functions.

A final luxury of the TPG is an availability of alternate outputs. The pulses are divided and sent

to two output jacks which can be separately monitored. By using only one of the two outputs, it is possible to cut the pulse rate exactly in half. The uses of such alternate outputs will be discussed in relation to gating techniques in chapter 6.

One of the most popular types of voltage sources is the "sequencer," or "sequential voltage source," or "sequential controller." The sequencer has an unlimited number of applications and consequently is probably the most complex of all the voltage sources. The main function of the sequencer is to supply the composer with a repetitious stage of preset voltages. The various designs may allow for as few as 2 or as many as 45 individual DC voltages to be produced in sequence at varying speeds. The basic design for a sequencer is illustrated in figure 5.9. Each individual voltage may be manually set by using the individual voltage pots. By controlling the speed of the sequencer with trigger pulses, it is possible to produce the voltages at a constant rate or the rate may be changed by varying the speed of the control trigger. The most commonly used source of trigger pulses with the sequencer are the timing pulse generator and the Schmitt trigger, because the rate of the pulses can be voltage controlled. Some sequencers are equipped with an internal speed control and do not necessarily have to depend on external trigger pulses.

An ostinato passage, as in figure 5.10, would very easily lend itself to sequencer applications. The sequencer would be patched to a voltage controlled oscillator and each increment of the se-

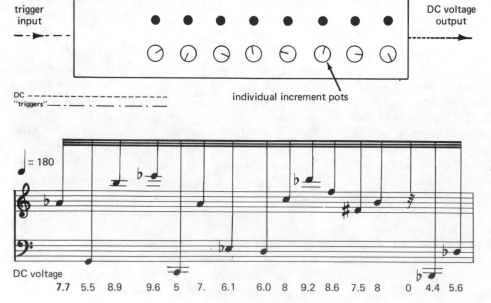

Fig. 5.9.   Sequencer

Fig. 5.10.   Notation and voltage relationships of a sequencer-controlled oscillator.

quencer would then be set to produce the desired frequency of the ostinato passage. The 14th increment would set at zero DC to allow for the 32nd note rest at that point. If the tempo is ♩ = 180, the 32nd notes must be at a speed of 24 per second. The sequencer can be programmed to fire at this rate by supplying it with trigger pulses at a rate of 24 Hz. The sequencer may continue to produce this pattern for any number of repetitions or may be programmed to stop after the first repetition. Sequencers with internal speed controls will produce the same tempo by manual setting of the pot.

A sequencer may have one output for the entire bank of increments or may have an individual output for each increment (fig. 5.11).

Just as with the voltage-controlled keyboards, the sequencer may have from one to three (or more) banks of individually controlled outputs. Each bank can have a different sequence of preset voltages, but the firing speed for all three banks will remain constant. When the first increment for the first bank fires, so does the first increment for all of the other banks. Whether or not the composer chooses to utilize the other banks is up to him. With multiple banks it is possible to program any sequence of frequencies with one set of pots and control the individual amplitudes with another set (fig. 5.12). By using a third output, it is possible to program very complex rhythmic patterns. Patching an output to sequencer's speed control, via a trigger generator or its own internal firing control, each progression to the next increment will change the speed proportional to the voltage of that particular increment (fig. 5.13).

Fig. 5.11. Sequencer with individual DC outputs.

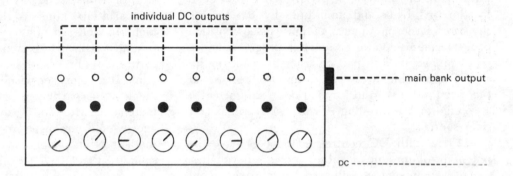

Fig. 5.12. Sequencer control of frequency and amplitude.

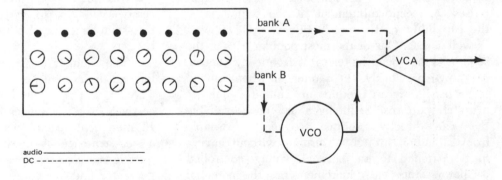

Fig. 5.13. Voltage loop to control sequencer's firing rate (period).

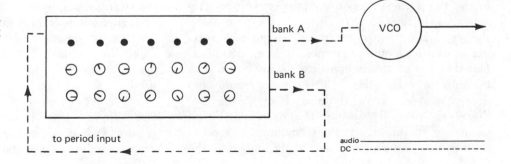

As an example, the relatively simple pattern below could be programmed in the following manner:

The first increment on the sequencer would be set to produce a voltage that, when applied to the sequencer's speed control, would advance to the next increment at a rate of once every 2 seconds. The second and third increments would have to produce a higher voltage which would advance the sequencer at a rate of twice in 1 second, and the fourth increment would have to advance the sequencer at a rate of every 1 1/2 seconds, continuing in the same manner for the time value of each note. If this process were being controlled by the third bank of voltages, with frequency controlled by the first bank and amplitude by the second, the three basic parameters of musical composition could be subjected to sequential programming.

Sequencers are particularly, but not exclusively, applicable to serial techniques because of the possibility of transforming any parameter to a voltage and controlling it with a sequential (serial) source.

Along with DC control, sequencers have the potential of producing other types of voltages. Since each increment will also fire a trigger voltage, the sequencer may be used as a type of trigger to control any other module that reacts to trigger pulses. A recent refinement of the sequencer is the capability of the production of AC voltages, as well as DC. One of the most popular uses of the sequencer has been in terms of frequency control. As shown previously, the sequencer when applied to an oscillator can produce an unlimited number of pitch patterns. Sequencers are now available that can directly produce frequencies variable from subaudio through ultrasonic, without having to be patched to an external, voltage-controlled oscillator. Since each increment has the potential of producing individual frequencies, it is possible to use the sequencer as a complex waveform generator. As discussed in chapter 2, complex waveshapes usually consist of several frequencies serving as non-harmonic overtones. It is an acoustical fact that the overtones can exist in any phase relationship to each other. (This phase relationship does, however, have a definite effect on the produced timbre.) By setting the increments of a sequencer to produce various frequencies and repeating this pattern at an extremely high rate, the individual frequencies will blend together and be perceived as overtones or sidebands. If the sequencer is firing rapidly enough, the individual firing times will function as different phase relationships of the total perceived sound. The individual amplitudes for the various components can be accomplished by using a second sequence bank to control an amplifier, as in figure 5.12. It must also be considered that the rapid change of frequency increments is actually a form of frequency modulation which will produce additional frequencies as FM sidebands. The switching from increment to increment will also produce various "clicks" and it may be desirable to remove them with a low-pass filter. By using longer pitch sequences, the perceived sound will become more complex and more sidebands will be produced.

The standard design of sequencers today consists of either 8, 12, or 16 increments. These are only arbitrary numbers decided on by the manufacturers and are of no special benefit to the composer. By using an "increment switch," it is possible to fire any number of successive increments in the bank. If a composer wishes to have only five increments in a particular pattern, he would set the increment switch to "5" and only the first five voltages would fire as a repetitive pattern. Another method of increment selection is with individual switches that allow for any number of individual voltages to be eliminated from the sequence. By switching out the unwanted increments, the composer is not always forced to use the preset successive voltages. In certain designed sequencers, this switching may be manual or controlled with triggers.

The number of increments may be extended beyond the normal range in several different ways. The simplest is to monitor each of the banks successively. If a sequencer has 3 banks consisting of 16 increments each, there is the possibility of a 48-set sequence. A more complex method of acquiring more increments involves the timing pulse generator and a voltage gate. This technique will be covered in chapter 6. If the sequencer is equipped with inputs for the voltage control of the voltage settings for the individual increments, the continuous variation of the control voltages will result in a continued variation of the output voltages, irrespective of the number of increments used.

The sequencer may be turned on and off by two different methods, depending on its manner of control. If it is being triggered by pulses from an external source, it may be stopped simply by stopping the source. Start-stop control of the timing pulse generator is extremely useful in this way. If the TPG is in the single pulse mode, the sequencer may be fired at will by the manual depression of the firing button. Sequencers with internal firing and control have self-contained trigger inputs for starting and stopping. The individual increments may also have a switch which will stop the firing action when that particular increment in the series is reached.

The sequencer is a relatively new innovation to the electronic music composer and its potential has not yet been fully recognized. Newer designs that allow for more modes of operation and faster repetition rates are providing the composer with many new methods of sound control.* Like any other technique involved with electronic music, the major part of the creative act is to find and exploit new methods of application. In the past few years most sequencer applications have been in terms of frequency control. As with any type of voltage control, sequential sources may be applied to any parameter, thus generating their own characteristic changes. The sequencer is capable of any type of repetitive or controlled series of events with a speed and accuracy dependent only on the programming voltages.

A sample/hold circuit is a special type of voltage processor which will also provide sequences of discrete voltage levels. Upon application of a trigger or pulse, the module will record the instantaneous level of an applied fluctuating voltage and will hold that particular voltage level until the next pulse is received. For example, if the sample/hold circuit were scanning a waveshape as illustrated by figure 5.14A, and received a trigger once every second (fig. 5.14B), the voltage output (usually DC) would be illustrated by figure 5.14C. If the triggers were spaced at irregular intervals (fig. 5.14D), the voltage output would be illustrated by figure 5.14E. Sequences of random voltages may be produced by scanning various bands of the white sound spectrum. If a sawtooth wave were to be processed by the sample/hold circuit (fig. 5.14F), the output would be a form of staircase wave (fig. 5.14G). The source of pulses may be external to the sample/hold module or it may have its own internal pulse source, commonly referred to as a "clock." Certain sample/hold circuits also contain their own internal white sound generator, which may be mixed with any input signal to provide varying amounts of unpredictability or may be used by itself in the production of steps of purely random voltage.

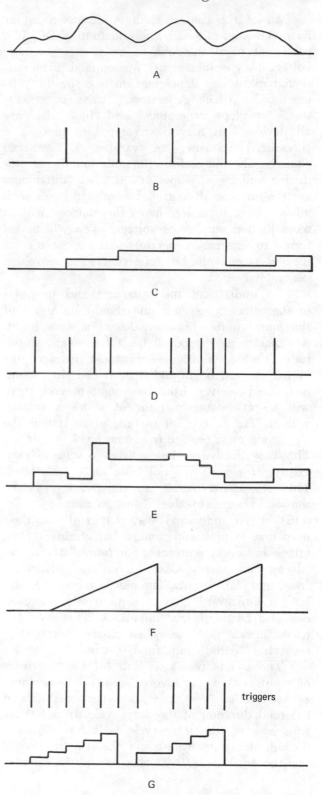

Fig. 5.14. Sample/hold processing

*Two examples of compositions using sequential voltage programming are *Silver Apples of the Moon* by Morton Subotnik (Nonesuch Records No. 71174) and *Joy Journey* by Warner Jepson.

All of the control voltages discussed so far have consisted of steady, non-fluctuating DC. If a particular parameter was to be changed, a new voltage (key or increment) was applied. Each particular event was dependent on one specific voltage level. "Attack generators," "transient generators," "envelope generators," and "bell gates" are all devices that may be triggered to produce a specialized sequence of varying DC voltage changes. They all perform the same function of producing voltage envelopes and the only differences are the number of controllable voltage levels each allows. For discussion here, the devices with a more limited number of voltage levels will be referred to as attack generators and the more complex devices will be referred to as envelope generators.

To understand the operation and functions of the attack generator, one should be aware of the more subtle characteristics of a sonic event. Any parameter of sound, be it frequency, amplitude, timbre, location, etc., must involve two events; it must begin and it must end. If a sound is to be perceived from beginning to end, there will be at least two transient states associated with it. The first event to take place is that the amplitude must change from one level to another. This may involve a change from a state of nonexistence or a rise or fall from an audible level. This "attack" may result as a constant level before the sound begins to "decay" into its next state (fig. 5.15). Even individual waveshapes derive their individual visual and sonic characteristics from attack and decay patterns. (The terms "attack" and "decay" are usually taken to represent respective "rise" and "fall" events. The inertia required to initiate a downward gliss or diminuendo, however, can also be considered an attack. Therefore, the terms "attack" and "decay" should be conceived as respective "initial" and "final" events.)

The instantaneous on and off characteristics of a pulse wave may involve an attack (sometimes referred to as "rise time") as long as 1/10th of the total duration of the duty cycle. In a 100 Hz square wave, the duty cycle lasts for .005 of a second (1:2 duty cycle) and the rise time could then be as slow as .0005 of a second. In complex waveshapes each frequency component may exhibit completely different attack and decay characteristics. Even the period between the attack and decay, known as the duration or "time constant," of the various frequency components is undergoing many subtle states of change. When triggered by a single pulse, the Attack Generator will usually provide three separate voltage states in sequence. The initial attack, in this case, is a voltage that rises from zero to a maximum DC level in a manually preset period of time. Controlled by a pot, the attack time may range from .005 of a second to 1 second or longer. The decay, or the voltage decrease, may range from .05 of a second to as slow as 5 seconds, also manually controlled by a pot. (These timings greatly vary, depending on the particular system design.) The time span, or duration between the attack and decay, can be manually set for a period of from .05 to 5 seconds. The duration can also be externally controlled as a function of the length of the trigger pulse. In using the attack generator, one must be aware that for normal applications the total attack, duration, and decay time must not be slower than the trigger frequency. If the attack generator is being triggered every second, and the total reaction time of the attack, duration, and decay is 1.5 seconds, there will be an overlap and certain programmed functions will not take place. Of course this characteristic can be used for some very definite advantages. If an attack generator with an attack time of 1 second, duration of 2 seconds, and decay of 2 seconds were applied to a voltage controlled oscillator, the following events would take place: after being triggered from any source of a trigger pulse, the attack generator would produce, via the VCO, a 1-second glissando to the maximum operating frequency of the oscillator. This frequency would remain constant for 2 seconds and then be followed by a glissando back down to the lowest operating frequency of the oscillator. (Methods of controlling the maximum and minimum voltage levels are discussed in relation to voltage attenuators and control voltage processors, see p. 35.) Applied to a voltage controlled amplifier, this same voltage pattern would produce a 1-second

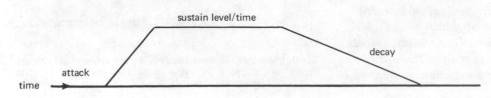

Fig. **5.15.** Control envelope produced by an attack generator.

crescendo, 2 seconds of sustained dynamic level, and a 2-second diminuendo.

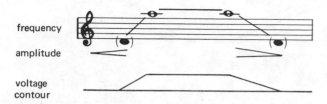

Fig. 5.16. Voltage contour controlling frequency and amplitude simultaneously.

If a second pulse triggers the attack generator while it is in the middle of an attack-duration-decay cycle, one of two things may happen, depending on the particular design. The voltage cycle may terminate at the spot where the new trigger is applied and a new attack beginning at zero DC will occur, or a new attack will occur beginning at the particular voltage level the cycle is at when the cycle is interrupted. By triggering the attack generator at various times during its cycle, many very unusual voltage contours may be generated. Various points of trigger applications are shown in figure 5.17.

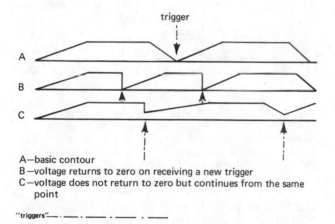

A—basic contour
B—voltage returns to zero on receiving a new trigger
C—voltage does not return to zero but continues from the same point

"triggers"— . — . — . — . —

Fig. 5.17. Interrupted voltage envelopes

The various voltage contours shown in figure 5.17 would have a congruent effect on whatever parameter it happened to be controlling. The same contours could be generated with a linear controller or with a voltage keyboard utilizing a portamento control. The use of the attack generator, however, makes fine voltage adjustments available at speeds that would be almost impossible to control manually.

More refined control devices have a greater number of voltage levels in their cycle. The envelope generator or transient generator is essentially an attack generator with another programmable voltage level. An "envelope" is the basic contour or outline of any waveshape, and figure 5.18 illustrates the envelopes of various waves. An ideal envelope generator would consist of an unlimited number of voltage levels which could be switched in and out to accommodate any desired waveshape. The most common design available

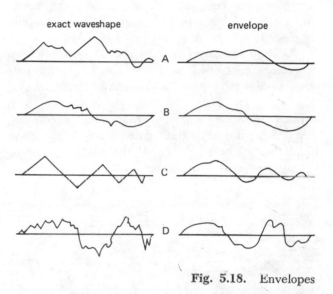

Fig. 5.18. Envelopes

today has four control devices. When triggered by an external pulse the envelope generator will produce a voltage which rises to a maximum DC level with a rise time as fast as 5 milliseconds or as slow as 10 seconds, again depending on design. As soon as the voltage level has reached maximum, it begins an "initial decay" which is also manually set to take between .005 and 10 seconds. During this time the initial decay voltage approaches a manually set "sustain" level that may range from zero DC to the system's maximum level. This sustain level will be maintained until the trigger voltage is released or for the duration of the remaining pulse length. The sustain control is not a temporal device like the rise time and initial decay pots, but is used to determine the amount or magnitude of the sustain voltage. The time period of the sustain voltage is dependent on the length of the applied trigger pulse. After the trigger voltage is released, there is a "final decay" which is also manually preset for any time period between .005 and 10 seconds. All four events

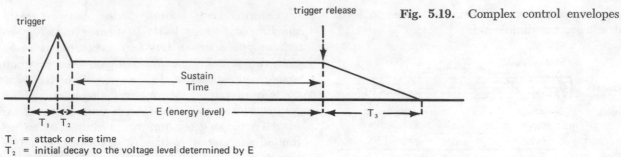

Fig. 5.19. Complex control envelopes

T_1 = attack or rise time
T_2 = initial decay to the voltage level determined by E
T_3 = final decay time
E = the length of E is determined by the length of the pulse

automatically take place in sequence upon receiving a single trigger pulse. Figure 5.19 is a graphic representation of a generated envelope.

If the envelope in figure 5.19 is applied to a voltage controlled oscillator, the frequency pattern shown in figure 5.20A may be produced. If the same envelope is applied to a voltage controlled amplifier which is processing a constant frequency, the amplitude pattern shown in figure 5.20B would be produced. If the envelope is used

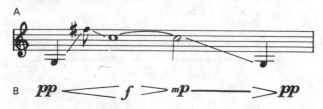

Fig. 5.20. Frequency pattern from a control envelope

to control both an oscillator and an amplifier the event shown in figure 5.21 would take place.

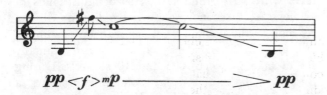

Fig. 5.21. Single envelope controlling both frequency and amplitude.

All of the above examples involve relatively slow time patterns. In actual usage, envelope generators are usually programmed to function at very rapid speeds. The onset behavior or attack of most acoustical events have different effects on the various components of a wave. Figure 5.22 shows the amplitude characteristics of the fundamental and first four overtones in the first 130 milliseconds of a violin attack (at a frequency of

435 Hz). It can be seen that the fundamental has a comparatively slow rise time as compared to the third overtone. The third overtone also has a very rapid initial decay time. In the electronic creation of attacks, the individual control of these various characteristics can be readily controlled with an envelope generator reacting on a voltage controlled amplifier. Observing the many amplitude changes in figure 5.22, one can imagine how an envelope generator with an unlimited number of program-

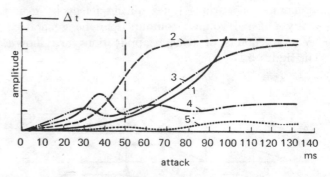

Fig. 5.22. Violin attack at 435 Hz. (Amplitude characteristics of a violin attack from *Music, Sound and Sensation: A Modern Exposition* by Fritz Winckel, Dover Publications, Inc., New York, 1967. Reprinted through permission of the publisher.)

mable voltage levels can be of great use in the control of transients. The various voltage levels of the initial rise times are achieved with the use of a voltage attenuator or a control voltage processor (see p. 35). By controlling a bank of envelope generators from a single trigger pulse, all of the components in figure 5.22 can be controlled. The delayed onset of the fifth overtone is accomplished by using a "trigger delay." A trigger delay will accept a trigger pulse from any available source and then produce its own output pulse at a preset time afterwards. This delay time may be from .002 to 10 seconds. In application to figure 5.22, a pulse would directly trigger four envelope

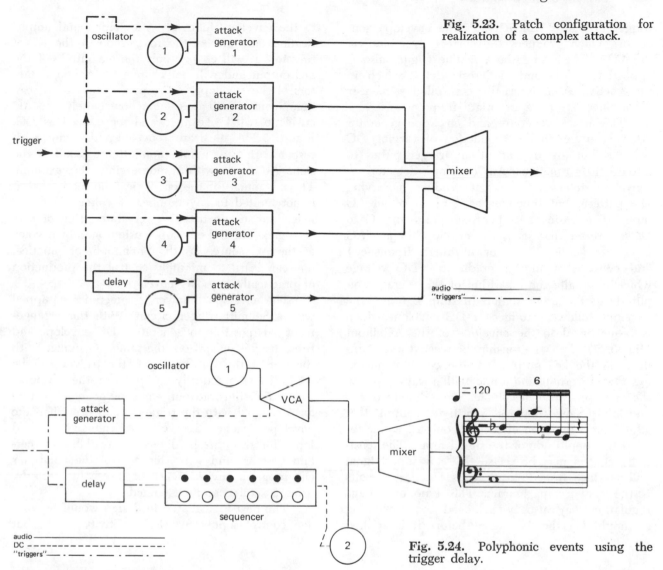

Fig. 5.23. Patch configuration for realization of a complex attack.

Fig. 5.24. Polyphonic events using the trigger delay.

generators and a trigger delay would initiate the fifth overtone about 22 milliseconds later (fig. 5.23). Each envelope generator would be programmed to produce the various rise, duration, and decay times for the particular wave component it is controlling.

Trigger delays may be designed as single units or they may be dual, with one chassis containing two individual units. In this case, the units may work independently of each other or they may be coupled together in one of two different manners. The "parallel" mode of operation will trigger both delays at the exact same time when one pulse is applied to either unit's input. The "series" mode will trigger the second delay at a preset time (.002 to 10 seconds) after the first delay fires. By using one initial trigger, it would be possible to produce three trigger pulses, all taking place at different

times. The initial pulse, from any trigger source, could be split to fire any module (attack generator, sequencer, etc.) and a dual trigger delay. After the preset period, one unit of the trigger delay will fire a pulse and, if in the "series" mode, fire the other delay unit after its preset period of time. By cascading several dual trigger delays together, it would be possible to simulate any number of sequential trigger pulses just as was done with the sequential voltage source. The trigger delay may be used to trigger any module that requires a trigger pulse and is by no means restricted to use with an attack generator. One manner in which figure 5.24 may be realized is to use a single pulse to trigger two events.* The initial

*This will serve only as an example of delay triggers, since there are much simpler methods that may be used to achieve this same event.

trigger in figure 5.24 activates the envelope generator, which produces the correct dynamics via the VCA (processing the C). The trigger also is applied to a 2 second (1/2 rest) delay, which, in turn, activates an internally controlled sequencer to produce the six appropriate frequencies.

The attack generator and envelope generator are very useful in the production of varying DC voltages but are dependent on trigger pulses to initiate their functions. An "envelope detector" or "envelope follower" also can produce a varying DC pattern, but functions as a result of an AC input. The basic envelope follower is an AC to DC converter that scans the envelope of any AC input (subaudio, audio or ultrahigh frequency) and converts it into a predictable DC voltage which is usually the logarithm of the average amplitude of the input signal. In simpler terms, the envelope follower produces a DC envelope which is proportional to the envelope of the AC input (fig. 5.25). The relationship between the AC input and the DC output may be constant, meaning that a certain amplitude will always produce the same proportional voltage. Some designs of the envelope follower have a "sensitivity control" that allows for a selection of the DC output, no matter what the ampltitude of the signal input. The sensitivity control may be set so that any input signal will produce from 0 to 15 volts DC (if 15 volts is the system's maximum). This type of voltage regulation may also be achieved by attenuating or amplifying the AC signal before it is applied to the envelope follower. Attenuation and amplification only affects the magnitude of the wave; therefore it will change only the magnitude of the DC output and will not change the temporal factors of the envelope. A "response time" or "decay time" control will determine how closely the AC envelope will be scanned and reproduced as DC. Figure 5.26A illustrates envelope following with response time at a minimum; figure 5.26B is the same AC input with response time at maximum. The advantage of the envelope follower is that it is not limited to any number of voltage levels or maximum sustain times. A very interesting process is to generate DC envelopes using one's own voice as the AC source. With a minimum of practice, one can learn to minutely control the production of practically any DC envelope.

The envelope follower is sometimes equipped with a Schmitt trigger circuit. With this arrangement it is possible to generate a DC envelope and fire a trigger pulse from the same AC signal. With the use of the threshold pot, the trigger can be set to fire at practically any point on the envelope. Figure 5.27 illustrates an envelope generation from an AC signal with the trigger set to fire when the envelope reaches 3.5 volts. A voltage-controlled input for this threshold level is available on certain designs, and with this control the composer can program any sequence of threshold levels by using a sequence of DC signals.

The next logical step in design would be voltage control inputs for the sensitivity levels, but

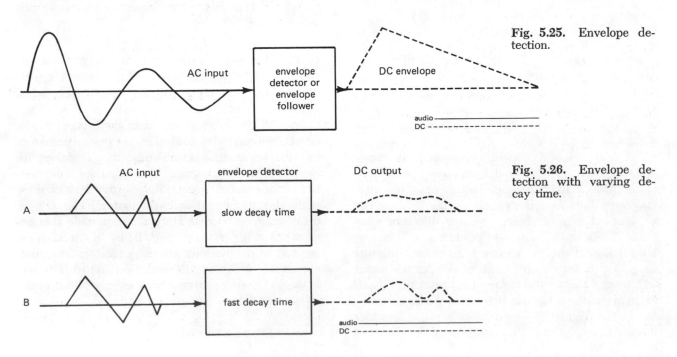

Fig. 5.25. Envelope detection.

AC input   envelope detector or envelope follower   DC envelope

audio ————
DC - - - - - - - -

Fig. 5.26. Envelope detection with varying decay time.

AC input   envelope detector   DC output

A   slow decay time

B   fast decay time

audio ————
DC - - - - - - - -

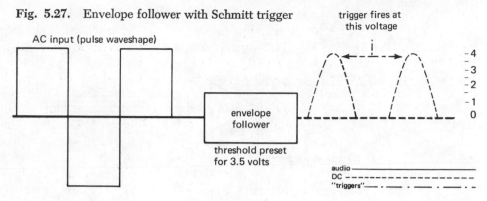

Fig. 5.27. Envelope follower with Schmitt trigger

even with all of the various kinds of control there are, there are many instances in which a composer cannot produce the correct voltage to control some special event. A device may produce the correct voltage pattern or contour but the magnitude may be too high or too low. In other cases the amount of voltage may be exactly right but the timing of the various level changes may be incorrect. These situations are often corrected by reprogramming, but many times the composer is limited to certain programming methods which cannot be altered. Because of these circumstances, certain types of control-voltage processing equipment has been made available. Since control voltages are usually in the form of DC, these processors can be thought of as attenuators and amplifiers for DC voltages. The simplest processor is a voltage attenuator. It consists of an input, an output, and an attenuation pot. An example of its application will explain its operation. Suppose the event in figure 5.28 is to be programmed with the use of an attack generator. By controlling an oscillator with the attack generator, there is no problem with the attack, sustain, or decay *times,* since they are all manually controllable by pots. The problem is that the attack voltage rises to a maximum peak every time the attack generator receives a trigger pulse. This, of course, sends the frequency of the VCO far above the desired pitch. The easiest solution to the problem is to put a voltage attenuator between the attack generator and the VCO. The attenuator will limit the magnitude of the voltage but will not affect any of the temporal parameters such as rise time, duration, or decay time. Figure 5.29

Fig. 5.28. Frequency control with an attenuated control envelope.

illustrates the program envelope before and after it is attenuated. (Certain designs of voltage attenuators will process AC as well as DC voltages in the same manner; these are referred to as being "AC-DC coupled.")

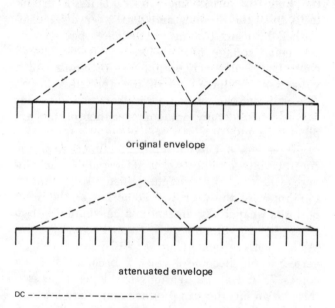

original envelope

attenuated envelope

DC

Fig. 5.29. Envelope attenuation

Another type of control-voltage processing device is commercially, and logically, known as a control voltage processor (CVP). This processor has a multiple of inputs and outputs and serves four different functions. First, the CVP is a source of internally produced DC voltages which may be manually controlled by a pot. Second, the CVP is capable of taking any external DC voltage and attenuating it as described above. Third, the CVP has a pot for creating mixtures between the internal and externally applied voltages. This is an indispensable tool for creating unusual envelopes. If a composer wishes to have a rising crescendo

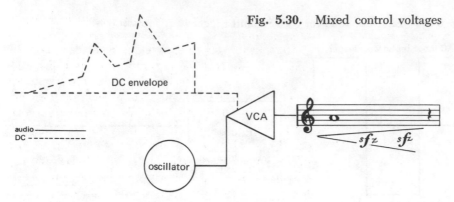

Fig. 5.30.   Mixed control voltages

with periodic amplitude surges (fig. 5.30), it would require a control envelope of a very specialized nature. Mixing a very slow rise time, zero duration, and zero decay from an attack generator with two faster pulses from some other DC voltage source will produce this envelope. Note that the first "sfz" attack must be of a lesser magnitude than the second, and this is easily accomplished by using the mixer attenuator pot for that particular voltage input. Many types of voltage-controlled devices have a multiple of inputs which will create a sum of all of the applied voltages. The value of the mixer pots is that they allow for the selection of any amount of either of the applied voltages.

The fourth and most unique function of the control voltage processor is its capability to "invert" voltages. Any voltage applied to the "inverting" input of the CVP will come out as the exact opposite shape. For instance, a maximum system voltage of 10 volts inverted would become 0 volts. With a voltage range from 0 to 10 volts, 1 volt inverted would become 9 volts, 2 becomes 8, 3 becomes 7, and so on. Various envelopes processed through an inverter can produce some very interesting controls. Since most voltage envelopes begin at 0, the inverted version will then begin at the maximum voltage of the system. This may be varied by either attenuating the output or amplifying the input to the inverter. Figure 5.31 illustrates several control contours and their respective inversions.

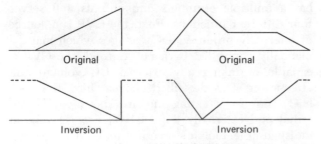

Fig. 5.31.   Inverted envelopes

An inverter is not necessarily part of a control voltage processor and may be found as a separate module on some systems.

Another method of producing constant or varying control voltages is with "photosensitive controls." In electronic circuitry there are many components that are used to limit or block voltage. Their rating (how much voltage or current they are capable of blocking) may be permanently fixed or may be manually controlled as with a potentiometer. Photosensitive devices will vary their rating in relationship to an applied light source. In simpler terms, a photosensitive controller is a light-controlled pot. A "photosensitive oscillator" will usually generate zero Hz when no light is applied to its light controlled resistor (pot). The photo-oscillator will generate a maximum frequency when a maximum amount of light is applied. A photo-amplifier will provide signal amplification in direct relationship to the amount of light applied to its photo-controller. (Photosensitive controls are very applicable to spatial modulating devices and will be discussed in detail in chap. 9.)

Direct voltage can be controlled with light by using "photodiodes." An absence of light to the photodiode may result in zero volts DC and an increase in the amount of light (usually measured in lumins) will produce a proportional increase in DC voltage. The amount of light can be controlled in two different manners. A change in voltage to the light source will change the intensity, but this method is usually inadequate because the control of voltage is the desired outcome. The most useful methods of controlling light intensity have been with the use of film. By placing film with varying levels of translucency between the light source and the photocell, it is possible to produce many voltage levels (fig. 5.32). By making lengths of film with various translucent patterns and driving it in front of the photocell with

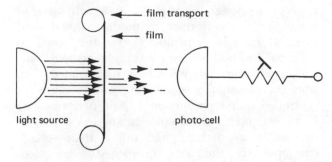

Fig. 5.32. Photo-control with film

a motorized transport system, it is possible to create practically any type of fluctuating DC (or AC) voltage pattern. If a film consisted of a series of transparent frames in alternation with opaque frames, the produced voltage would be a pattern of voltage pulses. The pulse speed could be varied by varying the speed of the transport system and the pulse magnitude would be a function of the translucency of the frames. Any voltage envelope could be produced in the same manner.

Punched tape control also uses a transport system. A strip of paper containing a series of perforations is passed over a switch by a transport system. The perforations are detected in one of several manners which either trigger a voltage on or off, usually by means of light-sensitive switches or relays. These voltages are usually preset and can be used to control any voltage-sensitive device. The "reader" usually has eight or twelve lateral switches which will accommodate a lateral series of perforations in the paper. Each series of punches can be used to control a different parameter (fig. 5.33).

The Coordinome, developed by Emmanuel Ghent at the Columbia-Princeton Electronic Music Center, is essentially a punched tape reader which can be programmed to control all of the parameters of sound as well as distributing cue signals to the performers for the coordination of live and prerecorded music. (See Emmanuel Ghent, "The Coordinome in Relation to Electronic Music," *Electronic Music Review*, no. 1, Jan. 1967, pp.

33-38, for a detailed discussion of punched paper programming.)

The advantages of film and punched paper programming are that the program is a physical entity which can be saved to be used at any future time; punched paper can control as many simultaneous sequences as there are switches on the reader; an entire composition may be programmed on film or paper and played in much the same manner as player pianos play rolls of music. The major disadvantage is the preparation of the film on paper. Using control pots, the composer can allow for a certain amount of experimentation in his compositional process and his only loss is the time it takes to turn a dial and listen to the results. With film and paper programming, however, there is a great deal of time involved in the actual physical preparation of the sequences, and if the composer wishes to recompose some particular event, it involves a complete physical reprogramming of that portion of the film or tape.

In certain instances the composer may wish to inject aleatory events into his music. Using all of the devices discussed so far, the programming of truly random magnitudes and occurrences of voltages could be a very involved process. A random voltage may be programmed by patching voltages through enough triggers and controllers that the composer could not accurately predict the outcome, but this usually will tie up most of the available programming equipment in the system. There are two ways in which random voltages may be achieved with a minimum of difficulty. The first method is simply with a "random voltage source." Upon receiving a trigger pulse, such a generator will produce a random DC voltage for as long as the trigger voltage is present. This is one instance in which pulse length is very important. A series of pulses at the rate of one every five seconds with a 50 percent pulse length will produce a series of pulses, each pulse lasting 2.5 seconds.

If random voltage is used to control an oscillator, the same effects may be produced by fre-

Fig. 5.33. Punched tape control

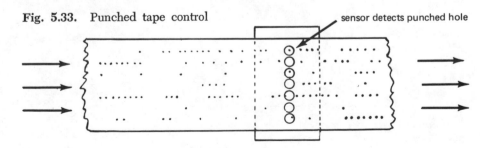

quency modulating with different bands of white sound. Since white sound is defined as a continual spectrum of all audio frequencies, an AC to DC conversion of this spectrum by means of a sensitive Envelope Follower will result in random DC voltages. The degree of activity and magnitude of the random voltages may be controlled by means of the sensitivity control on the envelope follower or by filtering the white sound before it is converted to DC.

Any audio or temporal art can never be fairly represented with words, and the only real representation of voltage control is in the actual practice of its application to a real time situation. A graphic explanation of voltage control may leave the reader with the opinion that the time spent on preparing the desired voltage is not justified by the end results. In acoustically produced music, all the composer is required to do is make the appropriate design on paper, and it will serve as a cue for the performer to produce the desired event. It must be remembered that the "standard notation" has been in use for many years and some people take its comprehension for granted. But would a person first embarking on the study of controlled sound production (music performance) find the standard music notation any less time consuming to comprehend and utilize than voltage envelopes? In the same manner, the composer working in the field of electronic music very quickly learns to use voltage programming in the same way that standard notation is used as a form of visual programming. And as the composer becomes more and more familiar with the music and acoustical counterparts of electronic manipulations, the production of the desired control voltages is no more a task than the copying of a score and parts.

gating

In terms of electronic music, the gate is a specialized type of voltage-controlled amplifier (VCA). A gate, in simplest terms, is a circuit which will block or pass information when cued externally by AC or DC voltage, light, manual operation, etc. In computer applications a gate is a logic circuit which has two inputs and one output. The presence of an output signal depends on which inputs are receiving a cue signal and the function of the particular gate. There are four basic types of gates used in computer design; AND, NAND, OR, and NOR. Figure 6.1 illustrates the basic gate functions for the two inputs. When

input pulse		output pulse			
A	B	AND	NAND	OR	NOR
			▭		▭
	▭		▭	▭	
▭			▭	▭	
▭	▭	▭		▭	

Fig. 6.1. Computer gating functions

dealing with an AND gate, both inputs A and B must be activated at the same time to produce an output pulse. NAND gates have just the inverse function and will exhibit an output pulse in every instance except when both inputs receive signals (cue pulses). The characteristics for the other two gate functions can also be observed in figure 6.1. (For more information on computer music see Max V. Mathews, *The Technology of*

Computer Music [Cambridge, Mass.: M.I.T. Press, 1969].) In electronic music applications, a gate controls signals by blocking or allowing their passage to the next step in their processing (audio amplifier, tape recorder, modulator, filter, etc.). Some type of control cue must be applied to the gate before it will pass the audio signal. Perhaps the simplest control is a manual switch such as a push-button or toggle switch. Each time the switch is depressed the circuit is closed and the signal is permitted to flow to the output. When the switch is released the circuit is opened and the signal does not reach the output. Although

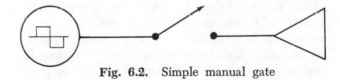

Fig. 6.2. Simple manual gate

this is a very simple device, it can save the composer many hours over a splicing block. If a rhythmic sequence of pitches as in figure 6.3 were to be produced by editing, the composer would have to calculate the exact length of tape required for each note and the amount of leader tape required for each rest. He would then record several seconds of the 82.4 Hz signal on tape and then cut the required lengths. Finally he would have to

Fig. 6.3. Pitch sequence

splice them in sequence interspersed with the corresponding lengths of leader tape. This process can be greatly simplified by routing the audio signal through the manually controlled gate and pressing the switch at the desired time for the desired duration, much like operating a telegraph key. The only precaution that must be observed with this type of gate is that the switch should be the shorting or make-before-break type or there will be an audible "click" on each attack as the circuit is closed.

In much the same manner, the volume control on an ordinary amplifier or pre-amp may be used to manually gate signals. The advantage here is that to a certain degree the amplitude level can be controlled. The operator will usually have the facility to gate the signal at whatever level he chooses. The disadvantage is that there can be no abrupt switching on and off of the signal. No matter how fast the operator turns the pot, there will always be an audible attack and decay time as part of the envelope. Of course there are many instances in which a definite attack and decay characteristic would be a desired part of the produced envelope. In such an instance the composer would probably use an envelope generator and a VCA as described in chapter 5. This raises a question concerning the difference between a gate and a VCA. In many cases the terms are interchangeable and this often leads to confusing situations. Usually the VCA is used to sustain the signal at a definite level (DC application), or in other situations it may be used as an envelope generator (varying DC or subaudio AC application), or as an amplitude modulator (AC application). A gate, on the other hand, usually has a more non-periodic function (compared with amplitude modulation) and is used to initiate various "one-time" events or to provide rhythmic or sporadic bursts of sound. Therefore, the difference between a gate and a VCA is not particularly in the circuit design but rather in the application.

Manually operated gates are often inadequate due to very high accuracy and speed requirements. Consequently, most gates found within an electronic music situation have facilities for voltage control. The simplest type of voltage-controlled gate is one that provides a signal or information* input and output plus one input for a gating pulse. Every time a pulse or DC voltage is applied to the pulse input, the information will be permitted to pass to the output. If there is no applied pulse, there is no information output. The duration that the gate is open depends on the pulse length and

the relationship is one to one. A pulse lasting for 1 second, when applied to a gate, will permit the information signal to be present at the output for 1 second (fig. 6.4), assuming an instant reaction time of the gate, which is very often not the case. By using a pulse-activated gate, it is possible to block or pass signals at any rate, depending on the

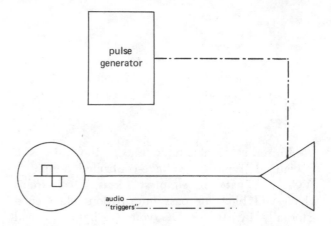

Fig. 6.4. Pulse-activated gate

rate of the cue pulses. The length of the information output signals can be varied by using a pulse generator equipped with a pulse length control (see chap. 5, p. 25). Keep in mind that this is a true gate which only allows for the abrupt on-and-off switching functions; there is no provision for any type of envelope shaping. Unlike a VCA, this type of gate has no way of controlling the amplitude of each gated output. The pulse is usually a trigger function and will open the gate to produce a maximum gain each time a pulse is fired. Due to this problem, some gate designs have a manual gain control that may be set before or during the gated events or sequence of events. With this design the pulse will open the gate to the maximum level set by the gain pot. In this manner it is possible to achieve gated sequences of varying amplitudes along with manually operated crescendi and diminuendi.

In many instances very rapid sequences of signals with individually varying amplitudes are required. Often the pulses are fired too rapidly for each signal output to be manually controlled. In this case a gate is needed which will react not just to the trigger pulses, but also to sequences of different DC voltages. A gated sequence of

*The term "audio input" is not used here, since subaudio and ultrasonic signals may also be gated.

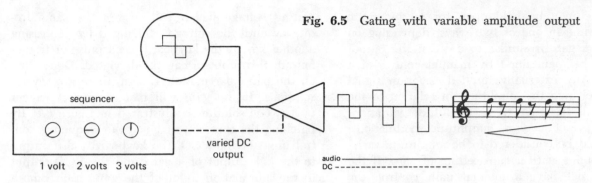

Fig. 6.5 Gating with variable amplitude output

sequencer

varied DC output

1 volt   2 volts   3 volts

audio ——————————————
DC - - - - - - - - - - - - - - - -

crescendoing frequencies could be produced by setting a sequencer with each successive increment having a slightly higher output DC voltage. If the sequencer output is patched to a gate control input, as each successive pulse voltage rises the output level of the gated information will be higher (fig. 6.5). Again, the length of each output signal would be dependent on the length of the DC pulse. If the sequencer is not equipped with a pulse-length control, there are still some possibilities for using other pulse sources to control duration. By using the DC output of a voltage keyboard, one could have direct control over the DC duration by how long the key was depressed (providing the keyboard had a "no-hold" function). But if circumstances, such as speed or number of consecutive pulses, dictate the use of a sequencer, a certain amount of duration control could be achieved by using one of the sequencer's output banks to control its own firing speed (such as with external control of a timing pulse generator or Schmitt trigger; see chap. 5, p. 25). This would vary the pulse length by varying the firing speed of the sequencer. Although this is a very useful technique, it requires careful programming to achieve the desired results.

The type of gating described above is an abrupt switching with the possibility of varying the switching rate and the output duration. This effect can be simulated with the use of a VCA and a square wave program. By setting the manually controlled gain of the VCA at zero, the VCA will provide no output unless an AC program signal is applied. Since a square wave exhibits an instantaneous change in polarity, it will periodically activate the VCA and provide a gating function similar to a pulse-activated gate. If the square wave is being generated by a pulse-wave oscillator, the gating speed could then be controlled by the pulse-wave oscillator's frequency and the duration could be varied by changing the duty cycle. In using this technique one precaution must be observed. Each half cycle, a positive pulse followed by a negative, may open the gate, thereby activating the VCA at a rate twice as fast as the program frequency, separated only by the instantaneous rise and fall time of the pulse wave voltage. With the manually controlled gain level set at zero, the VCA usually does not react to negative pulses. But in the event that negative pulses produce a rise in the output gain, there is still a solution to the problem. By routing the program signal through a special clipping circuit (see chap. 12), it is possible to eliminate the negative portion of the cycle but maintain the original frequency. Applying the clipped wave to a VCA, the absence of the negative cycle would result in the desired gating effect. The amount of space between the positive pulses can also be varied by changing the duty cycle.

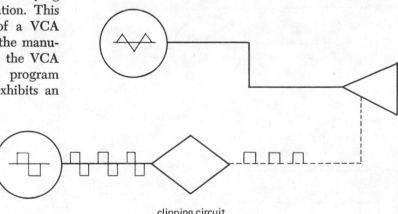

Fig. 6.6. Gating using a VCA and a clipped pulse wave (AC).

clipping circuit

A gate may be held open for an indefinite length of time in one of two ways, depending on design. If a gate is similar to a VCA, the output level may be maintained by manual control of a gain pot. Any externally applied program signal will then change the amplitude in relation to the preset level. In strict terms amplitude variations around a preset level is "amplitude modulation"; gating could be considered to be amplitude variations beginning with a gain setting of zero. If the gate does not have a manual gain control, the output may be sustained at a constant level by the application of an external DC voltage. Since DC is a non-fluctuating voltage, it will hold the amplitude level of the information signal at an intensity proportional to the applied voltage, if the VCA is operating on a linear or exponential scale. A good source of DC voltage for this application is the control voltage processor (see chap. 5, p. 35), since this leaves the keyboard sequencers, etc., free for other applications. Gates of this design may also be equipped with a gain pot and, in this case, it is a true potentiometer. The pot controls the full potential of the externally applied DC voltage. In other words, although a DC voltage may have the capability to produce a gain increase of 60 db, the manual pot can attenuate the output information to produce a gain level ranging from zero to 60 db (full potential).

The gate or VCA is not exclusively used to produce modulation effects. One of its most valuable uses is with a keyboard that sustains a particular output voltage until the next key is depressed—referred to as "hold-mode" or "hold function." If the output voltage is constantly applied to a voltage-controlled oscillator (VCO), it is impossible to get any temporal separation between the changes of frequency without the use of a gate. If a key is depressed, it will keep generating voltage which will sustain the same frequency until the voltage is changed by depressing another key. If the keyboard has a pulse or trigger output, this problem can be alleviated. Depending on the particular module design, there are several solutions. If the gate will react to direct trigger pulses, one solution is illustrated in figure 6.7. By patching the control voltage to the frequency control input of the VCO, the keyboard pulse output to the pulse input of a gate, and the VCO output to the information input of the gate, each time a key is depressed it will affect the output frequency of the VCO and at the same time will open the gate. The drawback to this arrangement is that the keyboard may not have provisions for controlling the pulse length so that the output duration is a direct function of the time the key is depressed. A second and perhaps more applicable solution is shown in figure 6.8. By using the pulse output of the keyboard to trigger an attack generator, which in turn controls a gate or VCA, the "on" time of the gate as well as controlled attack and decay times can be manipulated. (As soon as one becomes concerned with attack and decay times, a certain amount of envelope shaping is implied, however, and in the strict sense it cannot be called gating, but the composer is concerned with results and not with a strict categorization of techniques.)

Gating is also very useful in creating various types of percussive sounds. In order for the human ear to perceive a sound as a recognized pitch, the sound must have a duration of at least 4 milliseconds, depending on frequency. This duration is a standard for a 2k Hz sine wave at medium intensity. The duration threshold for pitch recognition actually depends on a combination of waveshape, frequency, intensity, and attack characteristics. Higher frequencies, up to about 2.5k Hz have shorter duration thresholds than lower frequencies. A 100 Hz sine wave may have to last for a duration of about 27 ms before the pitch can be perceived. The duration threshold is also affected by "onset transients." If a sound is suddenly gated with a zero

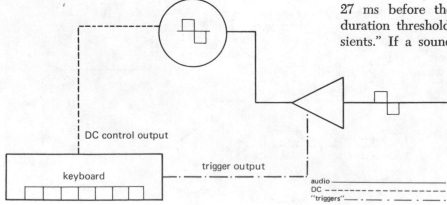

DC control output

keyboard

trigger output

audio ——————————
DC – – – – – – – – – – –
"triggers" –·–·–·–·–·–·–·

Fig. 6.7. Gating in synchronization with voltage-controlled frequency changes.

Fig. 6.8. Gating with synchronized frequency change using an attack generator.

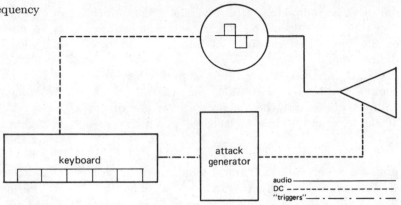

or instantaneous attack time, the switching will result in a great number of complex transients which will mask the actual frequency, requiring a longer duration for pitch recognition. A higher amplitude will also contribute to the production of onset transients. Under these circumstances the sound is perceived as a short "click" or "snap." By adding longer attack times to the gating function, the noise factor is reduced and the duration threshold is shortened. The gate can be pulsed with virtually no attack time, so by using a minimal duration time many interesting percussive sounds can be created. The gating of a relatively high frequency with a very short duration will produce a brittle click similar to the sound of a manual switch. By lowering the frequency of the gated signal, the sound will remain quite percussive but will have more resonance, much like the sound of temple blocks. It is possible to produce various types of percussive patterns by using a keyboard (or any other control voltage source) to determine pitch, and then gate the frequencies with a pulse output.

The type of waveshape used will also have a definite effect on the timbre of the percussion sounds, as well as on the duration threshold. A waveshape with many overtones, when gated with an instantaneous attack, will result in a multitude of onset transients and will therefore require a longer duration threshold for pitch recognition. Taking the inverse approach, the more complex waveshapes may be used to produce percussive effects with longer duration times than the more simple waveshapes. More complex waves also usually result in a sharper and more percussive sound when gated as described above. Even more variety can be achieved by using very complex waveshapes, such as modulation products. Acoustically produced percussion sounds usually consist of spectrums of non-harmonic overtones, so in attempting their re-creation it would make sense to begin with timbres which also contain non-harmonic overtones. Figure 6.9 is one possible method of using ring-modulated products gated by means of an attack generator and VCA controlled via a keyboard to produce percussive effects. The 20 ms

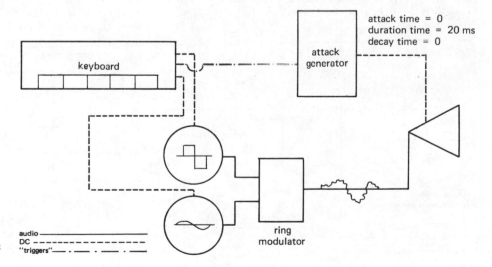

Fig. 6.9. Percussive effects

duration is completely arbitrary, since the duration time will depend on the frequency spectrum of the modulated product, its intensity, and the desired sound.

Carrying this concept one step further, the composer should also consider the possibilities of gating white sound, the human voice, or any other available sound source to achieve percussive effects.

A combination of two gates can be used to produce a very unusual sound which may be described as a "pulsed mix." In many communication systems it is a common practice to compress information by means of a specialized type of gating. It is possible to remove a certain amount of a message and still have it convey information. As an example, consider the conversational opener, "How are you?" It would be possible to eliminate a great deal of sound from that statement and still maintain the same level of intelligence. The sonic duration of the 'H,' the 'R' and the 'OU' could almost be cut in half and the sentence would still be recognizable in context. With these seemingly unnecessary sounds eliminated, the message could be transmitted in almost two-thirds of the time it would otherwise take. This type of compression can be accomplished very easily by gating. To carry the process one step further, it would also be possible to periodically eliminate a certain amount of information and still leave enough to allow it to be recognized. If conversation is being gated in bursts or durations of .9 seconds separated by a silence of .1 second, there would be very little information loss. This could be accomplished by using a VCA programmed by a 1 Hz pulse wave with a 9:10 duty cycle; the positive portion of the wave would pass information (A) and the negative portion would block information. The

next step in such a pulsed mixing process would be to insert other information (B) into the .1 second silence. This could be done by using a second gate which would react only to negative signals, or by routing the signal through a voltage inverter. By applying this portion of the pulse wave to a second VCA, the second VCA would open as the first gate is closed and vice versa. The final step would be to mix both outputs into a single line. The result would be a recurring cycle of .9 seconds of message A followed by .1 seconds of message B. By raising or lowering the program frequency (pulse wave), the gating rate would vary but the ratio between the two outputs would remain 9:1. The ratio could then be changed by changing the duty cycle of the pulse wave.

Depending on the nature of the two gated signals, the result of the pulsed-mix technique is an abrupt sampling back and forth between two signals. The resultant effect is dependent on the frequency of the program signal. If the gating is at a very slow rate, the ear may discriminate between each "on" and "off" portion of the two signals. If the program frequency approaches the audio range, however, the result is very similar to a combination of amplitude and frequency modulation. If the two gated signals exhibit exactly the same frequency and amplitude characteristics, but different overtone structures, this technique could be used as a specialized method of timbre modulation.

Using the same technique, a 1:1 ratio could be achieved by using the alternate pulse outputs of a pulse generator as described on page 26 of chapter 5. The main consideration here is that since the pulses are just alternations of a single pulse output, the firing time will be cut in half.

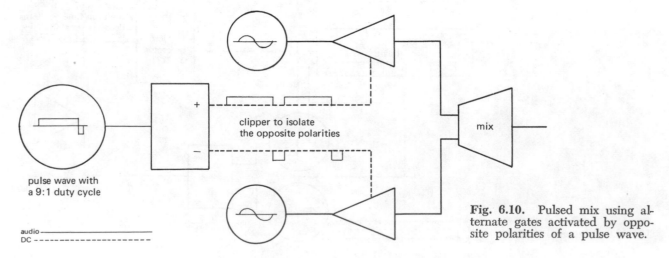

pulse wave with
a 9:1 duty cycle

clipper to isolate
the opposite polarities

mix

audio ————————
DC - - - - - - - - - - - - - - - -

Fig. 6.10. Pulsed mix using alternate gates activated by opposite polarities of a pulse wave.

Fig. 6.11. Pulsed mix using alternate outputs of a pulse generator.

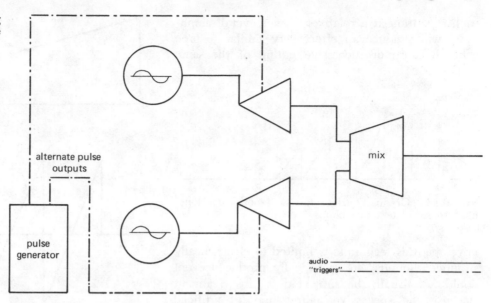

Gating with alternate outputs can also be used to double the number of increments on most sequencers. By using output bank A to control VCA-a and output bank B to control VCA-b, and then gating the two VCAs with alternate pulses from the same pulse generator used to fire a 5-increment sequencer, the following sequences would be produced due to the alternation of the pulses to the two respective gates. The output of gate A would be a repeated sequence of frequencies produced by increments 1a, silence because the gate is closed due to the lack of a pulse, 3a, silence, 5a, silence, 2a, silence, 4a, and silence. Gate B's output would be frequencies produced

by increments 2b, 4b, 1b, 3b, and 5b, with the corresponding silences. By mixing these two sequences down to a single line, the sequence would be 1a, 2b, 3a, 4b, 5a, 1b, 2a, 3b, 4a, and 5b. The application of this procedure to a 10-increment sequencer would produce a sequence of 20 different voltages and a 15-increment sequencer could produce 30 different voltages.

When working with electronically generated signals, the gate or VCA can be used to simulate "tape repeat" or "tape echo" (see chap. 10 for a detailed explanation of tape echo). If a particular sound is produced with an electronically controlled envelope, then repetitions of the envelope, with

Fig. 6.12. Extending the number of increments of a sequencer with a pulse generator and alternate gating.

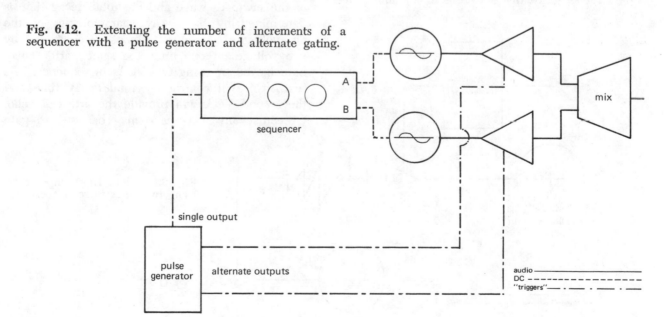

each repetition at a relatively lower overall amplitude, will produce an effect very similar to tape echo. Because of successive gating of the same

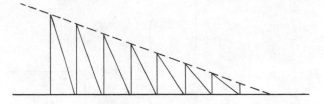

Fig. 6.13. Gradually decaying sawtooth envelopes used to simulate tape echo.

envelope, this technique is limited to electronically produced sounds; an acoustically produced event could not usually be subjected to this treatment because the successive gating imposes artificial attack and decay characteristics which are usually very different from the original.

The most successful method of producing multiple envelopes is by applying two control voltages to a VCA. The first voltage is the DC voltage which determines the amount of time the total successive attacks will take to fade to zero gain. This can be done with an attack generator or envelope generator set with an instantaneous attack time and a relatively long decay. If the decay time is 5 seconds, the controlled audio signal will gradually diminuendo over a 5-second period (fig. 6.14A). By exponentially adding a very low frequency sawtooth wave (fig. 6.14B) to the VCA, the combination will produce multiple attacks gradually decaying in a manner de-

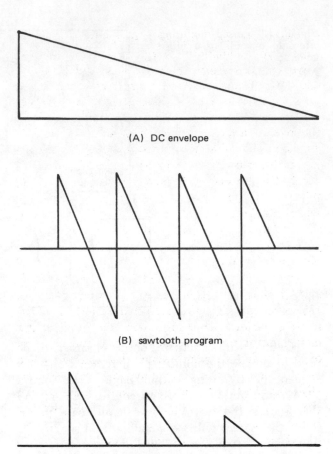

(A) DC envelope

(B) sawtooth program

(C) composite envelope

Fig. 6.14. Multiple envelopes

termined by the original envelope (fig. 6.14C). This technique, of course, requires an AC-coupled gate. The echo rate is determined by the frequency of the sawtooth wave and the total decay time is determined by the decay characteristics of the DC voltage. If the VCA cannot be controlled by two voltages at one time, the same pattern may be achieved by using two VCAs in sequence. The first VCA will control the total decay time and the second VCA will provide the artificial echo. Of course any waveshape may be used to gate

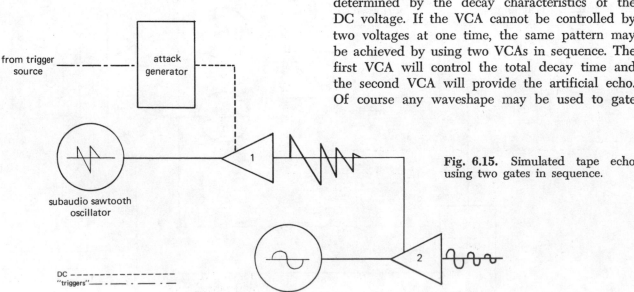

from trigger source

attack generator

subaudio sawtooth oscillator

DC ----------
"triggers" ---- · ---- · ---- · -

Fig. 6.15. Simulated tape echo using two gates in sequence.

the audio signal, but the sawtooth gives the closest approximation to true tape echo. A sine wave will provide a gradual attack and decay to each "repetition," while a pulse wave will result in abrupt bursts with sudden attacks and decays. By the same token, the composer should not limit the overall attack and decay pattern to the DC envelope shown in the previous examples. By using an inverse of the envelope described, an effect much like reverse echo may be produced (fig. 6.16A). In the same manner, a "sine" envelope will result in a gradual crescendo and diminuendo of the gated sounds (fig. 6.16B), and a more complex envelope will produce comparable amplitude changes (fig. 6.16C).

By using tape delay and loop boards, an effect of time distortion can be produced (see p. 121 in chap. 12). The recorded sound is monitored at various points on a loop board and is also monitored at the same moment that one or more of the heads is picking up sound at another place on the loop. Each of the playback heads is usually equipped with some manner of gain control (in the individual pre-amps) which permits the composer to mix the various playback points as he wishes. By subjecting each playback head to individual gating, an effect of "temporal shifting" can be produced.* As an example, suppose that the sentence, "Yes, I bet you can," is recorded and the tape is made into a loop and placed on a board with five different playback heads, each with their

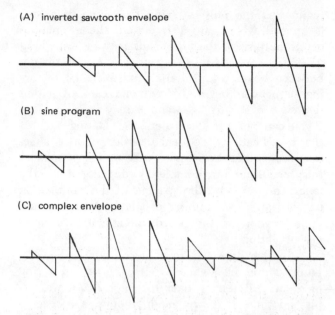

(A) inverted sawtooth envelope

(B) sine program

(C) complex envelope

Fig. 6.16. Other envelopes for producing unusual simulated echo effects.

own pulse-controlled gate (fig. 6.17). If gate 1 is pulsed at various intervals, the monitored output would be the elimination of various words in the sentence, depending on the length of the loop, the temporal spacing of the words on the loop, and the pulse speed and length. In much the same

*Composer Steve Reich makes extensive use of a similar technique in *Come Out* (Odyssey Records No. 32160160) and *It's Gonna Rain* (Columbia Records No. MS7265).

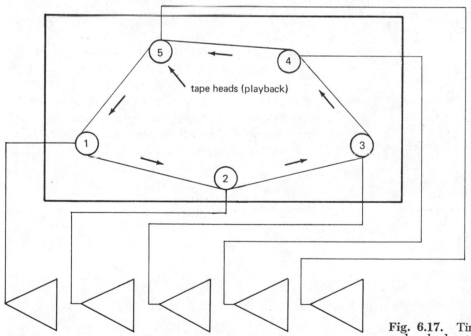

tape heads (playback)

individual gates for each playback head

Fig. 6.17. Time distortion using a tape loop and pulsed gates.

manner as the pulsed-mixing technique, if gate 5 is opened when gate 1 is closed, the alternation of the outputs of the two heads may be something like, "Yes you you I I can can," etc. An alternation between heads 3 and 5 could produce the following sequence, "bet you Yes I you can." A gating sequence of heads 2, 1, and 5 may result in "bet I you can bet Yes I can bet," etc. Gating each of the five heads in sequence could produce a sequence of "Yes Yes Yes Yes Yes." The results of this technique are completely dependent on the length of the loop, the spacing of the information on the tape, the number of playback heads, and their location on the board, along with the manner of gating.

Another approach to gating of which the composer should be aware is with the use of a ring modulator. Referring back to chapter 3, it was explained there that ring modulation was a specialized form of amplitude modulation involving the cancellation of the program and carrier frequencies, with the sideband spectrum consisting of sum and difference frequencies (see p. 11). If the ring modulator is "DC coupled" or able to accept DC as well as AC voltages, then it can be used to gate signals, with envelopes determined by the envelope of the DC voltage. This is explained by the fact that DC voltage is either positive or negative and is essentially non-fluctuating, and in these terms it can be thought of as a frequency of zero Hz. Therefore the sum and difference of an audio signal and zero is actually the same audio signal ($200 \text{ Hz} + 0 \text{ Hz} = 200 \text{ Hz}$; $200 \text{ Hz} - 0 \text{ Hz} = 200 \text{ Hz}$). And since the two applied signals operate in a manner to determine each other's amplitude, the AC signal will be heard as an envelope of the applied DC voltage. This technique works very well with attack generators and DC trapezoid envelopes.

Originally conceived as a simple switch, the gate has found applications ranging from envelope production to temporal displacement of sound. As with most "classical" techniques, the applications of voltage control and the curiosity of the composer have been major factors in expanding these electronic music techniques. This chapter has barely touched on the many ways in which a gate may be used. As the composer develops and refines his own techniques, it is certain that his familiarity with gating procedures will be just as important as his ability to make a good clean splice.

equalization and filtering

Any recorded or electronically reproduced sound is subjected to a certain amount of high and low frequency loss. While higher frequencies are usually the most readily audible, they also have shorter wavelengths and the least amount of energy content. Both high and low frequency loss can be compensated for with "equalizers." In simple terms, an equalizer is a "volume control" for certain selected frequency ranges. In order to better reproduce higher frequencies, they must be recorded at a higher level than the lower frequencies. The easiest way to do this is to attenuate the lower frequencies and then adjust the overall gain of the amplifier to bring these low frequencies back up to their original level. The overall effect is then an amplification or boost of the higher frequencies, while the lower ones are reproduced at their original level. When equaliza-

tion is used in a recording circuit it is referred to as "pre-equalization." If the equalization circuit is utilized in the playback stage, it is called "post-equalization." Effective reproduction is usually a combination of pre- and post-equalization. If certain frequencies are recorded at a higher than usual level, transmitted by disc, tape, broadcasting, etc., and then attenuated during the reproduction stage, the result would presumably be a faithful copy of the original. This approach to equalization will only be effective, however, if there is some sort of standard by which signals can be recorded and reproduced. By using a standard pre-equalization curve and an inverse post-equalization curve, the two curves would balance each other out and the result would be "flat" or accurate reproduction.

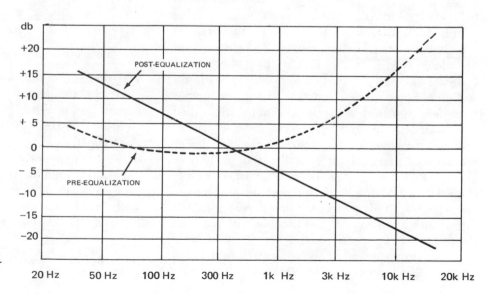

Fig. 7.1. Pre- and post-equalization curves.

At the present time there are three different equalization standards in use: these are those of the Record Industry Association of America (RIAA), the National Association of Broadcasters (NAB), and the Audio Engineering Society (AES). In dealing with tape recording and reproduction, the NAB curve is the most widely used. A professional-quality pre-amplifier should have the capability of being switched to any one of these standards depending on the curve used in recording. Most pre-amplifiers are equipped with additional equalizers, usually referred to as "tone controls," which are used to compensate for various environmental acoustic situations and to allow for variation in personal listening preferences. There are usually two separate pots: one for high-frequency attenuation and one for low-frequency attenuation. The term "boost" is often found on these controls but it is actually a misnomer. The controls are usually passive and do not provide for actual amplification, since a high-frequency "boost" is really an attenuation of the lower frequencies in combination with an overall rise in the total gain level. A typical "bass control" on a commercial hi-fi amplifier will produce maximum attenuation control of frequencies at about 50 Hz, while the "treble control" affects frequencies in a range of about 10k Hz. These frequencies are not standard and may vary according to different manufacturers.

Before a more detailed discussion of equalization techniques can take place, a standard unit of attenuation and amplification measurement must be established. Since loudness is a very subjective phenomenon, the acousticians and engineers have decided on a more objective type of measurement of intensity which is called the decibel (abbreviated *db*). In the early days of cable telephone transmission, the unit of measurement was "miles-of-loss," which referred to the amount of intensity lost by resistance in a "loop-mile" (which was actually two miles—one in each direction). Some time later this rather ambiguous term was replaced by a logarithmic ratio called the "transmission unit" and was later re-named the "bel" in honor of Alexander Graham Bell. For the sake of practicality, a smaller unit, 1/10th of a bel, or "decibel," has been established as the standard unit of amplitude measurement. The decibel is not a fixed value like an ohm or volt, but rather an expression of the notable difference of intensity between two sounds or signals. Consequently, db levels must be specified in relation to some fixed reference. In the past years many

different power levels have been used, such as 6, 10, 12.5 and 50 milliwatts.* In 1939 the electronics industries adopted a 1 milliwatt reference power in a 600-ohm line as the standard for zero db. When this .001 watt reference is used it is often expressed as dbm. The zero dbm rating also represents a level of 0.7746 volts. Figure 7.2 indicates the voltage-wattage and dbm levels for a 600-ohm line; —20 dbm indicates a level of —20 db referred to .001 watt, and +40 dbm indicates

dbm	wattage	voltage
60	1000 watts	774.6
50	100 watts	244.9
+40	10 watts	77.46
+30	1 watt	24.49
+20	100 mw	7.746
+10	10 mw	2.449
0	1 mw	.7746
—10	.1 mw	.2449
—20	.01 mw	.07746
—30	.001 mw	.02449

Fig. 7.2. Decibel scale with 1 mW/600 ohms reference

a level of +40 db also referred to .001 watt. As an objective measurement of loudness, a 1k Hz tone at 10^{-16} watts/cm^2 has been accepted as a standard. The reason for this is that that particular frequency at that particular level is very close to the threshold of audibility. Using these figures, a very accurate measure of intensity can be made:

$$db = 10 \log 1/I_0$$

$I = 10^{-16}$ watts/cm^2 and I = the intensity to be compared

therefore: $db = 10 \log I/10^{-16}$ watts/cm^2

The reason for this logarithmic scale to the base 10 is the tremendous sensitivity of the ear. The human ear is sensitive to pressure changes on a scale of 1,000,000,000,000 to 1. By using a log to the base 10, it is possible to express this on a scale of approximately 14 to 1, each unit representing a bel. By dividing this scale into units of 10, a decibel range of 0 to 140 is derived. A sound of 1 db is almost inaudible and a difference of 1 db is barely noticeable. Figure 7.3 lists various en-

*The watt (w) is a specified unit of electric power which is required to do work at a fixed rate, and 1 milliwatt of course is 1/1000th of a watt.

+120 db—Pain threshold
+ 90 db—Noisy traffic
+ 75 db—Orchestral brass instruments playing FF
+ 60 db—Orchestral strings and woodwinds playing FF
+ 45 db—Normal conversation at 10 feet
+ 30 db—Normal street traffic, residential district
+ 10 db—Normal whisper at 10 feet

Fig. 7.3. Average decibel ratings of normal environments.

vironmental conditions with their intensities rated in decibels.

Most professional recording and reproduction equipment such as mixers, recording and playback amplifiers, etc., are equipped with a meter which allows the decibel rating of the program to be visually indicated. These devices are referred to as VU meters, an abbreviation for "volume unit." VU meters are calibrated to a certain number of decibels expressing the ratio of the intensity of the signal being measured to the intensity of a .001 watt power signal in a 600-ohm line. The

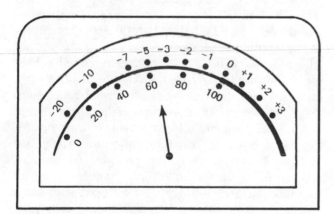

Fig. 7.4. VU meter

novice is often confused by the calibration of VU meters. The "0" level does not indicate zero db, but rather is an indication that when the needle reaches that point the signal is at the maximum level at which it can be recorded or reproduced without a certain amount of distortion. (VU meter calibration is dealt with in more detail in chap. 11.)

With this basic understanding of decibel ratings, a more detailed discussion of equalization is possible. Just as the conductor of an orchestra must balance the various sonorities of the sections

to achieve the desired sound, the electronic music composer learns to attenuate and balance various frequencies to achieve the desired timbre. Even the simple tone controls on the average hi-fi amplifier can be an invaluable tool for the composer. Although the concept of equalization was born out of a desire for accurate sound reproduction, the composer often uses it for very opposite effects. One of the simplest and most often used techniques in musique concrete and electronic music is the reproduction of sounds and speeds different from the original recording speed. The major difficulty with this technique is that the end result usually has a certain identifying quality about it that, in effect, gives away what has been done. A 7 1/2 ips recording played back at 15 ips sounds just like a 7 1/2 ips recording played back at 15 ips, and the same is true of the reverse process. The basic reason for this is that by changing the playback speed, higher and lower frequencies are affected which were not inversely treated in the recording stage. By observing the American (the European curve begins with about a 34 db response at 20 Hz) Standard Equalization Curve used in tape recording playback, it can be seen that a 1k Hz signal has a flat response while a 2k Hz signal is attenuated about 3 db. (The recording equalization would be the exact inverse of the

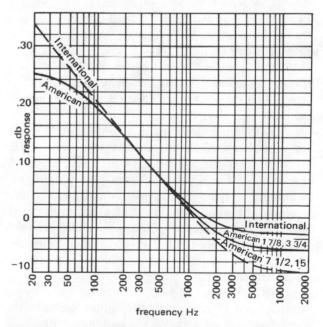

Fig. 7.5. Standard equalization curves for tape recording (curves shown are for playback). (From Norman H. Crowhurst, *Audio Systems Handbook*, Blue Ridge Summit, Pennsylvania, Tab Books, 1969, p. 33. Used by permission of the publisher.)

playback graph.) Therefore, when a 1k Hz signal is played back at twice the intended speed, it is equalized as a 2k Hz signal. This seems redundant, because a 1k Hz signal played at twice the speed would be a 2k Hz signal. The problems lie in the fact that this shift in the pre-equalization and post-equalization curves causes a noticeable loss in the high-frequency components of the recorded sounds. By using the tone controls on the pre-amplifier, this shift can be compensated for by boosting the high frequencies. A half-speed playback can also be greatly improved by boosting the lower frequencies. It would be possible to make these adjustments in pre-equalization, but this usually involves a bit of experimentation and could result in a great deal of recording time. Many recorders are equipped with an equalization switch for recording at various speeds. If one is recording at 15 ips and planning to play back at 7 1/2 ips, it might be possible to achieve better results by setting the equalization switch to record using 7 1/2 ips equalization. Equalization may also be used to eliminate a certain amount of tape "hiss." The hiss is strongest at the higher end of the spectrum, so high-frequency attenuation will reduce it considerably. The problem here, however, is that this will also result in considerable attenuation of other high frequencies. Artificial reverberation also attenuates many of the higher frequencies, consequently a certain amount of equalization is needed to restore the sound to its original balance. (Equalization in relation to reverberation is discussed in greater detail in chap. 10.) It should be said again that the composer use the controls to achieve whatever sound is desired. There is no right or wrong way to use equalization—it depends entirely on what you wish to hear.

Another type of equalizer sometimes found in pre-amplifier circuits is called a "presence equalizer" or "presence control." Many times a recording or other reproduction sounds very dull, lifeless. A presence equalizer provides a mid-range boost centered at about 3k Hz and sloping to about 1.5k Hz and 6k Hz on each side. Most presence equalizers provide for a 6 db maximum boost, but usually even a smaller amount of gain will result in a very noticeable change in the sound.

With the use of bass, mid-range, and treble controls, a composer has tremendous control over the frequency response of the audio spectrum, but this control is spread over three very general areas. Hypothetically, if attenuation is needed for a frequency band from 200 to 300 Hz, it would have to be done at the expense of most of the other low frequencies. To provide for more selective equalization, "graphic equalizers" have been developed. Graphic equalizers divide the audio spectrum into various band-widths (usually octave, half-octave, or one-third-octave bands) and then provide a certain amount of attenuation and/or gain for those bands which can be independently controlled. It is then possible to boost or attenuate practically any part of the spectrum without affecting any other frequency band. The amount of attenuation and gain is variable from about 8 to 12 db, depending on the particular manufacturer. Several groups of frequency bands are available, again depending on what particular unit is being used. The equalizer illustrated in figure 7.6 is divided into octave bands beginning with a low of 20 Hz. Each band is controlled by the use of a linear motion pot rather than the rotational design pot. Often referred to as "sliders," these pots together provide a graphic representation of the equalization curve being produced. The settings in figure 7.6 would produce a curve as illustrated in figure 7.7. A graphic equalizer with half-octave equalization could produce even more minute peaks and dips and might have such band divisions as 20 Hz, 40 Hz, 60 Hz, 80 Hz, 120 Hz, 160 Hz, 240 Hz, 320 Hz, etc. There are several multiband equalizers available, but they are not necessarily graphic in design; that is, the pots are not the slider type but of rotational design. This type of equalizer will produce the same results but without the advantage of having a visual representation of the curve. It is even possible to use a fixed filter bank as a multi-band equalizer (see p. 60).

Any equalizer or filter may be passive or active. A passive equalizer provides no amplification and requires no external power, while an active equalizer is designed to be used with some type of amplification. When a signal is routed through a passive network there is a certain amount of gain loss. This loss in gain is referred to as insertion loss and can be as little as 2 or 3 db or as much as 50 to 60 db or more, depending on the complexity of the circuit. The more components involved (resistors, capacitors, inductors, etc.) the higher the insertion loss. To compensate for insertion loss when working with passive networks, additional amplification is required. Large studio consoles with many equalizers have additional 20 db line amplifiers that are used precisely for that purpose. If the amplification circuit is part of the total equalization circuit design, it is then an active equalizer and usually no external amplification is needed.

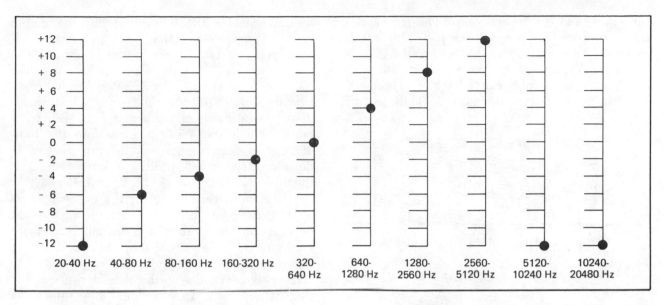

Fig. 7.6. Graphic octave band equalizer

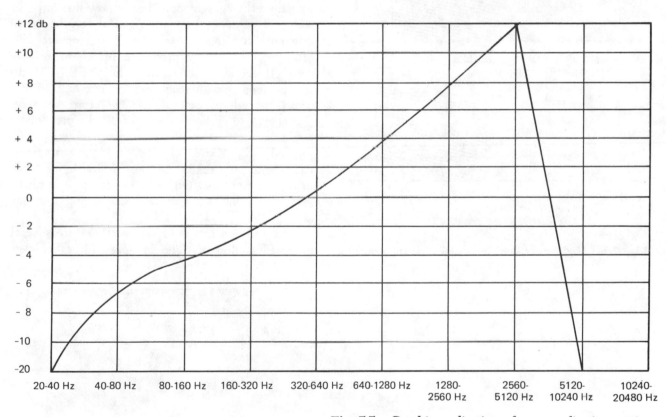

Fig. 7.7. Graphic realization of an equalization setting

While the function of an equalizer is to attenuate various parts of the frequency spectrum, it is a filter's job to totally eliminate various frequencies and frequency bands. In general, a filter is a circuit or network of circuits for the transmission and elimination of selected frequencies. In working with white sound sources, the use of filters makes it possible to divide the white sound into smaller bands of colored sound. In figure 7.8A, the white sound spectrum is represented with an overall amplitude of 60 db. With a "high pass" filter, it would be possible to eliminate the lower portion of this spectrum. The frequencies which are attenuated by 60 db are referred to as the "stop-band" or "reject-band." The frequencies left are referred to as the "band-pass." In general terms, the point at which the attenuation begins is called the "cut-off frequency," and with variable filters this cut-off can be set at almost any point in the spectrum. In figure 7.8B, the cut-off

frequency is 15k Hz. In more specific terms, the cut-off frequency is actually the point at which there is 3 db attenuation in the spectrum. The measure of a filter's effectiveness is known as the "Q" and is determined by dividing the inductive reactance of the filter's coil (a major component in the construction of a filter) by the DC resistance of the coil. Without going into the complexities of filter design and the problems of Q determination, it will suffice to know that Q is simply a measurement of the filter's efficiency.

It is much easier to observe the effectiveness of a filter in graphic terms. The ideal filter would provide an abrupt blockage of all frequencies beginning with the cut-off frequency as shown in figure 7.8C. This 90° "slope" is almost impossible to achieve, however, due to the characteristics of the filter's components. In very simple filters the slope is about a 6 db per octave "roll-off." This means that the efficiency of the filter is now measured in terms of rate of attenuation per octave. A more efficient filter may have a 24 db per octave roll-off. The terminology here is a bit confusing because this doesn't mean that the slope is 24 db per octave; actually the slope is one-half of the figure named for the roll-off. Therefore, a 24 db per octave filter has a slope of 12 db per octave beginning at the cut-off frequency. As will be explained later in this chapter, a high-Q or sharp cut-off filter is usually the most desirable for work in electronic music. On the other hand, a gradual-slope filter has the advantage of being used as an equalizer.

In addition to the high-pass, there are several other filter designs. The low-pass filter achieves

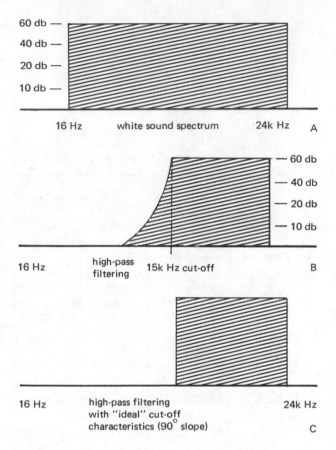

Fig. 7.8. High-pass filter applications to white sound

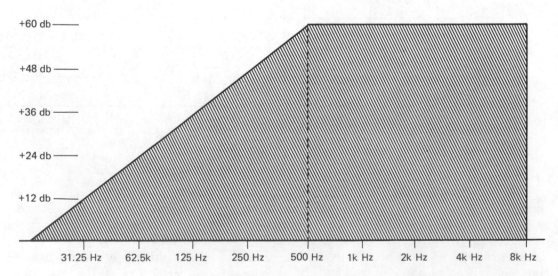

Fig. 7.9. 24 db/octave filter with a cut-off frequency of 500 Hz

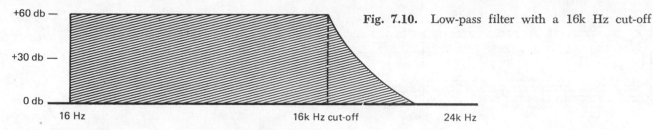

Fig. 7.10. Low-pass filter with a 16k Hz cut-off

the exact inverse effect of the high-pass filter. As with the high-pass design, the cut-off frequency of the low-pass filter can usually be set at any point in the audio spectrum. As a point of fact, a filter need not be limited to operation in the audio ranges, but the composer will find that audio filters are the most useful in studio situations. In using a low-pass filter, it would be possible to affect either end of the spectrum shown in figure 7.11 or to have a cut-off frequency at any point between these two extremes.

The most valuable application of high- and low-pass filters is in shaping various timbres by removing overtones. As a hypothetical situation, suppose a composer had produced a very complex timbre as notated in figure 7.12A. In this case the composer felt the sound was too "bright" or had too much "bite" for his preference. One process he might apply to reduce this is low-pass filter-

ing. By passing the timbre through a low-pass 40 db/octave filter with a cut-off frequency of 1.1k Hz, the top partials would be attenuated, thereby taking some of the "edge" off the sound (fig. 7.12B). An even sharper roll-off would remove these partials completely, without affecting the intensities of the lower partials (fig. 7.12C). Another method of eliminating the top partials is to set the cut-off frequency at some point lower than the lowest partials to be eliminated, perhaps 950 Hz. This will add more attenuation to the top partials but, due to roll-off, it would be at the expense of some of the lower partials (fig. 7.12D). By comparing the music notation with the accompanying charts in figure 7.12, one can readily see the advantage of a very high Q filter. At the same time there is the possibility of the need of a filter with a more gradual roll-off, as in the case of figure 7.12B. Consequently, an ideal situation would be a filter with a variable roll-off as well as a variable cut-off frequency.

All of the above treatments can also be applied in working with a high-pass filter. Beginning

Fig. 7.11. Low-pass filtering of white sound.

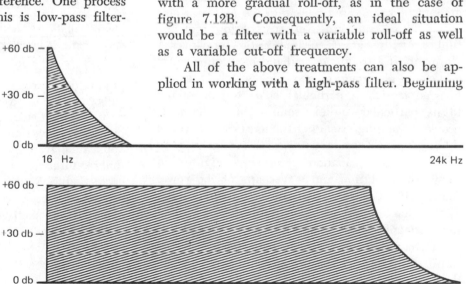

Fig. 7.12. Notation of low-pass filtering of a complex timbre. Relative amplitudes of individual frequencies are indicated by the size of the note.

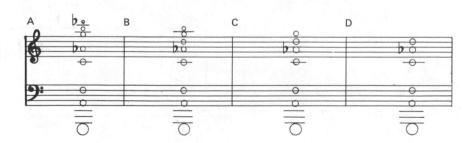

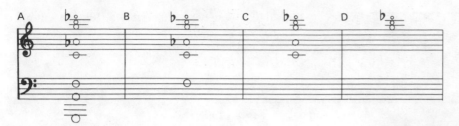

Fig. 7.13. Notation of high-pass filtering of a complex timbre.

with the same timbre as in figure 7.12A, suppose that the composer wished to attenuate or eliminate some of the lower frequencies. Again the cut-off frequency and roll-off must be adjusted to produce the desired timbre (fig. 7.13).

A very useful addition to the active filter circuit is a "regeneration" or "feedback" control. Filters with this provision are often referred to as "resonant" or "formant" filters. Usually controlled by a pot, the regeneration circuit has the capability of producing a resonant peak at the cut-off frequency. What takes place is that after the signal is passed through the filter network, the band-pass is fed back into the input of the filter. This provides further amplification, decreases distortion and gives resonance to the cut-off frequency. The amount of resonance may be controlled by a feed-back pot, which simply determines the amount of voltage fed back into the network. This regeneration control is very useful in producing timbres with various characteristic formants. A "formant" is a frequency or band of frequencies in a system (electronic or acoustic) which is always boosted to give a particular characteristic timbre to its particular audible sounds. Since formants provide the identifying characteristics for vowel sounds, speech production will serve as a good model for an explanation of formants. Figure 7.14 shows the spectrum and waveshape of the vowel sound 'ah' at 90 Hz (A) and at 150 Hz (B). Notice that even though the frequencies of all of the harmonics have changed, the frequencies of the formants (peaks) are unchanged. This is because the resonance or formants are produced by the shape of the vocal track, which remains the same for this particular vowel. Formants can be

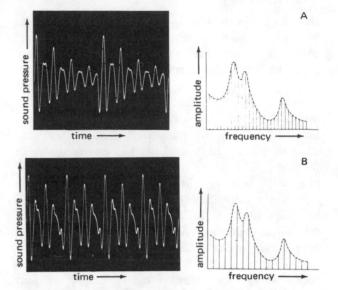

Fig. 7.14. Waveshapes and spectra of the vowel "ah." (From Cecil H. Coker, P. B. Denes, and E. N. Pinson, *Speech Synthesis,* Bell Telephone Laboratories, 1963, p. 69. Used by permission of the publisher.)

produced electronically by using regeneration circuits, and by imposing these formants on various parts of a particular timbral spectrum an unlimited number of new timbres may be produced. Another application would be to pass a series of complex timbres through a regeneration filter. Even though each timbre would contain different frequency components, each would be amplified at the same point in the spectrum if the cut-off frequency remains constant.

Regeneration may be simulated by patching an active filter and an active mixer (a mixer with output gain) in a feedback configuration as illustrated in figure 7.15. The signal to be filtered is

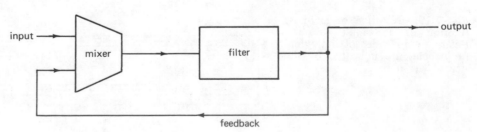

Fig. 7.15. External regeneration.

first routed through the mixer, and the output is patched to the filter input. The band-pass signal is then split, and one leg is routed back to a second input of the mixer. The gain control for this input then serves as a regeneration control for the filter. As with any other regeneration filter, the process is most effective when very narrow band-widths are possible.

A third filter design to be considered is the "band-pass." The high- and low-pass filters were limited to attenuating either the relative low or high ends of the spectrum. The band-pass filter has the function of attenuating or eliminating both ends of the spectrum at the same time. Referring again to white sound, the ideal band-pass filter could eliminate any amount of sound from each end of the spectrum. But of course this instantaneous transition from band-pass to band-stop exhibits less accurate slopes, such as those shown in figure 7.16. The frequency midway between

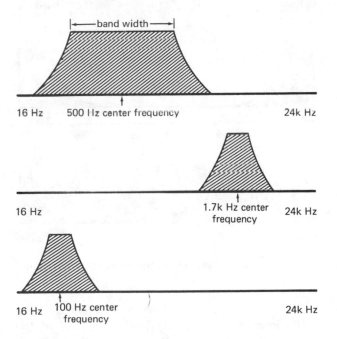

Fig. 7.16. Band-pass filtering of white sound

the high and low cut-off frequencies is referred to as the "center frequency." The band-pass frequencies are usually determined by two pots; one for the lower cut-off frequency (high-pass), and the upper cut-off frequency (low-pass). By adjusting these two cut-off frequencies, it is possible to produce various band-pass patterns ranging from a very wide "shelf" pattern to a very narrow "bell curve" (fig. 7.17).

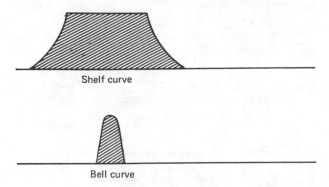

Fig. 7.17. Shelf and bell band-pass curves

Another control design for band-pass filters may be one pot for the determination of the center frequency and another pot for setting the band-width. The band-width is the spectrum of frequencies to be passed. There are several ways to indicate this. The first is by using a separate pot for the high and low cut-off frequencies; the second is to have a single pot with "maximum" and "minimum" settings. The latter, of course, tells the composer nothing about what the maximum and minimum settings represent. The minimum may be a 200 Hz band-width and the maximum may be a 300 Hz band-width—which isn't a great deal of variation. It would be much easier for the composer if the band-width pot were calibrated in Hertz with the minimum being 1 Hz and the maximum being 20k Hz or more. Some pots are calibrated with arbitrary numbers −1, −2, −3, 0, +1, +2, +3, etc. Again, this gives no information as to the exact band-width and the composer would have to refer to the manufacturer's specifications for information and would probably end up calibrating the pot himself. The fourth and most standard (in scientific terms) method of determining band-width is "percent band width." This is defined as $(f_h\text{-}f_l \times 100\%)/\sqrt{f_h f_l}$, where f_h is the cut-off frequency, the −3 db point, and f_l is the standard total attenuation point, −60 db. For compositional purposes it will suffice to indicate the high and low cut-off frequencies.

With the band-pass filter it is possible to "center in" on any partial or group of partials of any existing or constructed timbre. By beginning with a saw-tooth wave (fig. 7.18A) and subjecting it to band-pass filtering, it is possible to produce a timbre as illustrated in figure 7.18B. If the filter is a regeneration type, it is then possible to amplify the lower frequency (if the regeneration affected the lower cut-off frequency) and there-

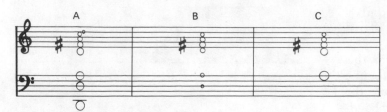

Fig. 7.18. Timbre modification with a band-pass filter.

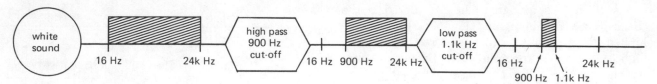

Fig. 7.19. Series connection for band-pass filtering

by create the effect of a new fundamental with non-harmonic partials (fig. 7.18C).

Minute inspection of timbres can be achieved by scanning a particular timbre with a very narrow band-width band-pass filter. With a high-Q filter it is possible to begin with the fundamental of a given timbre and, by gradually raising the center frequency, isolate each and every frequency component which contributes to the total sound. This technique would be analogous to the musician producing the natural harmonic series on a string instrument by lightly running his finger up and down the string from node to node.

If a studio or system is not equipped with a band-pass filter, it is possible to create band-pass results by using a low-pass and a high-pass filter in conjunction with each other. To achieve the bell curve shown in figure 7.17A, the signal would first have to be processed through a high-pass filter with a 900 Hz cut-off and then through a low-pass filter with an 1,100 Hz cut-off. A precaution to observe here is that both filters should have the same roll-off characteristics or the curve will be uneven and the center frequency will not be in the center. This manner of connecting the two filters is called "series" connection. In electronic terms a series circuit is one in which all component parts are connected end to end to form a single path for the signal or current. In this case the filters are treated as "black boxes"* and are patched in series.

The inverse of a band-pass function is the band-reject, band-stop, or notch filter (also sometimes referred to as "band-elimination" or "exclusion filters"). As the name implies, the function of this filter is to notch out a selected band of frequencies from the spectrum. Figure 7.20 illustrates

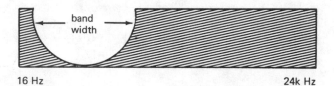

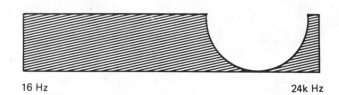

Fig. 7.20. Band-reject filtering of white sound

a few of the many band-reject functions. Figure 7.21 shows, in musical notation, the effect of the above curves on a single timbre. As with the band-pass filter, the center frequency and band-width of the band-reject filter may be controlled using two different pots. The difference is that the lower cut-off point determines the low-pass frequencies and the higher cut-off point determines the high-pass frequencies—thus producing a rejection of all frequencies between those two points. In the case of the band-reject filter, the center frequency re-

*A "black box" is any self-contained device that may be treated as a single functional device without an intricate knowledge of its components.

Fig. 7.21. Notation of the effects of band-reject filtering.

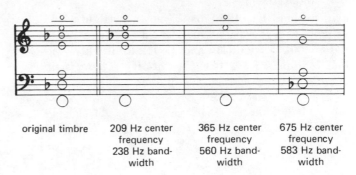

| original timbre | 209 Hz center frequency 238 Hz band-width | 365 Hz center frequency 560 Hz band-width | 675 Hz center frequency 583 Hz band-width |

Fig. 7.22. Parallel connection for band-reject filtering

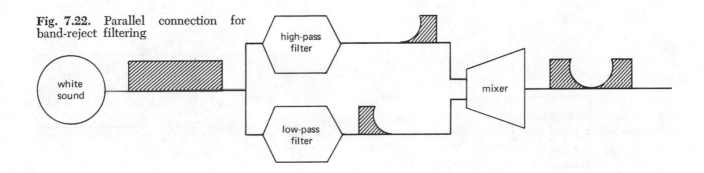

fers to the frequency in the center of the rejected band. In the same manner, band-width refers to the rejected band of frequencies.

Just as a high- and low-pass filter may be connected in series to produce band-pass functions, they may also be connected in "parallel" to produce band-reject functions. A parallel circuit is one in which the current is divided between two or more components. In this case the signal is split with a "Y" network* and then passed simultaneously through both filters and then mixed back together to produce a band-rejected signal (fig. 7.22).

In several commercial electronic music systems, the band-pass and band-reject functions are produced by series and parallel wiring. This can instantaneously be achieved by a "filter selector" or "filter coupler" switch. If the switch is off or in the "independent" position, both the high- and low-pass filters operate independently of each other. With the switch in "band-pass" position, the two filters are internally hooked in series, and in the "band-reject" position the filters are hooked in parallel. If a coupling switch is not available, the external patching is still relatively easy to accomplish.

All of the filter designs discussed so far have been variable in terms of band-width and center frequency. A non-variable filter is usually a band-

pass network designed to attenuate a particular fixed band-width. (Although fixed filters can be of any design, the band-pass is the most common.) As the name implies, these fixed filters cannot be varied except by internal component substitution and this involves a great deal of time, both in computations and in soldering. Many studios are equipped with 60 Hz and 120 Hz fixed filters which are usually used to reduce the 60 Hz and 120 Hz hum often caused by unshielded wiring or poor ground connections. (In the United States alternating electrical current is based on a 60 Hz supply frequency which is often audible as 60 Hz or 120 Hz hum—the 120 Hz hum being a result of the 1st harmonic.) By passing the signal through a 60 Hz and 120 Hz filter, this annoying hum can be reduced and often eliminated. In this particular case, the filter's Q is critical, since a wide band-width would attenuate other frequencies around the 60 Hz and 120 Hz center frequencies.

One of the most valuable tools for the composer is the fixed-filter bank—several fixed filters housed within a single chassis. One basic filter-bank design would consist of one input which is bussed to several individual filters, each with their

---

*A "Y" network or "Y" plugs have three branches usually used as 1 input and 2 outputs. Using "Y" plugs as mixers, 2 inputs and 1 output, is usually unsatisfactory; see chap. 8.

own output. The filter bank shown in figure 7.23 consists of a low-pass (400 Hz cut-off), two band-pass (400 Hz to 1k Hz and 1k Hz to 3k Hz), and one high-pass filter (3k Hz cut-off). There is no standard band-width or number of frequency

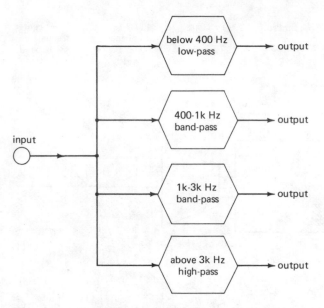

Fig. 7.23. Fixed-filter bank

bands employed in filter-bank design; this will vary greatly according to the individual manufacturer. A more complex filter bank could be designed with center frequencies as shown in figure 7.24.

With the use of a mixer, the fixed-filter bank may also be made to function as a high-pass or low-pass filter. By using the mixer illustrated in figure 7.24, and mixing all of the outputs above 1,280 Hz, the result would be a high-pass filter with a cut-off of 1,280 Hz. The inverse treatment would result in a low-pass filter with a similar cut-off frequency. In the same manner, the mixing of certain selected outputs could result in a notch or "multi-notch" filter. Figure 7.25 shows the result of white sound treated in this manner. The notches can be even more finely tuned by adjusting the relative amplitude levels of each frequency band by using individual gain pots on each output. In this manner each frequency band can be adjusted to the desired amplitude level and very exact timbres can be shaped (fig. 7.26).

Because of the many applications of output mixing and level control, many fixed filter banks are designed with amplitude pots for each frequency band and with provisions for internal mix-

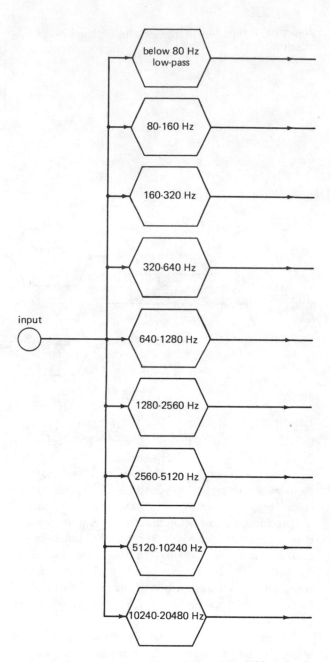

Fig. 7.24. Fixed-filter bank

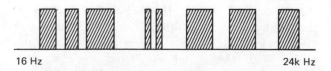

Fig. 7.25. Multi-notched treatment of white sound

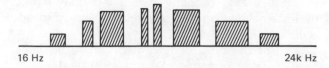

Fig. 7.26. Amplitude-shaped mix of band-pass outputs

ing. Therefore only one output is needed. This eliminates the need for an external mixer and saves considerable time usually spent with patching. The particular design shown in figure 7.27 has eight half-octave bands, with individual level controls for each band. The output for each band is routed to an internal mixer and the composite signal is taken from a single output. In the same manner, any fixed filter network may employ regeneration circuits to provide a fixed resonant filter or fixed formant filter.

By using voltage-controlled amplifiers in conjunction with fixed-filter banks, a specialized form of "timbre modulation" can be accomplished. By taking various frequency band outputs to individual VCAs, and then to a mixing unit, it would be possible to program very rapid selection of the individual band-pass frequencies. The programming could be done with a sequencer, attack generator, etc., depending on the desired effect. If the switching were to be done at a very rapid rate, the effect would be a combination of frequency modulation (modulation of the center frequency) and amplitude modulation, depending on the switching rate and the attack and decay characteristics programmed. As the switching rate approaches the audio range, characteristic AM and FM sidebands will be produced, adding further complexity (and perhaps interest) to the resultant sounds (fig. 7.28). If a formant filter were to be used in this manner, the FM characteristics would be even more pronounced and the method might be referred to as "formant modulation." This

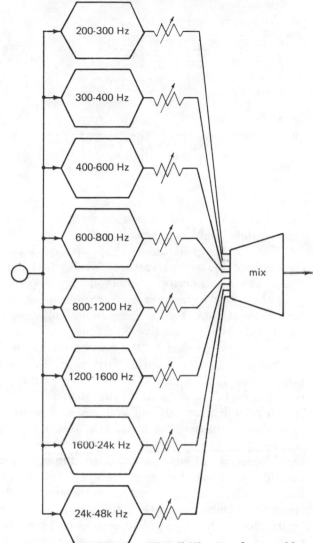

Fig. 7.27. Band-pass filter with internal band gain controls.

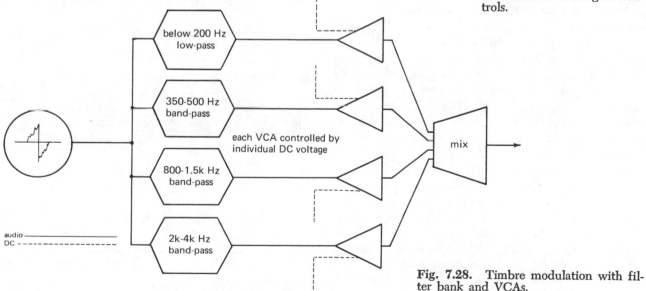

Fig. 7.28. Timbre modulation with filter bank and VCAs.

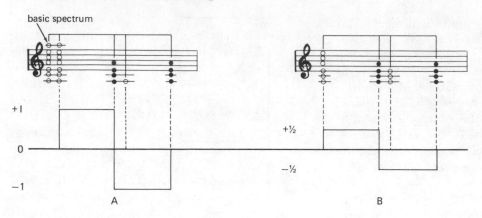

Fig. 7.29. Voltage control of a filter with a square wave.

technique is discussed further in relation to voltage-controlled mixers in chapter 8.

The filter and its innumerable applications in electronic music are so vast and varied that they could almost comprise a methodology separate from the other techniques of electronic music. In fact, filter techniques are sometimes collectively referred to as "subtractive synthesis," and have been greatly expanded by the application of voltage control. (For a brief discussion of this approach, see Jon Appleton, "Additive vs. Subtractive Synthesis," *Electronic Music Review,* no. 5, Jan., 1968.) Just as external voltages can be used to control frequency and amplitude, they can also be used to determine band-width, cut-off and center frequency in voltage-controlled filters. With currently available low- and high-pass filters, the only voltage-controllable parameter is the cut-off frequency. Once the cut-off frequency has been established, either by manual setting or by application of a DC voltage, an AC control voltage may be applied to modulate the cut-off frequency in accordance with the applied waveshape. The ratio of the control voltage to the cut-off frequency displacement varies with various systems. As a hypothetical example, suppose that an arbitrary ratio of 1 volt of applied voltage will produce 1 octave displacement of the center frequency. (This is in an exponential mode.) Therefore, a square wave control voltage with an amplitude of 1 volt, as applied to a low-pass filter with a 440 Hz cut-off frequency, would abruptly shift the cut-off frequency one octave in each direction once every cycle, as shown in figure 7.29A. If the control voltage was dropped to 1/2 volt the rate of modulation would be the same but the displacement about the center frequency would only be 1/2 octave (fig. 7.29B). By using a sine wave program signal, the effect would be a glissando back and forth about the center frequency (fig. 7.30). A ramp wave program would produce an upward glissando

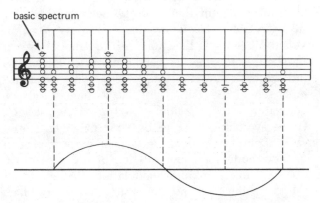

Fig. 7.30. Voltage control of a filter with a sine wave

to a point determined by its voltage, an abrupt shift to a point opposite the center frequency, followed by a glissando back up to the center frequency (fig. 7.31). If the control voltages were below the audio range, the ear could possibly distinguish between each of the spectral components as the cut-off frequency moves higher and lower according to the program signal. An approximation of musical notation of this effect is giv-

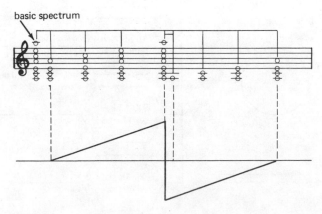

Fig. 7.31. Voltage control of a filter with a ramp wave.

en with each example. As the program frequency approaches the audio range, the ear will begin to hear sidebands produced by the rapid modulation. As explained before, this is a combination of frequency modulation caused by the modulation of the cut-off frequency and amplitude modulation caused by the fact that the slope of the filter is continually moving, causing crescendi and diminuendi as it affects various parts of the spectrum.

Voltage control of a high-pass filter works the same way, except that the inverse patterns would be produced, as shown in figure 7.32.

Another approach to voltage-controlled high- and low-pass filters is to bypass the preset cut-off frequency and make it entirely a function of the program voltage. The modulation is not then cen-

tered around a preset cut-off frequency. Rather, the highest point of negative program voltage would produce a cut-off frequency corresponding to the lowest frequency affected by the filter. Conversely, the highest point of the positive program voltage would determine the highest cut-off frequency to be produced. The higher the voltage of the program frequency, the wider the band-pass (fig. 7.33).

Band-pass and band-reject filters are also subject to voltage control, but in this case there are two voltage controllable parameters—center frequency and band-width. If a band-pass filter is thought of as a high- and low-pass filter connected in series, it is very easy to understand how both center frequency and band-width can be subjected

Fig. 7.32.   Voltage control of a high-pass filter

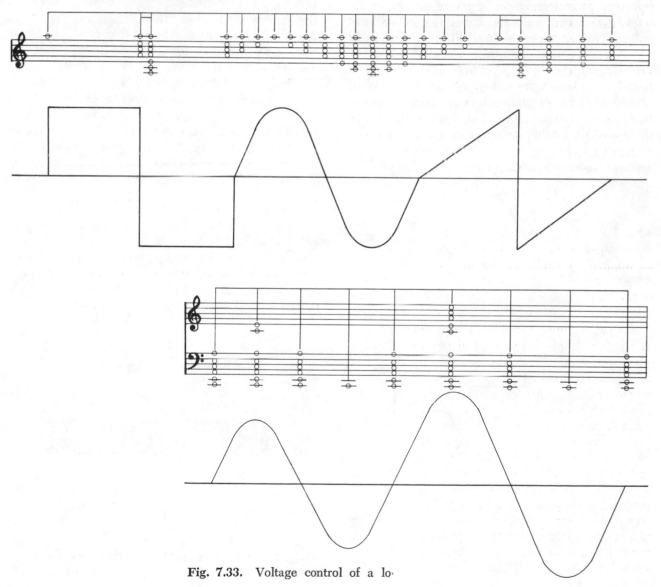

Fig. 7.33.   Voltage control of a lo·

to voltage control. By applying the same program voltage to both filters simultaneously, the cut-off frequencies will be shifted in an exponential manner, keeping the band-width between them the same. As a hypothetical example, suppose that the center frequency was 24 Hz with a half-octave slope on each side. This means that the cut-off for the high-pass filter would be 16 Hz and the cut-off for the low-pass filter would be 32 Hz. The ratio represented by this band-width is 16:32, or 1:2. By keeping this 1:2 ratio constant, there will always be a half-octave slope on either side of the center frequency. If the center frequency is 440 Hz, the high-pass cut-off would be 330 Hz and the low-pass cut-off would be 660 Hz (330:660 = 1:2). Since a band-reject filter is essentially a high- and low-pass filter connected in parallel, the treatment is the same except that the center frequency now refers to the point of maximum attenuation. In both cases the application of a control voltage is the same—a higher voltage will result in a wider shift in the center frequency, while the waveshape determines in what manner the frequency will move. As with the voltage-controlled high- and low-pass filters, the possibility of presetting a center frequency manually or by DC voltage is dependent on the particular design. Even if the center frequency is *strictly* a function of control voltage, there are still an unlimited number of applications.

By routing white sound through a voltage-controlled band-pass filter, it would be possible to "play" various sound bands by varying the control voltage with a keyboard or sequencer (fig. 7.34). Even more of a pitch effect could be produced if the filter were resonant. The same treatment with a band-reject filter would allow the composer to play "holes" in white sound or in a complex spectrum (fig. 7.35).

By voltage-controlling the center frequency, it is also possible to trace any portion of another voltage-controlled sound. If the following sequence of timbres were being produced by ring modulating (or any other type of modulation) two constant-ratio sine waves, any constant portion of each successive timbre could be continually passed or rejected in the following manner: set the band-pass or band-reject filter to affect whatever portion of the first timbre is desired, and then use the same voltage being used to control the oscillators, which in this case is a sequence of non-fluctuating DC voltages, to also control the center frequency of the filter. As the DC control voltage shifts the oscillators, it will also shift the center frequency of the filter, resulting in similar timbres no matter what range of frequencies are being produced by the modulation (fig. 7.36).

The band-width of a band-pass or band-reject filter can be controlled by varying the ratio between the high and low cut-off frequencies. In the

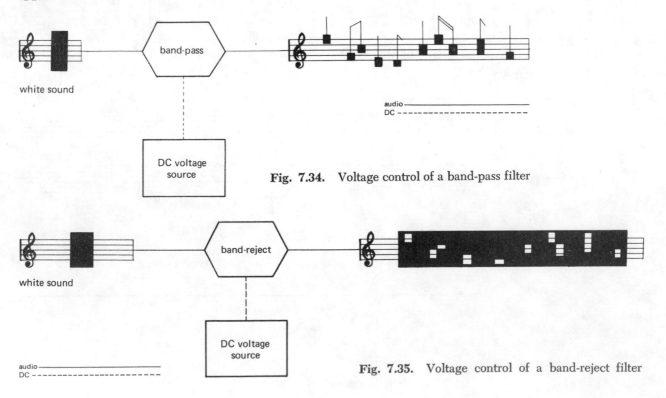

Fig. 7.34. Voltage control of a band-pass filter

Fig. 7.35. Voltage control of a band-reject filter

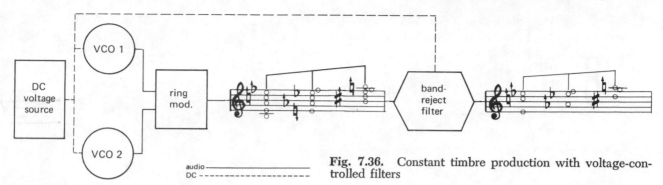

Fig. 7.36. Constant timbre production with voltage-controlled filters

earlier example, a center frequency of 440 Hz with a half-octave slope on each side represented a 1:2 ratio. If the high-pass cut-off is raised from 330 Hz to 395 Hz, and the low-pass is lowered from 660 Hz to 550 Hz, the center frequency would remain the same but the band-width would have narrowed to a ratio of approximately 3:2. This process can be voltage-controlled by exponentially moving each cut-off frequency for the high- and low-pass filters the same interval toward or away from the center frequency, depending on whether it is desired to narrow or widen the band-width. An application of a DC voltage would change the ratio according to the preset voltage. If the preset ratio is established with an X volt DC level, an application of a negative X DC voltage would make the ratio larger, thereby widening the band-width. Conversely, an application of a positive X DC voltage would make the band-width narrower. By using an AC program voltage, the band-width would change in accordance with the positive and negative changes in the program voltage.

It should be noted that the band-width can become so small that the signal is completely attenuated in a band-pass function. In a band-reject mode, a very narrow band-width could result in no noticeable rejection at all. Following the principles of voltage control, the amount of band-width modulation depends on the intensity of the program signal, with the modulation rate a function of the program frequency. It should also be pointed out that band-width and center frequency are independent functions and can be controlled by two separate control voltages. This means that it is possible to raise or lower the center frequency while widening or narrowing the band-width. By applying the *same* control voltage to both functions, it is possible to raise or lower the center frequency in direct proportion to the modulation of the band-width. By routing one of the control-voltage lines through a voltage inverter it would be possible to vary the center frequency and band-width in inverse proportions.

Since the initial musique concrete experiments of Pierre Schaeffer, the filter has become one of the most widely utilized devices of the electronic music composer. As new methods of sound modification were developed, more effective methods of design enabled the filter to hold its place as one of the composer's most useful tools. The whole concept of subtractive synthesis makes it irreplaceable in the electronic music studio. More recent voltage-control designs have opened an entire new realm for filter applications. Techniques of formant and timbre modulation are still in their infant stages and their full potentials in terms of sound modification have yet to be realized. In conjunction with various other modules and voltage sources, the filter affords the composer an endless number of sound-modification techniques.

Fig. 7.37. AC voltage control of band width.

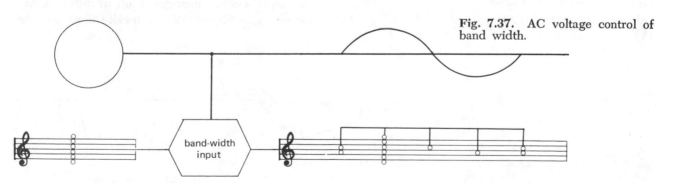

mixing

The previous chapter was based on a *subtractive* technique of sound construction. The mixer provides for an *additive* approach to the creation of sounds. A basic definition of a mixer is that it is a device which allows for the combination of two or more signals in any proportions into a composite signal. A composition may contain several simultaneous levels of activity being produced by independent modules, but for all of the produced signals to be perceived from the same source it is necessary to mix them down to a single output signal. Also, the construction of many complex timbres may involve the mixing of various proportions of several less complex signals into a single output. The mixer may serve other functions, such as gating, cross-fading, panoramic division, and signal distribution to several independent channels, all of which will be discussed in this chapter, but it is usually desirable when composing with a complex system to use the mixer as the final output terminal before the amplification or recording stage. This enables the making of sudden changes in balance and provides for making last minute additions or subtractions to the composite signal without the need for repatching.

There are two basic methods of mixing: linear and non-linear systems. In a linear system, equal changes in applied voltage continually result in equal changes in the current or rate of transfer of electricity (which is measured in amperes). This means that the output current of a linear mixer will vary in direct proportion to the number of signal inputs and their individual level settings. Linear mixing circuits are usually preferred by audio engineers because of the low percentage of distortion to the controlled signals. The output signal is an algebraic sum of all the input signals according to their various independent amplitudes. In other words, the composite output signal contains *only* the components of all of the input signals (fig. 8.1). Without going into detailed electronic theory, this linearity also means that the resistance in the circuit is essentially the same over the circuit's entire operating range.

With a non-linear device, the flow of current (which may be observed as resistance) is variable, since equal voltage changes result in different current changes. Figure 8.2 graphically illustrates the

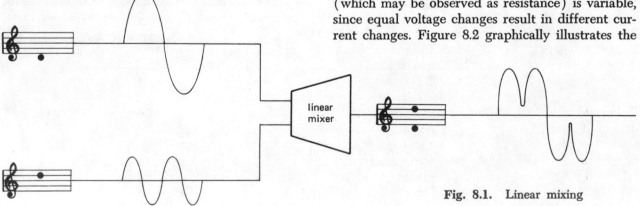

Fig. 8.1. Linear mixing

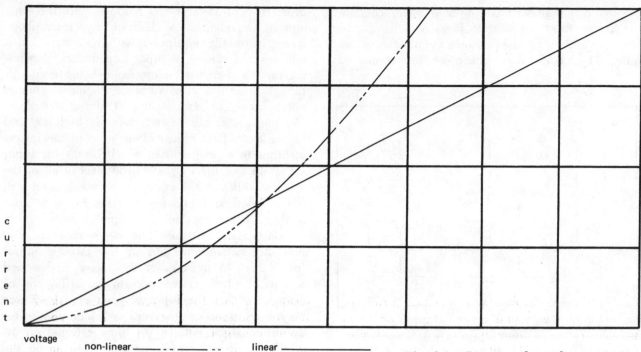

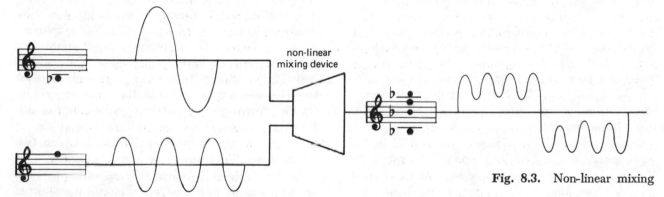

Fig. 8.2. Linear and non-linear reaction

non-linear — · · — · — · ·   linear ————————

Fig. 8.3. Non-linear mixing

difference between linear and non-linear response. The composer's concern for non-linear mixers is that it introduces additional frequencies into the final output which were not present as one of the inputs. These extra frequencies are the sums and differences of all of the input signals, as shown in figure 8.3, or heterodyning (see chap. 2), and is very similar to amplitude modulation. Although the audio engineer and hi-fi buff do everything in their power to avoid non-linearity, the composer may find it a very useful tool. When processed through a filter or reverberation unit, sum and difference frequencies take on a very eerie character and have a sound and direction very different from conventionally generated frequencies. Non-linear mixing may be achieved by simply connecting all of the input signals together without the use of bridging resistors. The number and strength of the sum and difference frequencies

produced will depend on the non-linearity of the particular circuit. The non-linearity can be controlled to a certain degree by inserting extra non-linear components, such as diodes or capacitors, into the circuit.

Most studios are equipped with patchboards and multiples which can be used for non-linear

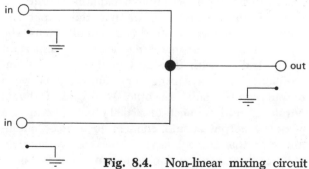

Fig. 8.4. Non-linear mixing circuit

mixing. A patchboard is simply a panel containing many input or output jacks which can be wired together as the various circumstances require (fig. 8.5). Any group of interconnected

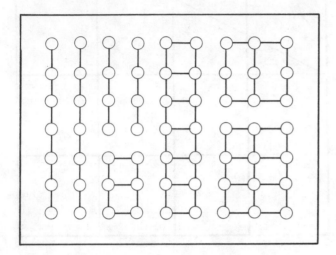

Fig. 8.5. Patchboard (lines indicate connected jacks)

sockets comprise a "multiple" which may be used as a non-linear mixing circuit. Any jack can be used as either an input or an output, so any number of signals may be connected together. Strategic location of patchboards and multiples within the studio or system permit it to be used as an extension device. Many times you will find that your patchcord is not long enough to reach the input of the next processing device in the system. If a long enough cord is not available, then two shorter cords connected via a multiple will—it is to be hoped—make connection with the next module. (The basic law with respect to the availability of patchcords—see epigraph—also applies to their length.)

Any circuit offers a certain amount of resistance to the flow of alternating current. This opposition, when a combination of resistance, inductance, and capacitance, is called "impedance," and is measured in ohms. For maximum transfer of power from one circuit to another, the output and input impedances of the two circuits must be equal. Impedance matching is most important when dealing with low-level devices such as microphones, or when using very long lines between outputs and inputs. In other words, a 600-ohm output should connect to a 600-ohm input and a 50k-ohm output should connect to a 50k-ohm input. For this reason, mixers are usually designed with a particular input impedance to be used

expressly with devices and modules with the same output impedance. A high-quality microphone mixer is usually equipped with a switch which will select a variety of input impedances, depending on the particular microphone being used. Although there is a great variance the most common microphone impedances are 50 ohms, 150 ohms, 250 ohms, 600 ohms, and even as high as, and higher than, 100k ohms. Many microphone mixers incorporate a preamplifier which brings the input signal up to a level equal to the level of all of the other modules in the system. The ideal mixer will have individual impedance switches for each input so that it can accept and mix signals from a variety of sources at one time. The same reasoning also may necessitate variation in the mixer's output impedance. In most cases the mixer is designed as part of a total system and its output impedance always matches the input of each module. There may be instances, however, in which the mixer output must be patched to some external circuit which has a different input impedance from the system.

Another consideration the composer should be aware of is the type of transmission line employed. A circuit that uses two output or input connection points is said to have an unbalanced or single-ended input or output. One of the connections is for the wire carrying the voltage, the other connection for the wire at ground potential. A balanced or differential line employs three different terminals. In this case the AC voltage is divided between two out-of-phase lines and the third connection is grounded (fig. 8.6). When working with very low-level or long lines, the balanced circuit is preferred because an unbalanced line is very susceptible to stray, unwanted signals and hum. Balanced lines are less susceptible because the circuit will react only to the difference between the two out-of-phase voltages. Without the use of a special transformer, it is not advisable to connect an unbalanced to a balanced line. Since microphones usually employ a balanced line, the microphone mixer is usually equipped with balanced inputs. On the other hand, most mixers incorporated within commercially available electronic music systems are designed with unbalanced inputs. The ideal situation would be a mixer with accommodations for accepting both balanced and unbalanced lines.

A final item to consider about the electronics of a mixer is whether it is active or passive. Just as with the various equalizers, a mixer may or may not employ additional amplification. Depending largely on the number of inputs in the circuit, insertion loss may be as high as 45 to 50 db. To

Fig. 8.6 Balanced and unbalanced lines.

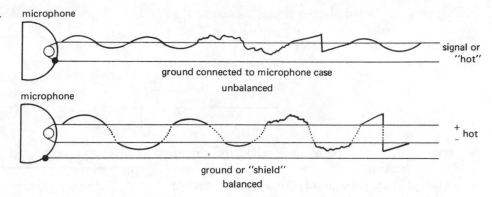

compensate for this loss, additional amplification is included in the circuit to bring the signal back up to its original level, or higher. Active mixers may provide for gain increases varying from 40 to 50 db, as with many mixer-preamplifiers. The passive mixer contains no amplification, and a certain amount of loss is to be expected, depending on impedance and the number of inputs. With active mixers there is often provision for controlling the total amount of gain produced by the circuit. This is accomplished by a special "adder" switch (see p. 72).

Once the composer has considered the results of linearity, non-linearity, balanced and unbalanced lines, and active/passive networks, he must choose a mixer design according to its application. The simplest mixer design is one that has two or more inputs and one output. Each individual input will usually have its own gain pot which will allow the mixing of the various input signals in proportions set by the composer. In creating complex waveshapes via a mixer, the composer will find that certain frequency components have amplitude levels higher or lower than other frequencies. If the amplitude of each input signal can

be independently controlled, the composer can then have complete control over the composite waveshape. The total amplitude of the composite signal can be controlled by raising or lowering all of the individual input signals, keeping their relative amplitudes at the same ratio. This, of course, is very difficult to do, and impossible to do instantly. For this reason a mixer is usually equipped with a master gain control which controls the total output level of the composite signal. This allows the composer to change the output level instantaneously without affecting the individual input ratios (fig. 8.7).

The more professional mixers usually have VU meters to indicate the total output gain for each channel. The meters are usually calibrated in terms of db gain from a specific reference point as described in chapter 6. VU meters are very helpful in maintaining constant levels. Since the output level is dependent on the sum of the inputs, a sudden change in any one of the inputs could greatly affect the composite output. This change will immediately register on the VU meter and the master gain or individual input levels can be adjusted accordingly (fig. 8.8).

A further refinement to be found on certain mixers is individual on/off switches for each input, making it possible to switch signals in and out of the circuit instantaneously. Just as with a gating switch, such switches must be of the short-

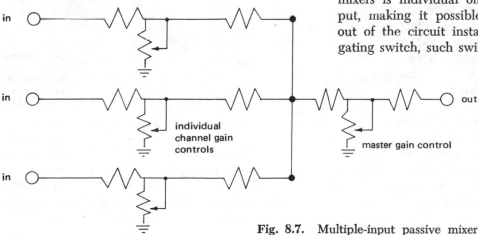

Fig. 8.7. Multiple-input passive mixer

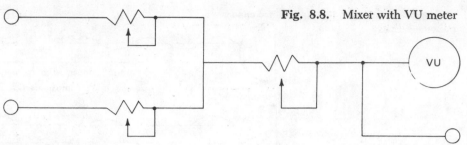

Fig. 8.8. Mixer with VU meter

ing type so there will be no click when the circuit is made or broken.

The physical design of the manual controls should also be considered when choosing a mixer. Many engineers and composers prefer slider pots over the rotary design. As with graphic equalizers, the slider pots provide a cybernetic model indicating the individual signal levels—the higher the slider position, the higher the signal level. At a glance, the composer can see all of the individual levels without having to read dial positions. With slider pots it is also possible to raise and lower several input levels with one hand, depending on the proximity of the controls. Some mixers are designed with slider pots which may be interconnected by means of a connecting piece as shown in figure 8.9. This allows several inputs to be controlled simultaneously from one slider and moved in parallel.

Stereo mixers are essentially two individual isolated mixer circuits housed within a single chassis. Each circuit contains its own respective inputs, gain controls, and outputs. Some stereo mixers provide a switch for the interconnection of the two circuits which results in a monophonic mixer with twice the number of inputs and outputs (fig. 8.10).

Since the mixer is often used to shape and create a combined complex timbre, it is desirable to have equalization controls which affect the total output signal. A good mixer will have separate high- and low-frequency filters, since these are of tremendous aid in achieving the desired output. A further refinement would be separate equalization controls for each individual input. In this way each input signal could be independently shaped before it is mixed with the other inputs. When mixing several sound sources, the composer will find that the more individual control he has over each component the more accurate he can be in producing the anticipated output.

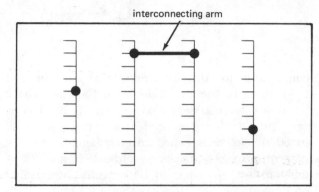

Fig. 8.9. Mixer with slider pots

The more combinations of input and output routing available in a mixer circuit, the more valuable it is in a studio or live performance situation. With multiple outputs, the mixer can be used to route various composite signals to various channels (inputs to different recording channels, amplifiers, sound processors, etc.). There are as many individual mixer designs as there are manufacturers and it is not within the scope of this book to try to describe each and every one of them. Figures 8.11 through 8.13 give some idea of the various possibilities of input/output/routing combinations.

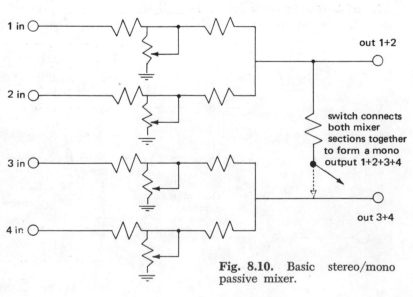

Fig. 8.10. Basic stereo/mono passive mixer.

Fig. 8.11. Multiple input/ output mixer.

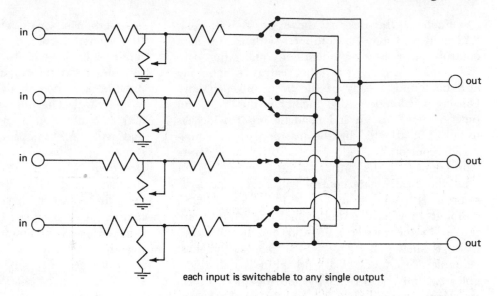

each input is switchable to any single output

Fig. 8.12. Multiple input/ output mixer.

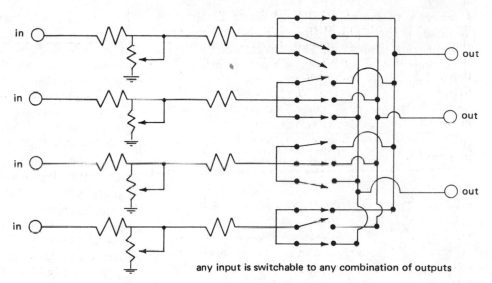

any input is switchable to any combination of outputs

Fig. 8.13. Matrix mixer

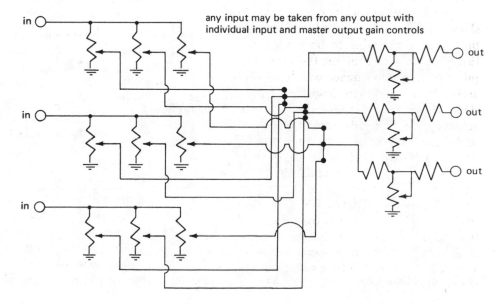

any input may be taken from any output with individual input and master output gain controls

Each of the designs shown in figures 8.11, 8.12, and 8.13 may be equipped with master gain controls and master or individual equalization controls. There are several other extras which may also be found on any of the basic mixer designs. One very valuable added facility is the "wild" input. A "wild" is an independent input which is usually not affected by the master gain or equalization control. The wild input also has no separate gain control, so the output to the bridging resistor after the master gain control will have almost the same level as the input (fig. 8.14A). Some wilds, although they have no individual gain control, are routed to the master gain and equalization controls, as shown in figure 8.14B. One of the most valuable advantages of a wild input is that it enables two mixers to be connected together to form one large mixer circuit. By connecting the output of mixer A to the wild input of mixer B, all of the inputs of both mixers form a composite signal at the output of mixer B. This can be done if the output impedance of mixer A is less than or equal to the impedance of mixer B.

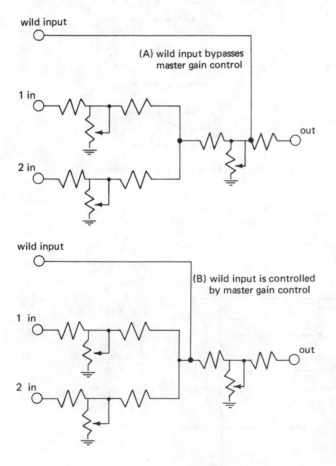

Fig. 8.14. Mixer with "wild" provisions

Certain mixer designs incorporate a gain function separate from the master gain control. The "adder gain switch" found on various mixers determines the total amount of gain the circuit can provide and thereby be controlled by the master gain control. The number of selection possibilities and amount of gain increase is not standardized and will vary according to design. A mixer designed and described by Robert Moog ("Construction of a Simple Mixer," *Electronic Music Review*, no. 4, Oct., 1967) has the possibility of zero db, +10 db or +20 db gain. If the particular mixer is a combination of normal mixing functions and preamplifier for microphone mixing, the adder switch will often not affect the preamplifier gain.

The large console mixers found in recording studios often incorporate facilities called "echo send" and "echo receive." Both facilities add artificial reverberation to the signal in an attempt to add more realism to the sound. The difference between the two facilities is that the echo send control determines the amount of signal being fed to the reverberation unit. The point at which the signal is taken can be either before or after the gain controls. The echo receive control determines the level of the signal after it has been processed through the reverberation unit. It is of added value if this mode is switchable to the external monitors only, so that it can be heard through the monitor speakers but not be present in the program output. It is desirable to have echo send and echo receive on each channel to provide for greater selectivity and control. (A more detailed discussion of echo and reverberation techniques will be found in chap. 10.)

Two additional devices often found on mixers are the "seque pot" and the "panoramic divider," "pan pot" or "direction control." A seque pot allows the composer to fade from one input to another in various degrees. The same effect could be achieved by turning down the gain of one input while turning up the gain of another. The seque pot accomplishes the same thing by using just one control (fig. 8.15). Crossfading may be between two separate channels or between two entire circuits of a stereo mixer. By reversing the inputs and outputs of a seque pot, a simple panoramic divider may be simulated. The pan pot has one input and two outputs and is used to simulate stereophonic movement of a signal from one output to another. As with the seque pot, panning can also be achieved using two pots. In this

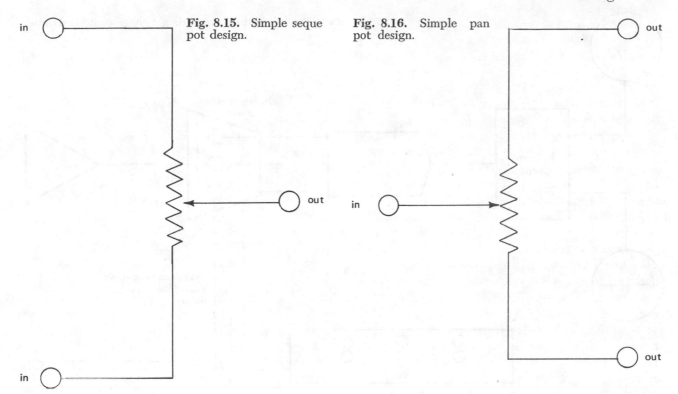

Fig. 8.15. Simple seque pot design.

Fig. 8.16. Simple pan pot design.

case the signal is fed to two identical outputs and then one is turned down while the other is turned up. The audible effect is that the sound seems to move between speakers or can be placed at almost any point in a straight line between two speakers. Panning has become a very valuable tool for the electronically oriented composer and various techniques and problems of panning are discussed in detail in chapter 9. Stereo mixers incorporating a pan pot will usually have one input for the signal to be panned and the panning will occur between the two individual outputs.

As with most other electronic music techniques, the range of applications of the mixer has been greatly extended by incorporation of voltage control. The voltage-controlled mixer is essentially a series of voltage-controlled amplifiers or gates with mixed outputs. As with many gates, there are two modes of control. The first is the applied control voltage. Whether the gate reacts to AC or DC or is coupled will vary with the individual manufacturer. In any case, the greater the intensity of the applied voltage, the higher the amplitude of the signal in that particular input. The second mode of control is the manual gain pot for each input which controls the potential of the applied voltage. One of the many advantages of the voltage-controlled mixer is its ability to switch

rapidly from one input to another at speeds which would be impossible manually. By applying the individual trigger pulse outputs of a sequencer to the control inputs of a voltage-controlled mixer, the switching speed is limited only by the firing speed of the sequencer. Many very unusual and complex envelopes can be produced by controlling the various input levels with program voltages from different attack or envelope generators. If each control voltage exhibited a different attack, sustain, and decay time, each mixer input would have a varying amplitude change. A perfect application of this technique is illustrated by the production of the complex violin timbre envelope in chapter 5, p. 32. Depending on how the times were set and how the generators were fired, the various attacks and decays of the inputs would overlap in a continually changing manner, resulting in a very complex combined output. A special technique of timbre modulation may also be achieved by using a voltage-controlled mixer. If a signal is patched to a filter bank, many of its individual and combined frequency components can be taken from the individual band-pass outputs. If the signal is then reconstructed via a voltage-controlled mixer, each component can then be brought in and out of the composite wave according to its own particular program voltage.

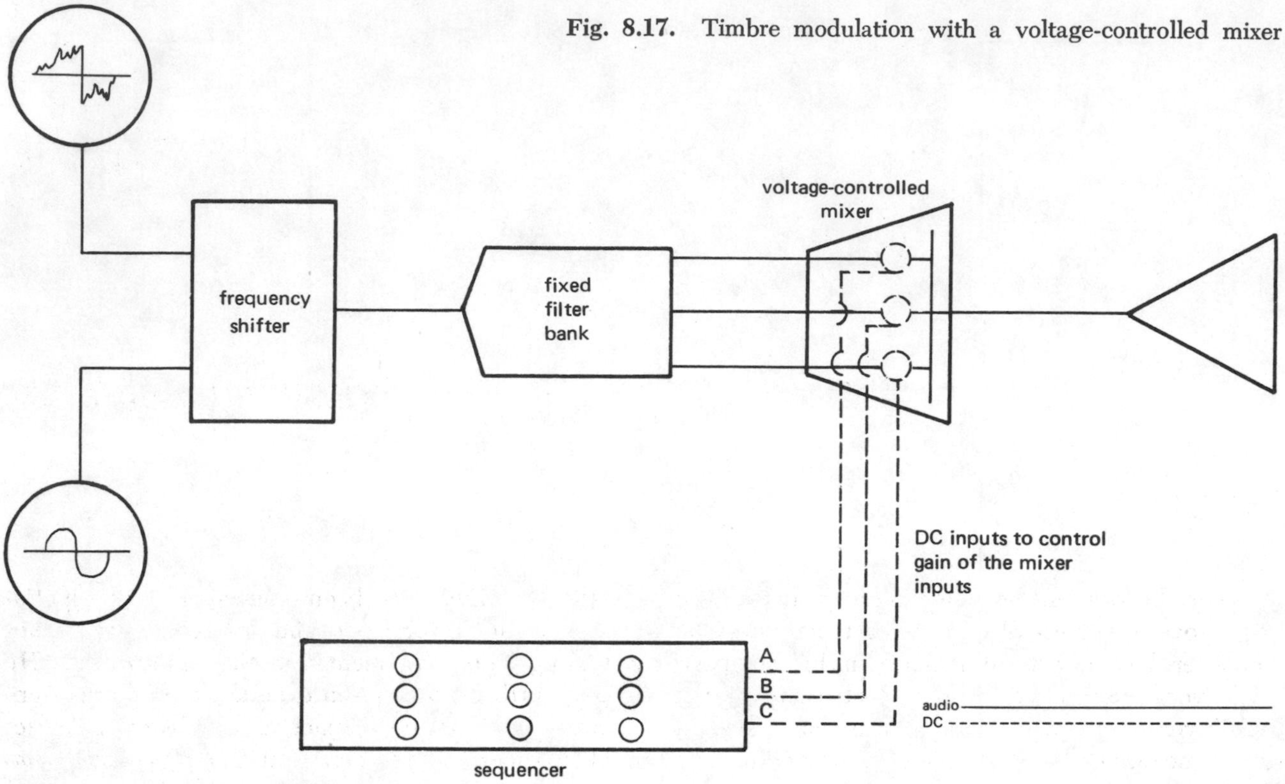

Fig. 8.17. Timbre modulation with a voltage-controlled mixer

As with all mixer designs, the voltage-controlled mixer may or may not be equipped with all of the extra facilities such as VU meters, master gain controls, equalization and so on. Such mixers are also available in mono or stereo design, with the possibility of interconnection of the two individual circuits of the stereo mixer. A logical step in mixer design would be to incorporate a voltage-controlled master gain. This would allow for instantaneous changes in the composite signal and would be very helpful in controlling the total output of a highly polyphonic situation. A voltage-controlled master gain can be simulated by routing the output to a single VCA and using it as the final level control. In applying the old adage of "the more one has the more one wants" to circuitry design, the *ideal* mixer should have the following: (1) any number of multiple inputs with the possibility of connection to any number of multiple outputs, (2) individual input and master gain control, both manual and voltage-controlled, (3) individual input and master equalization control, both manual and voltage-controlled, (4) the possibility of individual input and output impedance-switching to meet any situation, (5) the possibility of preamplification of any input for use with microphones, tape head outputs, phonographs, etc., (6) slider pots in close proximity to each other,

(7) VU meters for each output, (8) voltage- and manually-controlled echo send and receive, (9) voltage- and manually-controlled seque and pan pots, with the possibility of connection to any combination of inputs or outputs, (10) non-linear mixing inputs for heterodyning, (11) several wild inputs, (12) input and output switches which would allow for the use of balanced or unbalanced lines or both, (13) portability for use in live performance situations, (14) a moderate cost within the composer's budget.

At this stage in our technological development the last two criterion make such a piece of equipment impossible. As the field of microelectronics and integrated circuits progresses, however, such an instrument may someday become a reality. For the present, the composer must be satisfied with having several different designs available in the studio which may be combined to produce all of the required functions.

Since the mixer is often a switching center and/or final terminal before output to the audio amplifier or tape head, the requirement of high quality for it cannot be overstressed. The most beautiful and carefully programmed events can be totally destroyed if routed through a mixer with a poor frequency response and a high percentage of distortion.

location modulation

The history and development of music has been governed basically by what techniques the composer has chosen to include in his compositional vocabulary. The composers of early Church music were concerned with pitch as manifested in single melodic lines and two-part organum. The Renaissance composer began to add a more complex polyphony to his vocabulary. The music of the early Baroque began to utilize notated dynamics and new concepts of orchestration. Consequently, throughout the history of musical performance the musician has been required to become more and more concerned with finer aspects of sound production. Much of the music since the middle of the twentieth century has tended to isolate various parameters and to be composed basically with those aspects, leaving other parameters as sort of residual products. Many times the conventional hierarchy of parameters has been inverted—by, for example, concentrating mainly on timbre and using pitch and rhythm only as vehicle for timbral development.

A parameter which has been rediscovered in recent years is that of space. Spatial considerations are by no means new to the composer. Responsorial and antiphonal psalmody of the early vocal church music, the *cori spezzati* (divided choirs) of the sixteenth-century St. Mark's Cathedral, Mozart's "Notturno" in D Major-K 286 for four orchestras, Verdi's use of off-stage trumpets in his "Requiem" are all examples of interest in the spatial location of sound. In many twentieth-century scores the composers give very precise instructions for exact placement of individual and groups of instruments. A composer representative of this approach is Henry Brant. Since the middle of this century Brant has been concerned with spatial aspects of performance and his scores give exact seating and placement for the instruments. He puts forth his views and experience on spatial concepts in his article, "Space as an Essential Aspect of Musical Composition" (in *Contemporary Composers on Contemporary Music*, ed. Schwartz and Childs [New York: Holt, Rinehart and Winston, 1967]).

Early musique concrete and electronic music composers were limited in their approach to spatial considerations. With the development of binaural multi-track, recording-tape presentations were able to locate various sounds according to speaker placement, and the refinement of stereophonic recording and reproduction now enables the composer to locate a sound source at any point within a stereo field generated by only two speakers. If two speakers are reproducing the same program with identical phase and amplitude, the sound will appear to come from a point exactly between the two speakers. If the composer wishes the sound to appear to be generated at a point to the right of center, he lowers the gain to the left speaker and raises the gain to the right speaker. With only two speakers it is possible to simulate up to five or six individual sound locations at one time in a stereophonic field by adjusting the relative output gains. Figure 9.1 shows the relative gain relationships for the two channels of a stereophonic tape with five evenly-spaced tracks across the stereo field. The spatial image produced by these amplitude relationships would place tracks A and E at the extreme sides, track C in the exact center, track D right of center, and track B left of center. This could be accomplished by using several stereo-

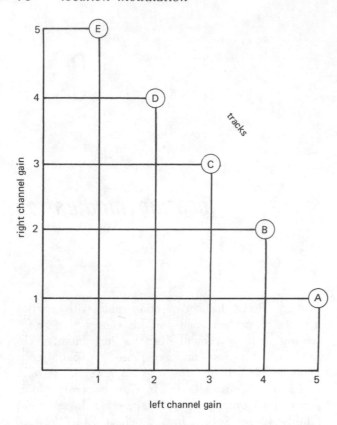

Fig. 9.1. Gain relationships between channels for stereophonic location.

phonic tape decks and a stereo mixer to reproduce five stereophonic tapes or, as more commonly done, dub down a composite mixture of the tracks with the correct amplitude relationships on each track. An available example of a five-track stereo image is Stockhausen's *Telemusik* (Deutsche Grammophone Records no. 137012).

In addition to being able to locate sounds precisely in a stereo field, stereophony can also be used to create the illusion of a sound source moving back and forth between two speakers. An excellent example of this simulated movement is in "Her Majesty" (Lennon and McCartney) on the *Abbey Road* LP by the Beatles (Apple Records no. SO-383). Paul McCartney's voice and guitar accompaniment are first heard on the left channel and over a 22-second period the whole track slowly moves across the stereo field to the right channel. The movement of an image across a stereo field is called "panning" and falls under the broader category of "location modulation." The term "panning" is usually taken to mean the perceptual movement of sound on an axis, while the term "location modulation" can refer to any type of sound processing which involves varying the spatial location of sound. As will be explained later,

this processing does not always result in perceptual sound movement and may also be used in the alteration of pitch and timbre. There are many different approaches to the technology of location modulation, ranging from very simple techniques to the use of very complex apparatus. The methods presented in this chapter will be directed primarily to use with equipment found in the average electronic music studio and with modules found on commercial electronic music systems.

The composer should consider that the electronic movement of sound is an illusion. The most effective manner of location modulation is to physically move the sound source during a live performance. At the same time, the composer should remember that a media must be dealt with for what it is and what it can do. He may spend a great deal of time attempting to "synthesize" the sound of a bassoon. If that sound is then used to do something a real bassoon could do just as well or better, then the time was spent only as a technical exercise. If that sound was used in a manner which is technically impossible with the bassoon, however, then the composer was certainly justified in its synthesis and any small flaws in its realism are often masked by the produced effects. By the same token, location modulation can go beyond what can be done by having performers move about an environment with sound sources. Although many of these modulation techniques are not 100 percent effective as a simulation of acoustical sound movement, they still present the composer with many new processing possibilities and provide him with a precise control over an often neglected parameter.

Perception of sound location involves four different kinds of information: horizontal angle cues, vertical angle cues, distance cues, and velocity cues. Horizontal or lateral angle cues are derived from the phase and intensity of a signal. As explained earlier (p. 75) the location of a sound can be judged largely by its loudness. If the sound is being produced at some point to the right of the perceiver, the sound will be louder in his right ear than in the left. Frequencies below about 1k Hz, however, have very long wavelengths and these sound waves are diffracted around the head so that in many cases the intensity is equal in each ear. In this case the perceiver must rely on other cues for sound location. For frequencies below 1k Hz, and especially those between 200 Hz and 800 Hz, the prime cue is phase. Even if a long wavelength is diffracted to reach both ears with equal intensity, one ear is going to receive the sound before the other. These time differences are so small that they are actually differences in phase. If a sound is being produced at a point to the right of the perceiver, the phase of the signal at the right ear may be x° of the phase of the same signal as it reaches the left ear. Higher frequencies display shorter wavelengths and the head acts as a "sound shadow" to make the shorter wavelengths more directional to one ear or the other. Consequently, higher frequencies are much easier to locate as far as point of origin is concerned, with intensity being the primary cue. This is especially true of frequencies around 5k Hz. But this information is a bit misleading when working with electronically manipulated sound. Location modulation within a stereo field in effect uses the relative loudness of the speakers to produce the relative loudness of the signal in each ear. Due to the extreme directionality of higher frequencies, more pronounced differences in intensity are required for them than for lower frequencies. Consequently, higher frequencies are often more difficult to pan than lower frequencies. Various experiments have also shown the sine waves are more difficult to locate than waveshapes with higher harmonic and non-harmonic overtone content. Sine waves in the range of 3k Hz are very difficult to locate because the frequencies are too high for effective phase discrimination and too low for effective intensity discrimination. There are several theories concerning cues for vertical discrimination of sound location. One theory set forth by Hans Wallach states that the direction of the source of a sound is cued by a sequence of lateral angles perceived by the listener as he moves his head toward the direction of the sound (Hans Wallach, "On Sound Localization," *Readings in Perception*, ed. Beardslee and Wertheimer, [New Jersey: D. Van Nostrand Company, 1958], pages 476-483).

The distance from a sound source is cued by the ratio of reverberated sound to the direct or non-reverberated sound perceived at a given point. If a sound source is some distance away, there may be X number of surfaces which can reflect the sound before it reaches the listener's ear. If the same source is moved closer to the listener, there will be less reflected sound perceived and more direct sound. Reverberation cues can also aid the angular placement of sound. If the source is located slightly to the left of center in the left channel, along with a higher gain, it should also exhibit slightly less reverberation. This, of course, will also give the sound the effect of being less distant in relation to its radial axis. John Chowning of the Stanford University Department of Music describes this as "local reverberation." (John

Chowning, "The Simulation of Moving Sound Sources," paper presented at the 38th Audio Engineering Society Convention, Los Angeles, California, May, 1970, Audio Engineering Society reprint no. 726). The overall reverberant signal is referred to as "global reverberation" and is one of the primary cues for simulating the overall space of the reproduced environment. Therefore, with increasing distance, the ratio of the local reverb to the global reverb becomes greater. This increase in local reverb is not linear, since the ratio increases at a faster rate as the distance increases. An increase in distance is also characterized by a gradual loss of low frequencies. This often presents problems because of the cut in response at the high end of the spectrum which is characteristic of artificial reverberation units (see chap. 10, p. 88).

The final dimension of sound location is its speed or rate of change on the lateral and vertical axis (angular velocity) and rate of change in proximation (radial velocity). A change in reverberation characteristics at various rates can be used to simulate a certain amount of depth. As the distance between a constant-frequency sound source and the perceiver diminishes, the sound pressure waves become more and more compressed and more frequencies are perceived in the same amount of time. The result is a rise in the perceived pitch. Conversely, as the distance increases, the distance between the pressure waves becomes greater and the perceived effect is a slight drop in pitch. This "Doppler effect" is the prime cue for radial velocity of a sound. A simulation of a sound source moving toward the perceiver would then require a very slight rise in the frequency along with the correct change in the local and global reverberation ratios. It must be remembered that the Doppler effect is only present when the sound source is in motion. At the same time a greater velocity and closer proximity requires faster and greater pitch changes. As the simulated sound source loses velocity and again becomes stationary, the pitch accordingly drops back to its original frequency. *Angular velocity* is cued by the rate of change of the gain levels of the reproduction channels.

The problem facing the composer is to develop proper controls for simulation of each of these dimensions using devices commonly found in the electronic music studio. Approaching the problem in these terms means that each spatial cue must be a function of some process commonly available to the composer and performer. Intensity is a function of amplitude between two or more outputs; reverberation ratios can be a function of the relative amplified gain of direct and reverberated signals; and phase and Doppler effect shift can be a function of phase and frequency modulation. All of these parameters can be subjected to electronic control which can be manipulated at will by the composer or performer.

The most common device used for moving sound is the "panoramic divider," more commonly referred to as the "pan pot," which consists of one input and two outputs with inverse gain functions (see chap. 8, p. 72). If the pan pot is turned completely to the left, channel A will exhibit full gain and channel B will have zero gain. As the pot is turned to the right, the gain to the left channel is slowly attenuated and the gain to the right channel becomes proportionally higher. At the center position, both channels are down 3 db and the sound source appears to be midway between both speakers. Pan pots are usually calibrated in steps, each step representing a certain number of degrees of shift. If the stereo field were 90°, a representative pan pot may have 10 positions of 9° each. A larger field may require more increments or larger angle changes. Figure 9.2 is a graph illustrating the relationship between the increments and the relative gain to each channel. Various stereo mixers are designed with a special panning input which allows one of the signals to be panned or placed at any point within the stereo field. A multi-channel pan pot provides for a number of channels to be panned individually or simultaneously. The 360° pan pot contains a wiper connection which continuously rotates 360° for circular panning effects. (The 360° pan pot will be

discussed later in relationship to Lowell Cross's "Stirrer.")

If the studio is not equipped with pan pot facilities, panning may be accomplished in a somewhat more cumbersome manner with a stereo mixer. If each channel of the mixer is receiving identical signals, the sound will emanate from between the two monitor speakers. By simultaneously attenuating channel A and raising the gain on channel B, the sound will pan to channel B at a rate determined by the rate of amplitude change on each channel. The obvious drawback to this technique is that it requires two hands, which may prevent the operator from simultaneously controlling other functions. This technique will also require quite a bit of experimentation to be able to manipulate the pots and maintain the correct relationship. Experience has shown that this type of manual panning is easier with slider pots, but many of the regular pan pots are also available in slider formats. If the slider is placed in a position horizontal to the operator, its position will provide the operator with a precise cybernetic model of the sound location. Figure 9.2 indicates that the relative amplitudes change in an exponential manner rather than linear; therefore, manual panning achieved in the above manner will be much more successful if done with exponential pots or with amplifiers set in exponential gain mode.

Another very common method of panning is done by using photo-sensitive resistors and photo-sensitive transistors. The amount of voltage allowed to flow through a photo-resistor is determined by the intensity and amount of light which is shining on its sensitized surface (see chap. 5, p. 36). If a photo-resistor were to be placed in series with an oscillator output and an amplifier, the gain to the amplifier could be controlled with a small, hand-held light source such as a pen flashlight (fig. 9.3). If two channels were to be controlled in the same manner with two individual photo-resistors, the relative gain to each channel could be controlled by passing the light source back and forth over the cells. By adjusting the relative position of each photo-resistor, the gain levels could be adjusted to produce very accurate panning effects. A four-channel photo-resistor panning device is illustrated in figure 9.4. With this configuration it is possible to continuously pan 360° around an environment, pan with figure-eight patterns or produce any other pattern, depending on how the light source is moved. Another advantage of this configuration is that it is a cybernetic model of the controlled environment. The position of each

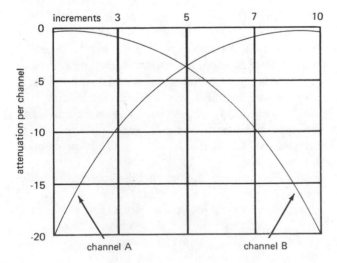

Fig. 9.2. Relationships between pan pot increments and relative channel gain.

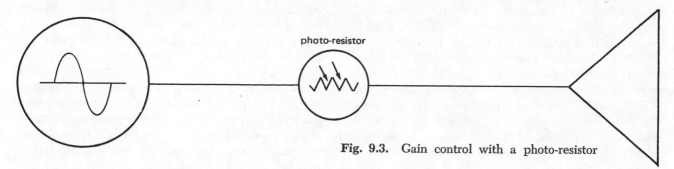

Fig. 9.3. Gain control with a photo-resistor

photo-resistor also represents the location of each speaker, so the panning patterns exactly coincide with the movement of the light source. The disadvantages are that this particular device is passive and there is a certain amount of insertion loss which may be enough to require additional amplification. Also, this being a light-sensitive device, one must contend with the ambient light in the room. The best solution to this problem is to cover the photo-resistors with two adjustable sheets of polarized glass or plastic. The relative positions of the polarized material can then be adjusted to block out any amount of light, thereby making the photo-sensitive device adaptable to almost any environment. Composer Frederic Rzewski has described the construction and provides component values for a very adequate photo-resistor panning device (Frederic Rzewski, "A Photo-resistor Mixer for Live Performance," *Electronic Music Review*, no. 4, Oct. 1967, pp. 33-34).

Photo-transistors are used in a somewhat same manner, but the circuits are active and necessitate

trol of voltage envelopes. This will be discussed later in this chapter.

A panning device used by many composers and performers is the "Stirrer," which was developed by composer Lowell Cross. Although this particular device is not commercially available, several have been constructed according to Cross's specifications and are currently in use. The Stirrer makes use of four specially-designed, continuous-rotation, 360° potentiometers controlled in synchronized movement by a planetary-gear arrangement, with the drive shaft being turned manually by a crank. Its configuration allows the composer

a power supply such as a battery. The advantage of photo-transistors is that they actually provide amplification and the relative gain levels can be finely controlled. Photo-transistors are often used in conjunction with light-emitting diodes, which produce illumination in relation to applied voltages. This of course necessitates very accurate con-

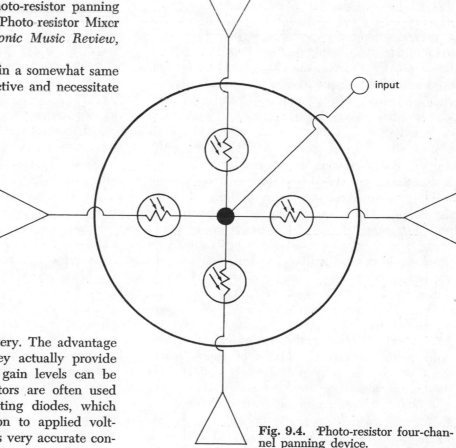

Fig. 9.4. Photo-resistor four-channel panning device.

or performer to pan four different signals around and through an environment, with the signals evenly spaced by a distance of 90°. The produced effect is that the four input signals follow each other around a space with the direction and speed determined by the direction of speed of the crank. The Stirrer is also equipped with a switching configuration which allows for several variations in the panning patterns. One such function could be to have inputs 1 and 3 moving in a clockwise direction while inputs 2 and 4 move in a counterclockwise direction. A similar function would allow for three inputs to move in one direction with only one input moving in the opposite direction. Other switching arrangements provide for various types of figure-eight patterns. (A detailed description of the Stirrer and its circuitry appears in Lowell Cross, "The Stirrer," *Source-Music of the Avant Garde*, no. 4, vol. 2, July 1968, pp. 25-28.)

All of the panning methods discussed so far have been controlled by manual means. The advantage to this approach is that the control is very cybernetic and the placement, speed, and direction can be directly determined by the operator. In live performance situations, manual control is the usually preferred method. There are various circumstances, however, in which manual control is less than satisfactory. The composer is many times so involved with adjusting frequency settings and riding gain levels that he lacks hands to simultaneously manipulate a smooth pan effect. Consequently an extra dub-down is often needed, especially for the production of spatial effects—and additional tape generations mean additional loss in fidelity. Another disadvantage is that the composer may wish to move the sound at speeds beyond the range of manual control. Without the use of switching controls, manual operation also limits the composer or performer from making truly instantaneous changes in the placement of the sound. The operator cannot manipulate the pots fast enough to avoid the movement of sound being perceived. An available solution to these problems is through voltage control, that is, making sound location, panning, and spatial modulation a function of voltage envelopes. The essential module for panning applications is the voltage-controlled amplifier. The application of various AC and DC voltages will then provide the composer with programable means of sound movement which can be instantaneously activated as they are needed.

The first method to be dealt with uses two VCAs controlled by opposite polarities of an AC signal. The information signal is split and each

leg is patched to the audio input of a VCA. The AC signal which is to control the gain of the VCAs is patched to a phase splitter, allowing the positive portion of the signal to be taken from one output and the negative portion from another. When these two opposing control signals are applied to the respective VCAs, the positive phase will produce gain in VCA-1 and at the same instant there will be zero gain from VCA-2. When the positive signal drops to zero volts, the negative phase then provides gain for VCA-2. If the VCAs are designed so that negative voltage does not result in positive gain, the negative control signal will have to be inverted, as shown in figure 9.5. Since the VCAs are operating with continu-

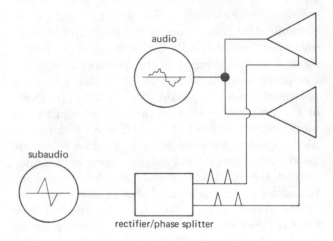

Fig. 9.5. Patch configuration for AC control of panning.

ally opposing gain characteristics, the monitored signal will appear to pan between the two channels. Although a triangle or sine-wave control may be used, the triangle waveshape seems to produce more realistic effects. If a pulse wave control were to be used as a control, the sound would instantaneously jump from one channel to the other. If the pulse were in a square-wave format, the pulsing between channel would be at an even rate. By varying the duty cycle of the pulse wave, it would be possible to control the on-off time ratio of each channel. A sawtooth control voltage would gradually pan the signal from one channel to the other as a function of the rise in voltage. The instant drop to the negative polarity would instantaneously place the signal back on the first channel at a speed which would be imperceptible as a pan.

The use of opposite polarities alone to control amplitude relationships is not completely effective, however. The problem is that there is no

Fig. 9.6. Use of phase shift with VCAs

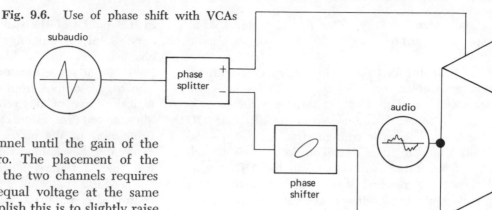

rise in gain on one channel until the gain of the other channel is at zero. The placement of the sound midway between the two channels requires both VCAs to receive equal voltage at the same time. One way to accomplish this is to slightly raise one VCA's reference voltage so that zero volts control voltage will still produce gain in the amplifier and a certain amount of negative voltage is required to produce zero gain. With this method, the negative cycle of the other control voltage will have to be inverted to make each VCA operate with the same characteristics. Another solution is to shift the phase of one of the polarities so that the rise in the negative cycle begins before the positive cycle has reached zero volts. This is effective with about a 60° phase shift, as illustrated in figure 9.6. The point at which the two voltages cross in time will be the point at which the gain is equal on both channels. Whether or not the signals must be rectified or inverted depends again on the operating characteristics of the VCA. As can be seen in figure 9.7A, this phase shift will produce the correct voltage relationship only once every two cycles. This also holds true for the previous method of changing the reference voltage. If the pan is to be a one-time event, these two methods will be very adequate. If the panning is to be a continuous modulation between two channels, however, negative clipping (see chap. 12, p. 115) is required to make the voltage envelopes cross at the same time with every cycle (fig. 9.7B). The negative clipping, in effect, shortens the time of the negative cycle, and used in conjunction with the 60° phase shift will produce the correct control voltage.

The panning rate is determined by the frequency of the control signal. With control frequencies below 7 or 8 Hz, the perceiver will be able to follow the sounds as they move back and forth between the speakers. With control signals above those frequencies, the sounds will move so rapidly that the ear will not have enough time to respond to the location cues. Consequently, the perceived effect will be a monophonic "wall" of sound and all panning movements will be imperceivable. As the control frequency approaches the audio range, characteristic amplitude-modulation sidebands will

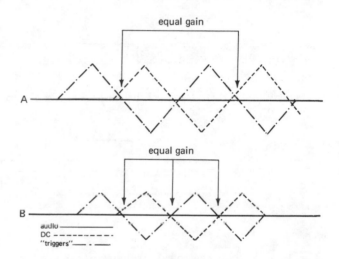

Fig. 9.7. Control voltages for panning

appear, because panning is essentially amplitude modulation of a single signal between two separate channels. It is even possible to pan at rates so high that the original audio signal will disappear. This is explained by the fact that a sound, depending on its frequency and overtone content, must last a certain length of time before it can be perceived. If a sound is being panned between two channels and only one of those channels is being monitored, the effect will be a gating on and off of the signal, with the gated envelope defined by the shape of the control voltage. If this gating is extremely rapid, the audio signal will eventually be heard only as a series of "pops" (see p. 42, chap. 6). If the other channel is also monitored, the number of pops is doubled. Therefore, as the control frequency becomes higher and higher, the original audio signal will tend to be dissipated into the energy of the sidebands and the prominent signal will then be the frequency of the control voltage. This duration threshold is especially critical with lower-frequency audio signals.

DC controlled gates, in conjunction with attack generators, may also be used to produce programmed panning effects. Alternate gates must be gradually opened and closed using alternate DC envelopes. The basic configuration for this method is illustrated in figure 9.8. The decay time of each attack generator must be set so the DC voltage has not yet reached zero volts when the other attack generator begins to generate the rising DC voltage. This is necessary to avoid the loss of gain

in the middle of the pan. This same technique is very useful for panning between more than two channels. For each additional channel, a separate pulse and attack generator and gate are required. The trigger output from a sequencer is the most logical source of the required pulses. If the sequencer requires external timing pulses, then the firing time of the pulse generator will indirectly determine the panning time by controlling the firing time of the sequencer. Figure 9.9 illustrates one possible patching configuration for voltage-controlled panning 360° around an enclosed speaker field. If the sequencer is allowed to continu-

Fig. 9.8. Patch configuration for use of attack generators for panning.

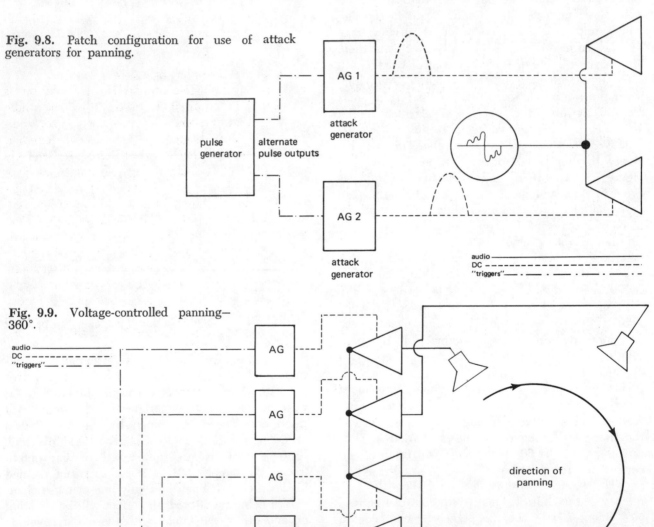

Fig. 9.9. Voltage-controlled panning—360°.

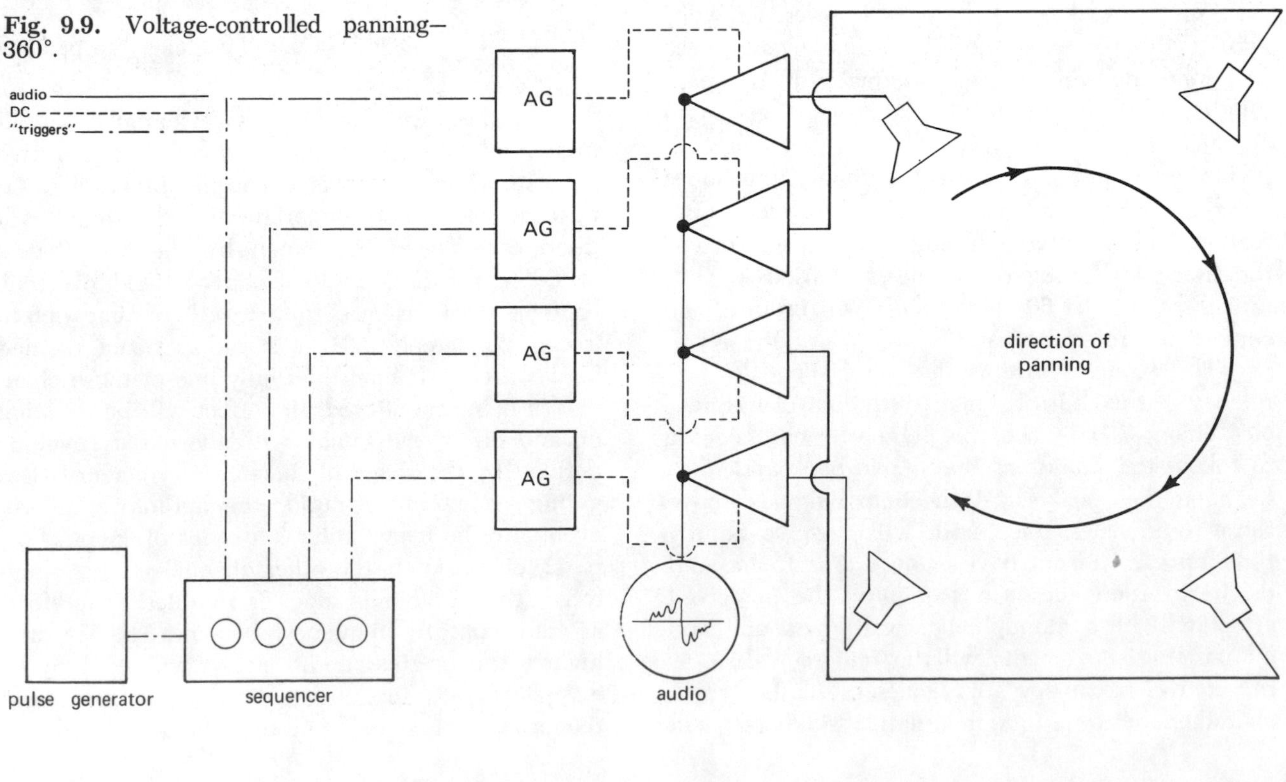

ously recycle, the sound will continue to spin around the audience. If the gates are designed with internal attack and decay controls, the attack generators may be eliminated and triggered directly from the sequencer. This configuration may also be simplified if the gates or VCAs can be connected in series with trigger delays, as described on page 33 of chapter 5. A single pulse is then used to activate the first gate and then each subsequent gate is fired at intervals defined by the delay times. If the panning is to be continuous, the initial pulse period must be equal to the total of all the attack and decay times.

The techniques discussed up to this point have only been concerned with moving sound on a single plane laterally in front of or around the perceiver. A sound which appears to be approaching from a distance involves a bit more complex technique. At the beginning of this chapter it was explained that reverberation and Doppler shifts are the prime cues for radial location. The farther a sound is from a perceiver, the more reverberation it will display. As the sound moves closer, the local reverberation becomes less as the intensity grows. At the same time, depending on the speed of approach, there will be a slight rise in pitch due to the Doppler effect. Figure 9.10 illustrates one possible configuration for controlling the radial effects of sound. Since the amount of reverberation is inverse to the gain, the control voltage to the reverberation unit must be inverted. The control signal to the frequency modulator must also be greatly attenuated, since the amount of voltage used to control the VCA would result in more of a frequency change than is needed to

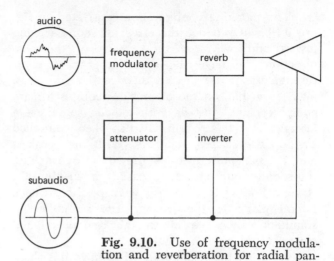

Fig. 9.10. Use of frequency modulation and reverberation for radial panning.

simulate the Doppler effect. If the reverberation unit is not voltage-controllable, one solution is illustrated in figure 9.11. In this case the audio signal is split and one leg is subjected to reverberation. Before the signals are mixed back together, the gain of the reverberated signal is inversely controlled by the same control voltage used to determine the final gain. If the mixer were voltage-controllable, the first VCA could be eliminated. A second reverberation unit could be added after the mix to simulate global reverberation. Another processing device which could be used is the high-pass filter. As the sound moves closer to the perceiver, the lower frequencies become more and more pronounced. As with the frequency modulator, the control signal would have to be considerably attenuated, since this shift in frequency response is very slight.

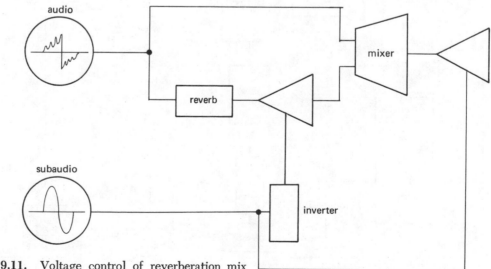

Fig. 9.11. Voltage control of reverberation mix

The patching configuration illustrated in figure 9.10 will produce the effect of sound moving toward and away from the perceiver in the same direction. To have the sound appear to move through the perceiver and then continue to move away from him on the other side requires a more complex patch. Just as with moving sound on a lateral plane, this requires two speakers controlled by opposite shifted polarities. With the speakers and listener positioned as shown in figure 9.12, the sound would appear to pass through him in a straight line. If the speakers were positioned on a lateral plane to the listener, the sound would simultaneously move left to right and nearer and closer, forming an arc pattern.

By using the techniques set forth in this chapter in various combinations, it is possible to place and pan sound in an unlimited number of patterns. The composer should experiment with all types of control envelopes and different patterns of speaker placement. Extreme care must be taken to be sure that the speakers are properly phased. Since the panning effects are dependent on relative amplitude levels of a monophone signal, improper phasing could result in very critical cancellation. The more speakers and channels used, the more precise the panning will be, and in a real-time performance situation one is only limited by the availability of the equipment. If the music is to be subjected to tape storage, however, the number of available channels is the limiting factor. The composer, in most cases, will find that four channels are usually sufficient for most panning requirements, since several different panning formats may be stored on a single tape at one time. One tape may contain information which moves in a figure-eight pattern, another information moving in a 360° clockwise pattern, and a third information moving in radial patterns. All three tapes may then be dubbed-down to a single tape without

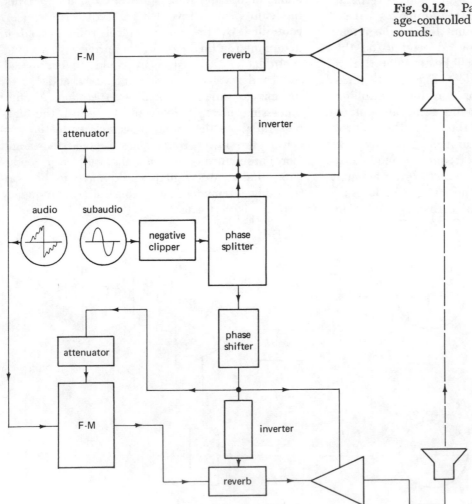

Fig. 9.12. Patching configuration for voltage-controlled panning for oncoming sounds.

affecting either of the panning patterns. The only limitation to the number of panning configurations that can be produced simultaneously is their composite effectiveness. Too many simultaneous patterns will not be perceived individually as pans, but rather the acoustical space will be perceived as being in an undefinable state of flux. Of course if this is the composer's intent, it may be used to create some very beautiful effects in itself.

The potential of the spatial aspects of composition has not yet begun to be realized. Just as the use of dynamics has been an evolutionary process of a parameter realized in the seventeenth century, the technology of the twentieth century has revitalized an aspect of sound which will continue to develop with the composers' and performers' methods of control.

10

reverberation, echo, and feedback

It is often said that electronically generated sound lacks "life," or is less "humanistic" than acoustically-produced sound. The novice composer working in the electronic medium will often overuse reverberation and echo in an attempt to compensate for the lack of acoustical "realism." It is true that a certain amount of reverberation will give an electronically-generated sound the sensation of being reproduced in a larger acoustical space, but it will not aid the composer in his quest for a true, "acoustically-generated" event. The phenomenon which creates this apparent difference between the sound produced by a square-wave generator and the sound produced by a clarinet is that the acoustically-produced sound is almost continually in a transient state, resulting in many minute variations that give it its characteristic "life," while the frequencies produced by an oscillator are much more stable and, excepting the artificially imposed attacks and decays, there are very few if any transients. Therefore the use of excessive echo and reverberation does nothing to add transients to a sound and often even masks whatever transients do exist. If the composer does require the illusion of an acoustically-generated event, he will usually have more success by using acoustically-produced sound as the basic source. True reverberation is the result of variations in arrival time of a particular sound caused by multiple reflections from several surfaces. In many cases an electronically-generated sequence can be greatly enhanced by re-recording the playback with an air microphone in an acoustically live environment.

The terms "reverberation" and "echo" are often used interchangeably, but when working in the electronic medium there is a distinct difference between these two effects. Reverberation is the sum total of all reflections of a sound arriving at a given point at different times. The onset of the attack is prolonged for the perceiver until all of the reflected sound has reached his ear. By the same token, all of the decay characteristics of the sound are extended until the final sound-wave reflection has reached the ear of the perceiver. In more general terms, reverberation is characterized by the prolongation of the total sound event for a certain time period which is determined by the distance from the sound source and the perceiver's proximity to the source and the reflective surfaces. Reverberation time is defined as the time lapse between the instant the sound is initiated and the instant the total envelope has decayed to a level of 60 db below its original amplitude. If the individual reflections of the sound are at intervals greater than 50 milliseconds, each individual attack can be perceived and the phenomenon is classified as "echo." Although each individual attack can be distinguished, the succeeding attack(s) may or may not take place before the sound has totally decayed. The number of repeated attacks, or "peaks," along with the repetition rate will vary according to intensity, number of reflective surfaces, and all of the same factors which contributed to the effects of reverberation. It is also known that the decay envelope formed by the individual energy peaks does produce an exponentially decaying pattern and this too might be considered in attempting to recreate natural echo effects.

The most natural sounding reverberation or echo is achieved by using an actual echo or reverberation chamber. This is an acoustically "live" room which contains a speaker and microphone. The sound to be subjected to reverberation is routed to the speaker at one location in the room and is then received by the microphone at another location in the room and finally routed back to the recording or monitoring circuit. The obvious advantage here is that the reverberation is produced under natural conditions and will thus sound very natural. But there are a number of disadvantages to be considered. First, since each chamber is a monophonic system, every independent channel of sound will require a separate chamber if echo is added during the final dub-down. If two binaural channels are routed through the chamber at the same time, even if taken through two separate microphones, most binaural effects will be lost. (Binaural and stereophonic sound is discussed in chap. 12.) Also, the necessary size of such a chamber does not allow it to be located in the immediate proximity of the recording amplifiers. Consequently, very long lines and line amplifiers are required to keep the signal at the proper level. The size and shape of the chamber will also determine the reverberation time and the sonic characteristics of the resultant signal. The reverberation time may be altered to a certain degree by changing the placement of the microphone and speaker within the chamber, but this takes a bit of experimentation and changes cannot be made during the

final recording or playback sequence. The character of the reverberation may also be altered by changing the angles of the reflecting surfaces or by positioning various objects about the chamber to break up the reflected waves. This is also a very experimental situation and cannot be done during mastering sequences. The amount of reverberation can be varied a bit by controlling the amount of the reverberated signal to be mixed with the direct signal, either via the echo-send or echo-receive pots (fig. 10.1).

Most electronic music studios are equipped with devices for the electronic simulation of reverberation. Artificial reverb, although less natural than acoustic reverb, is often preferred by the composer because of the direct and immediate control over reverberation time it gives. Artificial reverb may be produced using either of two devices: the reverberation plate or the more common spring reverb. The reverberation plate, or "thunder-sheet," is a large flexible metal sheet to which is attached an output transducer which transmits the signal from the system output to the metal sheet and an input transducer or contact microphone which is used to receive the signal. As the signal is transformed into vibrations traveling in various directions along the plate, the fluctuations of the metal simulate the reflections in an acoustical reverberation situation and are received as such by the output transducer. The normal maximum re-

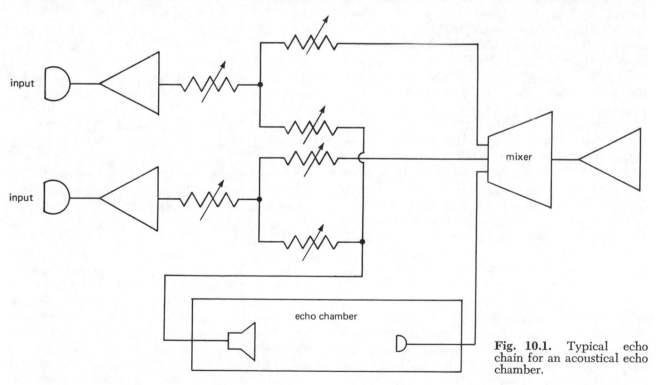

Fig. 10.1. Typical echo chain for an acoustical echo chamber.

verberation time for such an echo plate is about five seconds. This can be varied a great deal by placement of some sort of damping material adjacent to the plate. This damping can be electrically controlled and varied from a state of complete damping to its maximum reverberation time. The spring reverb is more common to the electronic music studio but is also less accurate and adds more of its own coloristic shading to the output signal. Operating on the same principle of input and output transducers, the signal is fed to a small spring or series of springs which cause the characteristic redundancies in the signal envelope. As with the echo chain illustrated in figure 10.1, the amount of reverberation may be controlled by the intensity of the reverberated signal which is mixed with the direct signal.

Due to the characteristics of any particular system, the subjection of a sound to artificial reverberation will result in additional signal modifications. One of the most noticeable effects of artificial reverb is the critical loss of high frequencies. To compensate for this loss, the more professional reverberation systems employ equalization circuits which provide boosts at various high frequencies. Although there are no set standards for this type of equalization, it is most effective at frequencies around 2k, 3k and 5k Hz. The composer will find that in conjunction with reverberation the boosting of these various bands will restore much of the original timbre to the sound, as well as providing possibilities for a minimum amount of timbre modification. Another consequence of artificial reverb is a definite amount of gain loss. When mixed with the direct signal, this loss in gain is not so apparent. If the composer is working with totally reverberated signals, however, he may find there is as much as 10 db loss in gain. To compensate for this loss, many reverberation systems provide a variable gain pot to boost the output signal. Although the amount of reverb can be controlled by the ratio of mixture with the direct signal, several of the professional systems also provide control over reverberation time by switching the signal to springs of proportionately varying lengths. These reverb times will vary from less than .5 second to a maximum over about 5 seconds.

As with most audio equipment, artificial reverberation was originally designed to add more realism to a reproduced signal. And as with most composers working in the electronic medium, the concern is very often with the production of sounds not to be found in a real acoustical situation. Depending on the desired effects, the com-

poser will require different reverb characteristics for different situations. If he wishes to simulate the reverberant characteristics of a particular environment, it is possible to compute the optimum reverberation time according to the simulated room size, nature of the produced sound, and its frequency band. This is a very complex computation carried out by first finding the average absorption coefficient of the environment to be simulated at the desired frequency. John Backus in *The Acoustical Foundations of Music* (New York: W. W. Norton, 1969) provides charts of absorption coefficients for some of the more common environments. These figures are arrived at by dividing the total number of absorption units by the total surface area (measured in square feet). Once this figure is found, the optimum reverberation time may be computed using the formula

$$T = \frac{.05V}{S \log_e (1\text{-aac})}$$

where T = the optimum reverb time in seconds, S = the total room size measure in square feet and *aac* = the average absorption coefficient. The type of music being monitored will also determine different reverb times. It has been found that the average reverb time for a large symphony orchestra in a full hall may be as long as 2.2 seconds, while the average chamber music situation needs only a 1.4-second decay for optimum reverberation. Unless the composer is attempting to recreate a live acoustical situation, he may still have more success by leaving the formulas to the engineers and acousticians and relying on his own ear and judgment. Reverberation can even be carried to the extreme of routing a signal through several reverb units in series, resulting in an almost total "smear" of the final output signal. It must be kept in mind, however, that artificial reverberation does result in a definite amount of coloration to the sound and, unless this is the desired result, it must be compensated for by mixing with a direct signal or by means of equalization.

A final precaution which should be observed when working with reverb units is their handling. The metal sheets or springs must exhibit a certain amount of flexibility in order to produce the required redundance in the signal. If the chassis of the reverb unit is suddenly jarred, the sheet or spring will be put in motion, resulting in a very loud "crash." If done with care, this effect can be used as a very unusual sound source. (The old thundersheets used for sound effects in theaters are very similar to the reverberation plate described earlier.) Very fine control of the "rum-

Fig. 10.2.   Spectrum selective reverberation

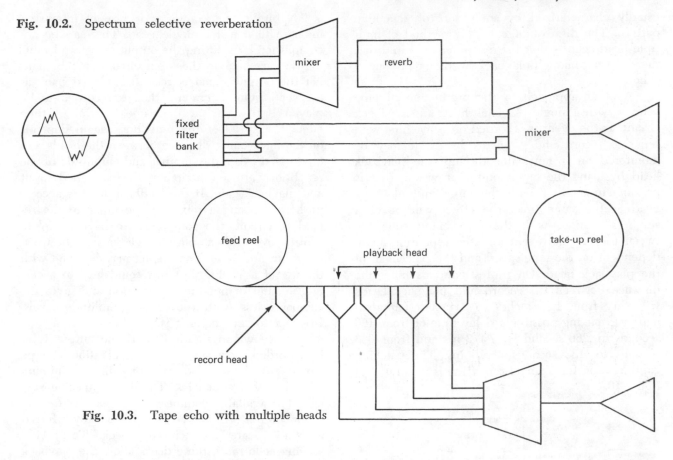

Fig. 10.3.   Tape echo with multiple heads

bling" can be achieved by patching only the reverb output to various types of filters, without using any signal to the reverb input. In this manner the very harsh output signals produced by jarring the unit can be split into various "thunder bandwidths."[*] A minimum amount of movement will cause a great amount of disturbance to the sheet or springs, so great care must be taken not to damage the unit or overload the output.

The filter may also be used in conjunction with a reverb unit in another unusual manner. Instead of subjecting the total signal to reverberation, it may be divided into various frequency bands with a band-pass filter or filter bank, in which case the composer has the option of routing individual bands to the reverb. Then, in mixing the bands back down to the original spectrum, some of the frequencies will exhibit reverberation while other frequencies will not (fig. 10.2). If the composite signal is the result of an additive process, each component could be subjected to reverb with an echo-send provision on the mixing board. But if the signal is a modulation product, there is no prior band separation and the method illustrated in figure 10.2 would be required. This technique in conjunction with voltage-controlled filters offers the composer many variations in application.

Electronically-produced echo is possible from a variety of sources, all of which operate on the same principle of delayed reproduction of recorded events. By recording an event on magnetic tape and then subjecting it to playback via several individual and evenly spaced playback heads, a fairly accurate simulation of natural echo can be produced. As the recorded event comes in contact with each successive playback head, it is repeated and gives the effect of being a reflection, as in acoustically-produced echo. The speed of the echo is a function of the speed of the tape and the distance between the playback heads. The number of echoes or repetitions depend on the number of playback heads being monitored. If the purpose is to simulate natural echo, the output gain of each successive head will have to be set in an exponentially decaying manner as are the successive reflections of natural echo. Care must also be taken to ensure that the playback heads are spaced at precise regular intervals so that the repetition rate will be constant (fig. 10.3). This is not to imply that irregular echo patterns are not always effective; only to say that natural echo is

[*]This technique was utilized by Allen Strange in the production of the pre-recorded tapes for *Vanity Faire* (Champaign, Ill.: Media Press, 1969).

usually characterized by some sort of repetitive pattern. The disadvantage to this method of multiple head echo is that the composer may find that there are not enough playback heads for prolonged echoes.

Another approach to the production of tape echo is with a single playback head and feedback circuit. If the event is recorded on a machine with separate record and playback heads, it may be monitored an instant later through the playback head by using the tape-monitor provision. If it is possible to monitor both the input and playback head at the same time, the effect will be of a single reflection, with the intervening time between the original event and the repetition again dependent on the tape speed and the placement of the playback head. On professional machines the distance between the record and playback heads will vary from 1.25 inches to 2 inches (approximately), making possible a delay time of from .166 seconds to .266 seconds at 7 1/2 ips and from .083 seconds to .133 seconds at 15 ips. The patching configuration for a single repetition is illustrated in figure 10.4.

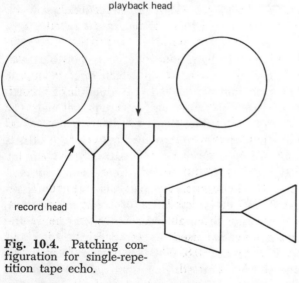

Fig. 10.4. Patching configuration for single-repetition tape echo.

Naturally the composer is usually interested in more than just a single echo. This can be accomplished by splitting the output signal and routing one leg back to the input circuit. In this manner the output signal is recorded, played back at a given instant later, and then re-recorded to be played back again at the same interval of time later. The speed of the repetitions again depends on the intervening distance between the heads and tape speed. Also, the number and amplitude of the repetitions are a function of the combined input and playback gain. If the feedback loop is accomplished by using a mixer at the input to the recording circuit, the composer can have complete control over the amplitude relationship between the input and echo. The mixing may be done with the use of a Y plug, but this could lead to a certain amount of non-linear distortion and gives the composer less control over the amplitude levels. In order to save tape, it is possible to use a tape loop as shown in figure 10.5. If the output is to be recorded, however, another generation of tape would still be needed, resulting in a minimum loss of high frequencies. This entire mechanism/circuit is available commercially especially for the production of artificial echo and is usually referred to as a "repeater" or "echo loop deck." To provide varying echo rates, these decks allow the playback head to be positioned various distances from the record head by sliding the head along a guide. The composer may even choose to calibrate the echo rate along the playback head guide. It is most useful to have the calibration in terms of repetitions per minute, in the same manner as conventional tempo-marking or in fractions of a second indicating the length of time between each repetition. If it is possible to have more than one repeater, many very interesting repetition patterns may be produced by patching them in series with

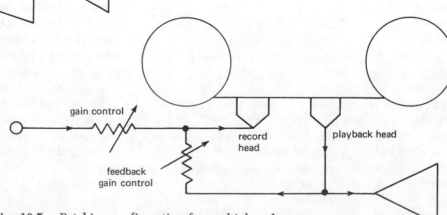

Fig. 10.5. Patching configuration for multiple echoes

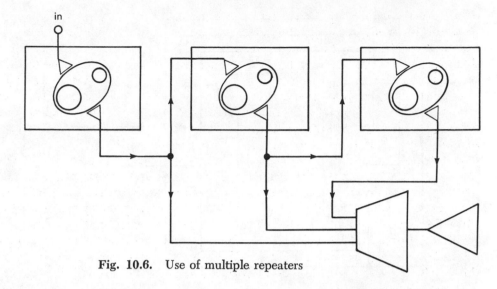

Fig. 10.6. Use of multiple repeaters

each set at a different repetition rate (fig. 10.6). If the playback head is moved along its guide path while the repeater is in operation, the result will be an exaggerated simulation of the Doppler effect. Depending on the rate and amount of displacement, the composer will find a wealth of modification possibilities which are not possible any other way except by variation of the tape speed (as explained on p. 90).

If one is recording from an acoustic sound source with an air mike, tape echo may be produced by simply splitting the line output and patching one leg back into the line input. The amount of echo can then be controlled by using the line input gain control as shown in figure 10.7A. Another method of working with acoustical

sources is to set up an acoustic feedback loop, with the monitor speaker providing the delayed input to the microphone (fig. 10.7B). A necessary precaution to observe is the critical placement of the microphone and monitor speaker. If the microphone sound field overlaps with the speaker sound field, an acoustically-induced howl may be produced. (This type of acoustic feedback can be put to very creative uses and is discussed on p. 96.) Even the electronic feedback/delay loops can result in unwanted resonances if the gain is not carefully controlled. In this case the build-up is so great that the original signals may become masked in a surge of white sound caused by too high a feedback gain. This can be controlled to a degree by careful equalization, but it will also have a definite effect on the frequency response of the output signal.

With the use of a stereo tape recorder, the tape echo can be made to have each successive repetition emit from alternate channels. The patching configuration used to accomplish this is illustrated in figure 10.8. This patching will pass the signal back and forth between the two channels with the repetition rate dependent on twice the

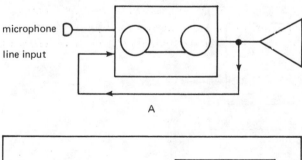

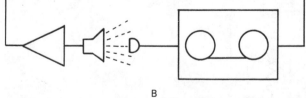

Fig. 10.7. Tape echo using acoustical feedback and simultaneous microphone and line inputs.

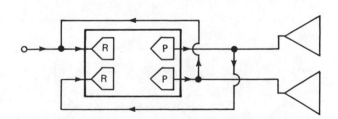

Fig. 10.8. Tape echo on alternating channels

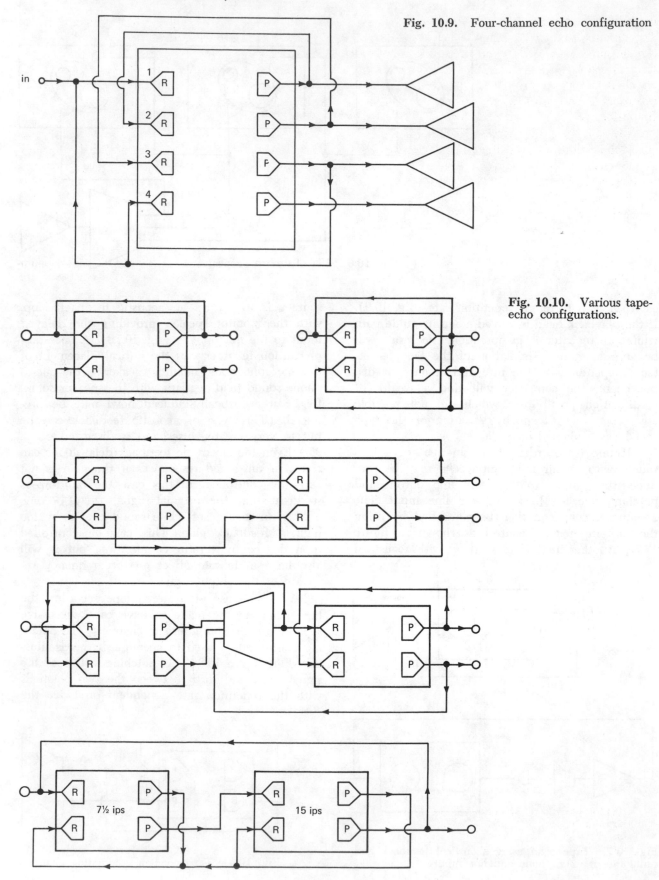

Fig. 10.9.   Four-channel echo configuration

Fig. 10.10.   Various tape-echo configurations.

distance between the record and playback heads. This time can be cut in half by simply monitoring the second channel from the input and not from the playback head. Similar cross-coupling of the channels can also be utilized with multi-track tape recorders as shown in the four-track feedback configuration in figure 10.9, a configuration that provides the composer with many possibilities of tape-echo patterns, depending on whether the individual channels are monitored from the playback head (as shown in fig. 10.9) or from the input, which would halve the repetition rate to the next channel. The composer should also consider the possibility of splitting the outputs of other channels and also patching them back into the first channel or any other channel.

The use of two or more machines with the possibility of using varying speeds provides the composer with an unlimited number of tape-delay configurations. Figure 10.10 offers some other possible patchings which may stimulate the imagination. With these examples, keep in mind that the echo rate can be varied by switching from input to output monitoring. More complex patching also requires careful gain control to avoid excessive build-up or overloading.

The composer could utilize even more complex configurations which also take advantage of different tape speeds and varying distances between the heads, as shown in figure 10.11.

Very slow repetition rates may be produced by using two or more tape recorders playing back a single continuous tape. The set-up in figure 10.12A illustrates how the tape is fed from tape recorder 1 to the tape-up reel of tape recorder 2. In using this technique, one must make sure that the tape follows the normal threading path on each particular machine so that the automatic stop is not activated nor the tension arms bypassed. The distance between the machines determines the repetition rate, which is 1.6 seconds delay for every foot of distance between the record head of tape recorder 1 and the playback head of tape recorder 2 at a speed of 7 1/2 ips and .8 second delay at a speed of 15 ips. Therefore, the echo rate produced by the set-up in figure 10.12A is one repetition every 4.8 seconds. Figure 10.12B illustrates one possible configuration using a combination of multiple machine-delay and electronic feedback. It is even possible to utilize three or more tape recorders for delay as shown in figure 10.12C. Composer Alvin Lucier calls for seven or eight (or more) machines for a very complex multiple delay/loop in his composition *The Only Talking Machine of Its Kind in the Whole World*.

As the composer becomes more and more familiar with delay and feedback loops, he will find that they can be a valuable tool for achieving sound modification. The mixture and superimposition of attack and decay transients will also serve to produce a certain amount of timbre modification if the levels are carefully controlled. This effect is even more noticeable on sustained tones where the feedback results in varying amounts

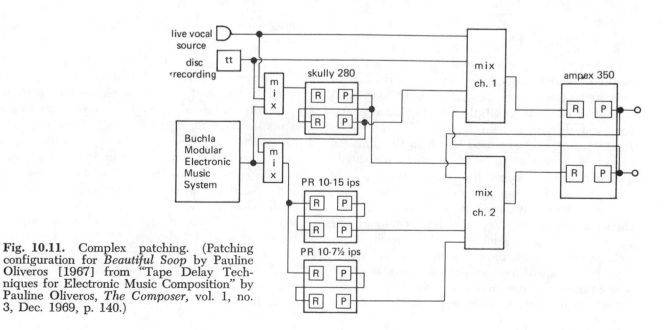

Fig. 10.11. Complex patching. (Patching configuration for *Beautiful Soop* by Pauline Oliveros [1967] from "Tape Delay Techniques for Electronic Music Composition" by Pauline Oliveros, *The Composer*, vol. 1, no. 3, Dec. 1969, p. 140.)

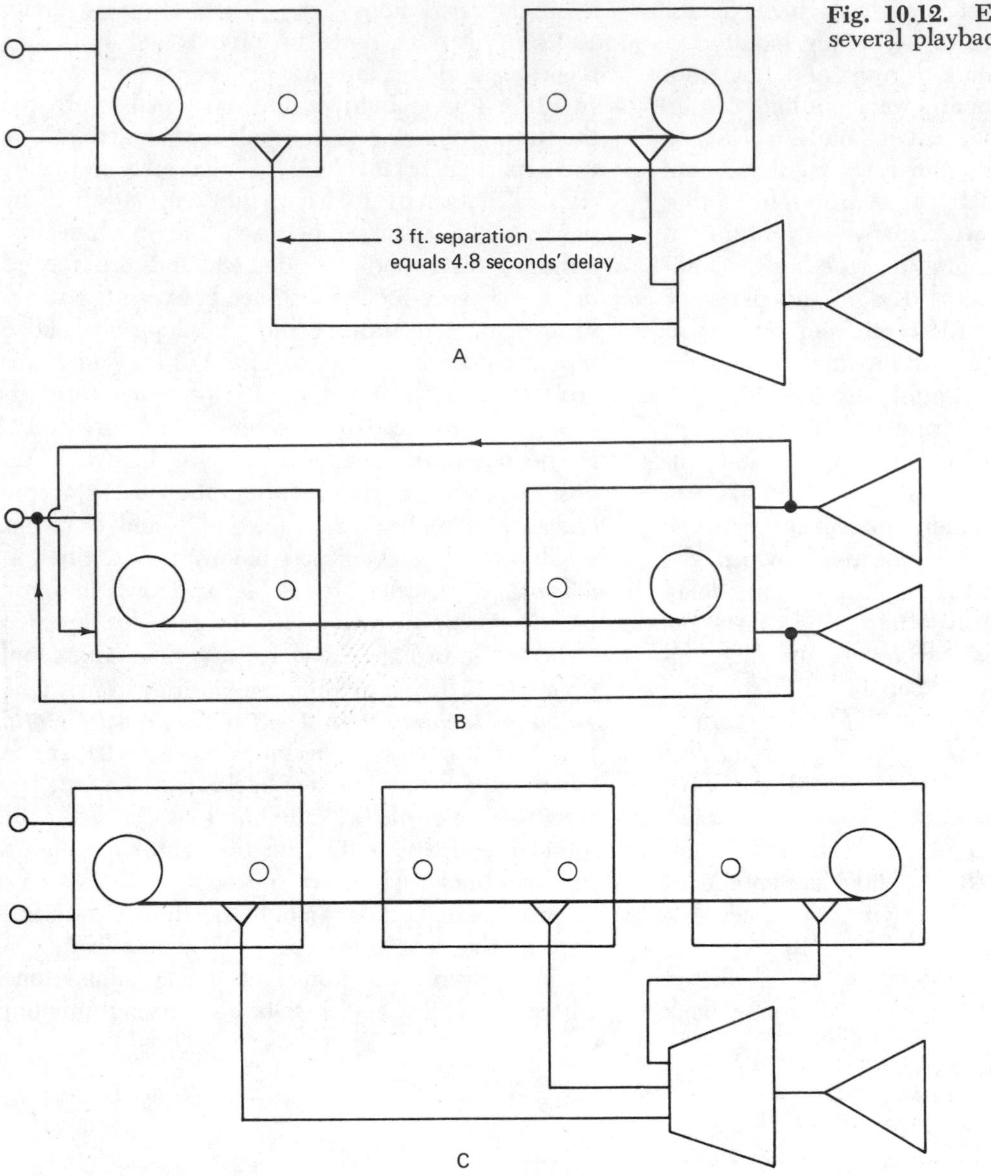

Fig. 10.12. Extended tape-delay using several playback decks.

3 ft. separation equals 4.8 seconds' delay

A

B

C

of phase modulation, along with the repetition of transients. Even with the use of only two channels, the maze of multiple attacks, decays, and temporal distortions will seem to fill the sound field with a cloud of sound in which the direction of origin is not apparent. The composer should also consider the possibilities of patching any of the feedback legs through any type of processing module (filter, gate, modulator, reverb, etc.) and then patching it back into the delay configuration, or using it as an output channel by itself. Tape-delay configurations produced by a variable-speed tape recorder will also provide the composer with quasi-Doppler effects, much like the results of the technique of using a moving playback head.

"Reverse echo" may be produced with either of two methods. In one, first record the sequence of events to be subjected to reverse echo in the normal manner on tape recorder 1. Next, exchange the position of the reels so the tape can be played in reverse on the same machine. Patch the output of tape recorder 1 to the input of tape recorder 2 and re-dub the original sequence, playing backward while adding tape echo as shown back in figure 10.5. Then, if this generation of tape is played in reverse, the sequence will be in the original direction with the echo preceding the initial sounds. But this can be done with a single half-track stereo tape recorder with a bit more ease. Record the sequence on one channel and then turn the tape over to play it in reverse. By reversing the tape, the recorded track will now appear on the second channel. Then patch the output of the second channel to the input of the first and add echo in the usual manner, as illustrated in figure 10.13. Finally, turn the tape back

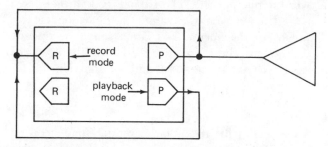

Fig. 10.13. Patching configuration for reverse echo

over and play the dubbed sequence in its original direction, with the echo preceding the original events. If the half-track tape recorder is equipped with sound-on-sound, this technique is further simplified by letting the S-O-S switch make the connection from the output of the second channel back to the first.

Due to the increased use of tape echo, many home machines are manufactured with a built-in feedback circuit which may be switched in and out as the operator desires. Certain mixing consoles are now built with inputs and outputs especially designed for use with delay loops and provisions for additional extended delay inputs. Because of the relative ease of use of these techniques, they have come to be somewhat of a cliché with the less innovative person. This is not meant to imply that the use of tape echo and feedback is an indication of a lack of creativity, because—as described earlier—they can provide the composer with many different and unusual means of sound modification. But the composer should extend his techniques beyond some of the simple configurations illustrated in this book and become familiar with all of the delay/feedback configurations that his particular studio situation will allow. The reader should also refer to Pauline Oliveros' article, "Tape Delay Techniques for Electronic Music Composition" (*The Composer,* vol. 1, no. 3, Dec. 1969) for even more ideas and information on the subject.

Almost everyone who has ever worked with a public address system has experienced the effect of acoustic feedback or "microphone howl." This howl is the result of standing waves and the in-

terference of the microphone field with the field of the monitor speaker, as shown in figure 10.14A. The feedback may be eliminated in one of several manners. The easiest thing to do is to reduce the size of the respective fields by lowering the output gain. If a higher gain is required, relocation of either the microphone or the speaker may be required. For best results it is suggested that the speaker be placed on the opposite side of the microphone, as illustrated in figure 10.14B. Even with this logistic arrangement, feedback will oc-

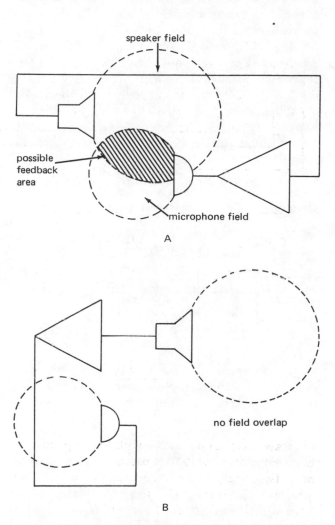

Fig. 10.14. Microphone/speaker feedback fields

cur if the gain is excessively high. The most effective method of feedback elimination is by producing a slight phase-shift (see chap. 12, p. 116) in the output signal, thus putting the speaker output out of phase with the microphone input and eliminating any standing waves. This method is used in large auditoriums and such shifting circuits are now even being built into many podium amplifiers and public address systems. A very similar technique is to actually effect a very slight frequency shift of about 5 Hz. Working in the same manner as a phase shift, this will also prevent acoustic feedback.

Under control, microphone howl can serve as a unique sound source. It is a technique most evident with the many rock guitarists who use feedback to sustain and modify the sounds produced by their guitars. Since a guitar transducer is a magnetic or contact pickup, it is also susceptible to the influence of the field produced by the monitor speaker. If the gain is high enough, almost any plucked string may be kept in motion by acoustic feedback. Various frequencies will be more receptive to acoustical feedback depending on the distance between the sound source and the speaker. It has been found that this type of feedback is most effective if the source is at a point which lies at a node of the particular wavelength of the frequency being produced. The wavelength of a particular frequency is found by dividing the velocity of the wave, which in air is 1120 feet per second, by the frequency in question.

$$\lambda = \frac{1120}{f}$$

The wavelength of A, 440 Hz, is:

$$\lambda = \frac{1120}{440} = 2.58 \text{ feet,}$$

so the optimum placement of a string vibrating at 440 Hz for feedback is about 2 1/2 feet from the speaker. For very long wavelengths, good results will be achieved at distances of one-half and one-fourth of the wavelength.

In much the same manner, the feedback frequency of the howl produced by a microphone can be controlled by its position within the speaker field. The feedback frequency can also be changed by placing lengths of ordinary cardboard tubing over the microphone. The frequency will then have a tendency to be the same as the resonant frequency of the open tube. The resonant frequency of an open tube is found by dividing the speed of sound (c) by twice the length of the tube (2L):

$$f = \frac{c}{2L} .$$

Along with frequency production, acoustic feedback can also be used as a modification process. The gain is usually so high that it in itself will result in a certain amount of distortion. Producing feedback with an air mike and singing various other frequencies can result in some interesting heterodyne effects. Robert Ashley, in "Wolfman" (Sacramento, Calif.: Composer/Performer Editions, 1968), requires a very high gain level to produce feedback and asks the performer to adjust his oral cavity in such a manner to produce specific sounds which result in a particular kind of mixture with the feedback. (The score and recording of "Wolfman" also appear in *Source-Music of the Avant Garde*, no. 4, vol. 2, July, 1968.) The composer should also experiment with other types of acoustical instruments to find what possibilities they offer when amplified with very high gain levels. The composer will find that the type of microphone used will also be a major factor in controlling acoustical feedback. This area will be discussed in chapter 13.

tape recording

The production of an electronic composition is a sequential process in most cases. A signal may originate with an oscillator but then it usually passes through several stages of transduction and transformation before it reaches the ear of the perceiver. Consequently, the quality of the final product is almost entirely dependent on the quality of each and every black box in its processing sequence. Even in live concert situations the tape recorder and reproduction facilities can determine the result of the composer's intent. The most carefully controlled sounds and the most painstakingly conceived processing can be destroyed by a poorly mastered tape or inadequate recording equipment. Even during the process of creating a composition a poor monitor system will add its own sonic characteristics to the sound, and under these circumstances reproduction over a better system may produce sounds quite different from what the composer monitored in the studio. For this reason the first concern of a studio should be the recording and reproduction system. An investment in the best available pre-amplifiers, amplifiers, tape decks, and speakers is the prime requisite for a successful studio.

Tape recording is very often the final process in producing an electronically conceived work. Moreover, with the development of the art of live electronic composition/performance, the tape recorder has now achieved the stature of a performance instrument to be used with as much care and artfulness as a fine violin. This chapter will therefore be devoted to providing a basic knowledge of tape machines, the recording process, and some suggestions on approaching the craft of tape editing.

Magnetic recording tape is a ribbon of acetate, polyester, mylar, or polyvinyl chloride (PVC) on which is bonded a very thin and even coating of minute magnetic particles or "domains." During the recording process these domains are aligned and realigned in various manners in response to the input to the tape recorder. During playback these imposed domain patterns induce an almost identical current, via the playback head, which is eventually perceived as a reproduction of the original input signal. (For a detailed coverage of tape recorder circuitry, see Burstein and Pollak's *Elements of Tape Recorder Circuits* [Blueridge Summit, Pa.: G/L Tab Books, 1957].) Since there is a transfer of power from the sound source to the recording circuit to the tape, and from the tape to the playback circuit, the tape must be considered as one of the prime factors in the transduction/transformation process of creating an electronic composition. Thus, the choice of high-quality tape is just as important as the choice of high-quality equipment. In choosing tape there are several factors to consider. With most professional recording tape, one has the choice of either acetate or polyester backing. Professional tape must be resistant to physical changes under a variety of temperature and humidity conditions and it must also be able to withstand the stress of a great deal of handling. Tests conducted by 3M, Magnetic Products Division, have shown that temperature and humidity have far less of an effect on the expansion and contraction of polyester tape than on acetate tape (see "Polyester and Acetate for Magnetic Recording Tape Backings," *Sound Talk*, vol. 2, no. 1, 1969). Tests also reveal that polyester withstands breakage under temperature and humidity variations better than acetate, but this is a bit misleading. Polyester, due to its ability to stretch almost 100 percent, can absorb sudden stress and is less likely to break. One of the major causes of tape breakage is sudden stops and starts of the tape deck with the feed and the take-up wheel out of adjustment. With polyester tape these sudden stresses stretch the tape a great deal before breakage. Once a tape has stretched beyond 5 percent, however, it is useless and very little can be done to salvage the signal which happens to be imprinted on the distorted portion. Acetate tape will break under much less stress and the elongation of the tape is usually not quite so critical. In many cases the break is very abrupt and a clean splice can be made without excessive distortion to the recorded signal. It is to be hoped that tape decks are always in good adjustment and the composer is always very careful in handling the tapes. Under these circumstances polyester is usually the preferred backing because of its ability to better withstand environmental changes during storage.

A second and very important consideration is tape thickness. Measured in mils, tape is available in 1/2-mil, 1-mil and 1 1/2-mil thicknesses. The advantage of thinner tape is that it is possible to store more tape on a reel, hence more recording time in the same amount of storage space. The disadvantages of thinner tape are (1) it is very difficult to handle and makes editing more of a major process than it already is, and (2) it contributes to the problem of "print-through" or "signal transfer." Print-through occurs when the magnetic flux on one layer of tape transfers its signal to the adjoining layers, resulting in the pre- and post-echo heard so often on commercial recordings. Although heat and long periods of storage contribute to this problem, a thinner tape will be more susceptible to print-through than a tape with a thicker backing. A preventative measure which can be taken against the effects of print-through is to keep the tapes stored in "tail-out" position— that is, with the beginning or "head" of the tape closest to the hub. (The tape must be re-wound before it is played.) This does not prevent print-through but any transfer that takes place will appear as a post-echo and will often be masked by the sound already on the tape. Another advantage of tail-out storage is that a more even and tighter winding is achieved if the tape is wound slowly, as it is when being played. Getting into the habit of storing tapes in this manner is no problem. It is just a choice of when you wish to

rewind the tape, before or after playing. (Another good practice in tape preservation is to store master tapes in aluminum tins in a place of constant room temperature. This protects the tape from stray magnetic fields and excess humidity.)

A second processing device to be considered is the recording and playback head itself. With extended use a tape head will build up a collection of magnetic fields and a certain amount of dirt will be collected on it. For the best possible head performance, the composer should periodically de-magnetize and clean the record and playback heads, following the directions supplied by the manufacturer. Low-quality tape is also a consideration in head wear. A rough coating not only causes undue wear but also prevents consistent contact with the heads, resulting in a certain amount of distortion.

Recording at higher speeds passes more tape by the record head in the same amount of time as recording at a lower speed. Consequently, there is a higher signal-to-noise ratio and a higher frequency response. (Signal-to-noise ratio is an indication of level of the inherent tape noise in relation to the recorded signal. Professional recordings should have a SNR of between 56 and 60 db.) Most professional recording is done at a speed of 15 inches per second and almost never at speeds less than 7 1/2 ips, unless it is intended to reproduce the recorded material at higher speeds. This, of course, means that greater amounts of tape must be sacrificed for purposes of quality and fidelity. Tape is available on reels ranging from 3 inches to 16 inches in diameter. Because of the need for longer recording time, along with high recording speeds, the studio machine should be able to accept at least a 10 1/2-inch reel of tape. The 14-inch reel, although less common, is available if longer playing time is needed. In order to provide adjustment in the tension arms for constant tape/head contact, a professional machine is usually equipped with a switch for varying tension according to reel size.

There are usually two different inputs to the tape recorder. A high-level 600-ohm line input and a low-level input usually used for microphones. Depending on the type of microphone being used, low-level inputs should be able to accommodate both high impedance (5k- to 50k-ohm) and low-impedance (50-250-ohm) microphones. Professional machines usually have separate gain controls for the line and microphone input. This allows mixing and simultaneous recording from both an electronic music system (providing that its output level is 600-ohm) and from a live acoustical source. The individual or combined input levels should be monitored via VU meters, as described in chapter 7. A standard VU meter has two different calibration scales for the indication of gain levels. The "A" scale is a decibel rating from −20 to +3 db; the "B" scale reads from zero to 100 percent, with the 100 percent mark coinciding with zero on the "A" scale. Both "A" and "B" VU scales are illustrated in figure 11.1. The zero db or 100 percent mark is actually 4 db above 1 milliwatt, indicating the optimum level the signal can be recorded without the possibility of causing distortion. Extreme care should be taken not to allow the VU meter's needle to suddenly pin against the right edge of the scale. This causes inaccuracies in calibration and could result in permanent meter damage.

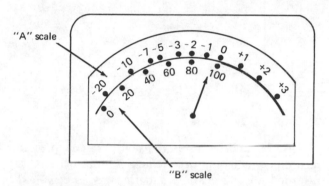

Fig. 11.1. VU meter scales

It is essential that studio machines have separate record and playback heads. The average home machine may have dual purpose heads which are used for the combined function of recording and playback. The major disadvantage of these is that the playback output function is not as high as it could be with separate record and playback heads. Consequently, most professional machines are designed with three separate heads; erase, record, and playback as shown in figure 11.2. As well as presenting possibilities for tape echo, the separate heads allow for monitoring of the signal either before it enters the recording circuit or after it has been recorded on the tape via the playback head. This comparison between the input and output signal is referred to as "A-B" comparison. This is accomplished by means of a switch that allows for monitoring before the signal is recorded or from the playback head. For optimum recording quality, there should be very little difference in the signal levels with an A-B comparison.

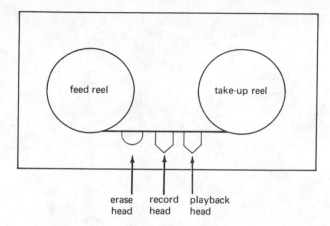

Fig. 11.2. Head format for three-head decks

In constructing a composition, the process many times involves recording several different channels for sound and then mixing them down to one single channel; this is the dub-down. The recording process involves recording one channel or sound, rewinding the tape, and recording the next channel while monitoring the previously recorded channel, and then repeating this procedure for as many channels as are needed or allowed. Because the playback head is usually located about two inches beyond the record head, exact synchronization between the input and playback signals is almost impossible. If the machine is equipped with only dual purpose heads, and if it is possible to record and playback on each channel independently, exact synchronization is possible in the following manner. After recording on one channel, the tape is rewound and information monitored by having the first channel in playback mode, the second in record. The output of the first channel and the input to the second will be in sync since the heads are stacked in line with each other. If the recording is being done with an air mike, then the monitoring should be done through earphones to prevent any first-channel sounds from being picked up by the second channel microphone. Synchronous recording on a machine with separate record and playback heads must be done on a deck with special circuitry called "selective synchronization" or "sel-sync." Sel-sync allows the record head to function temporarily as a playback head when put in operation by a special switch. By doing this, one can monitor the signal on any channel(s) while recording a signal at the same temporal place on any other channel. While monitoring from sel-sync, the fidelity isn't as high as it would be from the normal playback head but it is quite adequate for sync

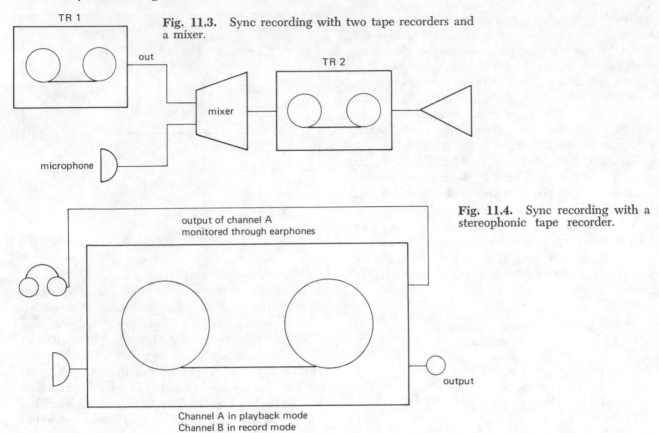

Fig. 11.3. Sync recording with two tape recorders and a mixer.

Fig. 11.4. Sync recording with a stereophonic tape recorder.

purposes. (Be sure to switch the monitor back to the playback head for the final dub-down.)

Two separate tape recorders may be synced together with the use of a mixer. The process involves recording information on one tape recorder and then rewinding the tape and patching the output to a mixer input. The new source of information is then patched to another input of the same mixer and the mixer output is patched to the input of a second recorder. Now tape one can be monitored as part of the total input signal to recorder two. All of the information ends up on a single channel and, depending on the mixer design, the mixer inputs will usually have to accept the same impedance. A block diagram of this technique is shown in figure 11.3. This same method may be simplified with the use of a stereo tape recorder. By patching the output of tape recorder one directly into one channel of tape recorder two and adding the new information on the other channel, the need for a mixer is eliminated. Of course, if tape recorder two has independent record and playback for the separate channels, the necessity of the first tape recorder is eliminated.

The procedure as described above is designed directly into recorders with sound-on-sound pro-

visions. (Sound-with-sound usually refers to sync recording with multiple tracks.) Information is recorded on one channel and the tape is rewound and set to record on channel two. If the sound-on-sound circuit is activated, the information on channel one will automatically be mixed with the input signal to channel two, resulting in both signals being on the same channel. The same process can then be repeated with three sequences ending up on channel one. This procedure can be repeated up to about five takes. After that there is a great deal of loss in the previously recorded tracks.

Sound-on-sound may also be accomplished using two other approaches. On some professional machines it is possible to switch out or unplug the erase head. This allows the composer to record sequence one and then rewind the tape and record sequence two over the original sequence without erasing it. This can be simulated by placing some non-inductive material, such as celluloid film, over the erase head to defeat its function. A major drawback to this technique is that there is a great amount of high-frequency loss with each successive overlay. There may be a total gain loss of up to 18 db or more in the original takes. Therefore, if one uses an erase head defeat method, it is ad-

Fig. 11.5. Additional play-back head for sound-on-sound recording.

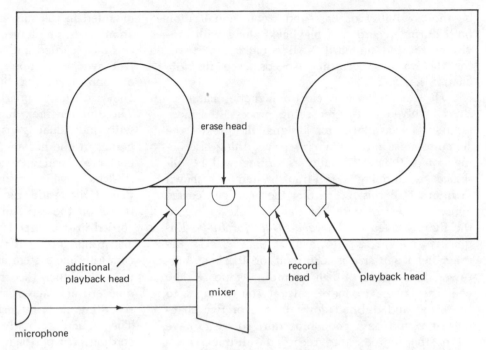

visable to record the sequences made up of the lower frequencies first and also record the first takes at a slightly higher level. Sound-on-sound may also be achieved by the placement of the playback head preceding the erase head. This configuration allows the recorded signal to be added to the input signal before it is erased. As illustrated in figure 11.5, this method is a single-channel version of the sound-on-sound technique described previously. The addition of the extra playback head provides sound-on-sound possibilities without the gain or high frequency loss encountered with the erase head defeat method.

Figure 11.6 shows the unequalized record-playback response of a professional quality tape recorder operating at 7 1/2 and 15 ips. A comparison of the response curves shows that each recording speed requires a different equalization pattern. Generally speaking, the required treble or high-frequency boost varies inversely with the tape speed. On most machines the change in equalization is accomplished with a simple switch with speed indications. The actual location of the equalization circuits within the total record/playback circuitry is very important. The guiding principle is to get as much undistorted signal on the tape as possible. The recording process, although it affects both the high and the low frequencies, most sharply attenuates the high end of the spectrum. If the high-frequency boost were located in the playback circuit, there would be a marked increase in audible tape hiss and the signal-to-noise

ratio would also be adversely affected. Therefore, the high-frequency boost is a function of the recording circuit. In figure 11.6 it can be observed that up to 30 db boost is required at the lower end of the spectrum. This amount of boost in the recording process would produce a tremendous

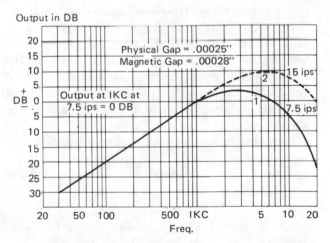

Fig. 11.6. Record/playback response, unequalized. (From Herman Burstein and Henry Pollak, *Elements of Tape Recorder Circuits*, Blue Ridge Summit, Pennsylvania, Tab Books, 1957, p. 94. Used by permission of the publisher.

amount of distortion on the tape, so bass equalization is usually a function of the playback process. At times the composer may be concerned with producing deliberate distortion in the recorded signal, so an ideal studio situation would be the possibility of bass and treble equalization both during record and playback, along with provisions for the standard NAB equalization curves for the various recording speeds (see fig. 7.5, chap. 7).

Due to the various electromagnetic characteristics involved in the recording process, the more tape surface available for a signal the greater the signal-to-noise ratio. Therefore, everything else being equal, the best quality recording will be obtained by utilizing a full-track system. As shown in figure 11.7, this means that the head gap covers almost the entire width of the tape. According to the figures given in *Reference Data for Radio Engineers* (New York: Howard W. Sams, 1968), the exact head gap size is .238 inch, or .012 inch narrower than the 1/4-inch recording tape. If the composer plans to make several source tapes to be mixed and dubbed down to one or two channels, it would be a good procedure to try to have all of the source tapes recorded full-track. Full-track recording also makes many more editing possibilities available, as will be discussed later in this chapter. Half-track heads cover .082 inch of tape area and are available in monophonic or stereophonic configurations. The half-track mono system has only a single record head, making it possible to record on the upper half of the tape and then turn the tape over and record independent information on its lower half. Since the head only affects .082 inch of each edge, there is approximately a .07-inch separation between the two tracks, which prevents excessive signal leakage or "crosstalk" between the two channels. (A certain amount of crosstalk is to be expected, but this should occur at a level of about 60 db below the information on the track being monitored.) A stereophonic half-track format involves two in-line half-track heads stacked one above the other

mounted in the same housing. With this configuration, two simultaneous channels of information can be recorded and played back together in perfect synchronization. Because of the availability of more recording time, the average home machine utilizes a quarter-track head configuration. The quarter-track format has two in-line heads with individual gaps of .043 inch stacked together in one housing. The measurement from the center of head one to the center of head two is .134 inch, which means two other tracks can be placed alongside the original tracks. With four tracks on the tape, one stereo system may be recorded in one direction and a second in the other. The usual format for this is tracks one and three comprise one system and tracks two and four comprise the other (see fig. 11.7). The advantage of quarter-track stereo is the availability of twice the recording time by using both sides of the tape. The numerous disadvantages include (1) less recording area per channel, resulting in a lower signal-to-noise ratio and less fidelity, (2) less separation between adjacent tracks resulting in more crosstalk, and (3) the fact that if both directions of the tape were used, splicing would be impossible without cutting into the other system. For these reasons most studios incorporate half-track stereo systems. If for some reason a source tape were to be recorded with a quarter-track format, it should not be played on a half-track machine. The half-track head will also cover the adjacent track on the quarter-track format and, assuming that that particular channel is blank, will result in excessive tape hiss during playback. For this reason many tape decks, although they employ exclusive half-track recording, have provisions for both half- and quarter-track playback. This is accomplished by having two sets of playback heads and switching in whichever format is needed, or by

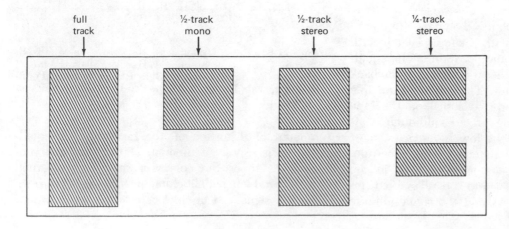

Fig. 11.7. Common head formats for 1/4-inch tape.

using only quarter-track playback heads and, by means of a lever, shifting them down so they are placed right in the center of the half-track playback path.

By careful planning it is possible to use full-, half-, and quarter-track machines together to achieve a very unusual full-track mix. Up to five channels of information may be reproduced on a single full-track tape by following this procedure: record information A on a full-track machine and, using the same tape, record information B and C on the two respective tracks with a half-track machine. (Usual stereo format designates the left channel as channel 1, the right channel as channel 2.) This of course will erase part of information A's signal but it will still be present in the .07-inch gap which separates the two half-track heads. What is now on the tape is, starting from the top edge, information B, information A, and information C recorded at approximate gaps of .09 inch, .07 inch, and .09 inch respectively. Now, using a quarter-track stereo machine, record information D and E on the tape's two respective tracks. The final tape will then contain five different tracks of information located, in order from the top edge, B, D, A, E, C. All five tracks may then be monitored by playing the tape on a full-track deck. This is not the most effective way of mixing, but it has been used very successfully many times by composers with limited mixing equipment. One precaution to be observed is that the individual machines have erase heads which only affect the particular tracks being recorded. A full-track erase head on the half- or quarter-track machine makes this technique impossible.

A more effective method of multi-track recording is with regular multi-track machines with the required number of tracks all running in the same direction. The most common multi-track format is the four-track tape recorder. Utilizing 1/2-inch tape, the head format is four in-line record heads, each with a .082-inch gap and the same amount of separation as the half-track stereo format. Some four-track home machines, referred to as "quadraphonic," use 1/4-inch tape and have the same formats as quarter-track stereo, but with all four tracks running in the same direction. The reason for the 1/2-inch tape is that it allows for wider tracking and better separation of the individual channels. Because the four-track machine is used primarily for building up various layers of a composition, it is necessary that it have sel-sync operation. Eight, twelve, sixteen and twenty-four-track formats are available using 1- and 2-inch

tape. There have even been reports of a 72-track machine in operation owned by Apple Corporation in London. This particular system is actually four individual tape decks, each having 18 tracks driven in synchronization from the same power source. Although the composer can find a justified use for a great number of tracks, he must keep in mind that each channel adds to the number of mixer inputs and equalization circuits required to make that channel usable. Except for very special situations, the composer will find that an eight-track machine will be sufficient for the normal studio requirements. In most cases the four-track machine is all that will be required and this is the usual multi-track deck found in the average studio. A well-equipped studio, however, should have two four-track machines to allow for four-track dubbing plus the availability of as many half-track stereo and full-track machines as possible.

Playback at speeds different from the recording speed, if used with taste, can result in some very intriguing sounds. The provisions for speed changes at ratios other than 2:1 (3.34:7.5 and 7.5:15) gives the composer even finer control and provides many other variations in sound. In the event that two tapes must be synced together, minute variations in speed allow the composer to make very fine adjustments in timing and tuning. There are several tape machines available today with provisions for limited speed variation. By means of a rheostat, the playback speed may be varied within a range of from 20 to 30 percent. (Some of these commercial decks provide for speed variation both in record and playback mode, while others operate only in playback mode.) With more professional machines that utilize a "hysteresis synchronis" motor, the basic record/playback speed is determined by the voltage frequency, which in the United States is a 60 Hz standard. With these machines it is then possible to use other frequencies than the standard 60 Hz and achieve speeds other than the standard 7 1/2 ips and the 2:1 multiples and divisions thereof. Several studio model tape recorders have a special input jack which allows an external oscillator to determine the speed. With this manner of control, speed will vary in direct proportion to the input frequency. The usual speed range is variable from 1-7/8 ips to 60 ips, or a 32:1 ratio. This means that a frequency recorded at the slowest speed could be raised five octaves during playback at the fastest speed. The composer must also remember that this also causes a 5:1 change in the tempo of the recorded material. With experimentation it will be found that speed changes can also be very useful in achieving very unique timbre changes. Some of the newer tape decks have the control oscillator built into the deck chassis and no external oscillator is needed. The advantage of an external oscillator is that it would be possible to use various frequency-modulated signals to control the tape speed, providing the composer with an unusual approach to sound modification. Because of the various loop techniques used by the composers of musique concrete, the loop machines also had provisions for a certain amount of speed variation. Even in the more modern studios these loop machines can be very useful in various multi-deck set-ups and were discussed in relationship to tape delay and feedback techniques (chap. 10).

Voltage control has several times over reduced the task of tape editing which was once the major job in creating electronic music. But still the composer will find that a basic knowledge of editing procedures can be a very useful tool. Repairing broken tape, adding leader, adding or deleting bits of information after the major sequences have been recorded, making loops, etc., all require a certain amount of skill with the splicing block. The guiding factor in making a good splice is to create as little disturbance as possible to the recorded signal. If possible, all cuts should be made at an angle somewhere between 45° and 60°. A cut above an angle of 60° will begin to cause an excessive amount of electrical disturbance as the splice passes the playback head, and a cut at an angle below 45° may cause the tape edges held by the splicing tape to bend back and wear loose. In the event a 90° splice must be made, the noise and disturbance can be kept at a minimum by following procedures discussed below.

A deck with an edit button frees the transport system so the tape may be manually moved back and forth across the playback head. (The composer might experiment recording by manually moving the tape by the record head while the transport is free.) This enables the operator to pinpoint exact sounds and silences at any point on the tape. Of course as the tape is moved more slowly, the pitch is proportionally lower. Consequently, the novice editor may at first find it very difficult to recognize a particular sound due to speed and pitch distortions. He will soon learn how various attacks, transients, decays, and timbres sound under editing conditions, however. As soon as the particular point on the tape is found, it is marked with a wax pencil. The tape should be marked on its shiny side at a point directly on top of the playback gap. A machine specially designed for editing locates the head at a very accessible point just for that reason. If the head is in an inconvenient position for marking, the common procedure is to locate the portion to be clipped with the playback head and then mark the tape at some other consistent and convenient point along the tape path. The editing block should have a cue mark located at the same distance from the razor guide as the cue mark is from the playback head, as shown in figure 11.8. When the cue mark on the tape is lined up with the cue mark on the editing block then the exact portion of the tape which was against the playback head will line up with the razor guide. This procedure also protects the playback head from dirt and grease from fingers and marking pencil. The cut should be made as close to the beginning of the sound as the editing technique allows. If this is carefully done, then the disturbance caused by the cut is masked by the attack transients of the recorded sound and the splice will be less noticeable. If the composer plans to edit silences into acoustically recorded events, it is good practice to record a minute or so of silence from the same environment and save it for editing purposes. If a silence must then be added to a final recording, the extra tape will contain the same level of background noise and apparent acoustical characteristics. When adding silences to a recording from an electronic sound source, it is desirable to use leader tape because of its complete lack of a recorded signal. Most composers prefer to use paper leader, since plastic leader is capable of holding a slight amount of static which is often audible as it passes the playback head. The composer should also take care that the razor blade used for cutting the tape does not become magnetized. A magnetized blade will induce stray magnetic fields onto the tape and this electrical disturbance will be audible as the splice passes the playback head.

The most important factor in making a good splice is cleanliness. A professional splicing block will hold both pieces of tape firmly yet will allow them to be easily butted together with a minimum of handling and without any overlap. Any oil or dirt on the tape will prevent the splice from holding firmly and could result in noise. Once the two pieces of tape are in position, they are joined by a short piece of splicing tape. The shorter the splice, the better. Very long pieces of splicing tape affect the pressure pads which hold the magnetic tape flush against the playback head and may re-

Fig. 11.8. Set-up for "off-the-head" editing.

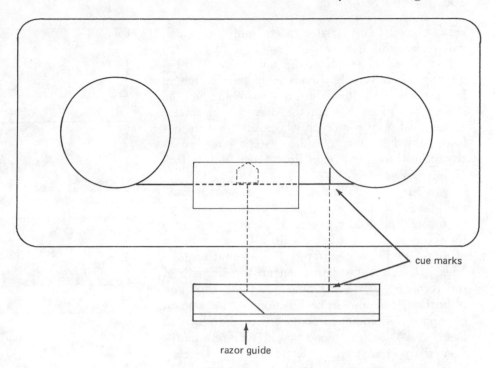

cue marks

razor guide

sult in a 3 to 4 db signal loss. The preferred splicing tape is 7/32 inch wide, or 1/32 inch narrower than the recording tape. The reason for this is that after long periods of storage the adhesive may "bleed" out from under the splicing tape and cause the adjacent layer to stick. If the splicing tape is the same width as the recording tape, the problem is magnified because of the possibility of the adhesive seeping over the edges of several layers of recording tape. (The hourglass splice pictured in figure 11.9 really doesn't solve the problem and the indentation could result in momentary gain loss if it cuts into the recorded signal.)

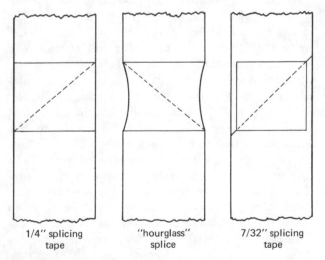

| 1/4" splicing tape | "hourglass" splice | 7/32" splicing tape |

Fig. 11.9. Splicing tape formats

To avoid direct handling of the magnetic tape, the master tape should have leader at both ends of the recorded portions. At the head the leader should extend right up to the initial attack, and tail leader should be added as soon after the final decay as possible. This is done to eliminate any tape hiss which may proceed or precede the recorded signal. As an added aid it is a good practice to have a minute or so of a 1k test signal recorded at zero db according to the VU meter preceding the head leader tape. This allows the player of the tape to set the playback gain at the level intended by the composer, ensuring accurate reproduction. As mentioned earlier, the tape should be stored in aluminum tins in a tail-out position to prevent pre-echo. An added precaution is to provide about 1/4 inch of bumper tape between the center reel hub and the head leader. The guide holes in the reel hub cause tension fluctuations in the tape wound in the first 1/4 inch nearest the hub and may result in periodic gain fluctuations at those points which line up with the holes. The bumper tape acts as a cushion between the hub and the leader to prevent these gain fluctuations. All extra bits of unused tape should be salvaged for this purpose, since it is much less expensive than leader.

For the unexperienced editor all of these precautions and procedures may seem very time-consuming and even unwarranted. True, tape editing is at first a very tiring and often frustrating process. A good editing habit to get into—one which will make editing an easier task—is to always lay out tools and materials in the same way. The beginning editor usually spends more time searching for a razor blade than he does searching for the right place to cut. As for the necessity of careful editing, ask any composer whose master tape has been ruined because of splicing tape ooze, excessive print-through, or gain fluctuations due to lack of bumper tape.

In the modern studio, splicing is usually used for adding or deleting various parts of the tape or for adding leader. Various splicing configurations can also be used to create a limited number of attack and decay patterns. The amount of playback gain, although dependent on the strength of the recorded signal and amount of playback amplification, can also be a function of the amount of tape which comes in contact with the playback head. A 90° splice into a sound will result in a very sharp attack which is boosted by the electrical disturbance caused by that particular cutting angle. A more gradual attack would be achieved if the cutting angle were only 10° or 15°. As the tape passes the playback head, more and more of the recorded surface would come in contact with the head, resulting in a rise in output gain. As mentioned earlier, less than a 45° cut will eventually affect the stability of the splice, but these artificial attacks are usually made on source tapes and re-dubbed onto a master. If a splice such as the one shown in figure 11.10B is made on a stereo tape, the effect would be an attack and crescendo on channel B followed by a later attack and crescendo on channel A. To achieve a simultaneous attack pattern on both channels of a stereo tape, a splice such as the one shown in figure 11.10C would have to be made. The editor may even carry this technique to the very complex manner of creating amplitude modulation, as shown in figure 11.10D. In the same manner, decay patterns can be created using the opposite angles. With this technique, attack and decay times are a function of angle and tape speed, so if fidelity permits, some of these effects are easier to achieve at slower speeds. Another problem with this technique is that unless the editor has an editing block suited for these unusual cuts, the accurate fitting of the leader and magnetic tape is very difficult. This, along with possible gain losses due to very long patches of splicing tape, further demonstrates the value of voltage control.

One of the most important considerations in terms of recording and playback equipment is its

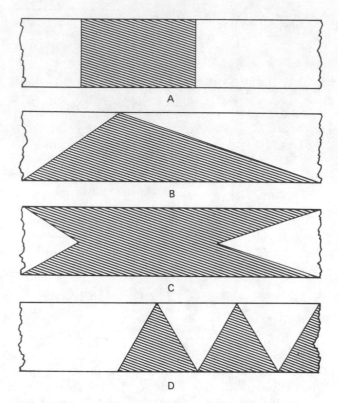

Fig. 11.10. Envelope generation with splicing patterns.

location within the studio. It can be very time-consuming if the composer must continually move back and forth across the studio to press the record button and then back to the output system to control what is being put on the tape. If the tape machines cannot be situated in a place convenient to both the system output and tape input, remote control devices may be used. Tape decks intended for studio applications are available with provisions for remote-controlled playback, record, fast forward, and rewind. Unless manual cueing is required, this gives the composer full control over the tape transport system and he still has immediate access to the signal sources. In commercial recording studios, the tape decks are usually built into a large panel and their placement is quite permanent. The obvious advantage to this situation is that there is less chance of maladjustment or damage due to excessive movement. In the electronic music studio many composers prefer to have all equipment, including turntables, tape decks, mixers, amplifiers, etc., fastened to chassis with portable rollers. Because of the many unusual and unpredictable uses to which a composer may subject equipment, the added advantage of portability is very important. This also makes the equipment available for use in live electronic situations which may occur away from the studio. A tape machine which is intended for use in concert situations, in addition to all of the other requirements discussed thus far, should be designed in such a way that all parts are very accessible for maintenance purposes. It is not unusual to have to repair a machine during the intermission of a concert where time is of the essence. (The ideal situation would be to have a machine so rugged and dependable that no maintenance is ever required, but here the artist is waiting for technology to make the required advances.)

The electronic music composer realizes that the tape recorder is used for more than just storing information. The tape recorder is an instrument which must be treated with just as much care and knowledge as a fine violin and must constantly be kept in optimum condition. Many times the studio budget does not provide for a full-time technician to make sure that the machines are properly cared for. For this reason the composer should carefully study the operation manual, specification sheet, and maintenance manual of all tape recorders in the studio. Even if he doesn't have the technical ability to repair a machine, he should at least be aware when it is not operating up to the standards set by the manufacturer, so that professional maintenance can be summoned.

12

miscellaneous equipment

The majority of the modules and equipment discussed in this book have been classed and dealt with in terms of function. At the same time, most of these devices were either incorporated as a module of a total electronic music system or were an integral part of the recording/playback chain. Even though oscillators, frequency modulators, ring modulators, filters, etc., are now being manufactured specifically for use by the composer and performer in the electronic medium, they were originally intended for use as communications and electronic test equipment. As composers became more and more familiar with the technology, they found they were able to make use of this equipment as a unique method of processing sound. The technological age of the composer is just beginning and as the field of communications and electronics continues to grow, the composer will continue to find uses for newly developed equipment. The purpose of this chapter is to familiarize the reader with some of the more common equipment found in an electronic music studio which is normally not part of present commercial systems.

One of the major processes of electronic music is that of "transduction," the transfer of power from one medium to another. A transducer is a device which reacts to one type of wave (voltage, light, pressure, current, etc.) by transforming that wave into an analogous wave of another medium. Transduction may then take place between any two mediums, such as light to voltage, voltage to frequency, pressure to frequency, voltage to pressure, etc. The ideal transducer is one that transfers the maximum possible power from one medium to another. Unfortunately, the ideal transducer is a hypothetical device; there is always a minute percentage of non-linearity or power loss.

The most commonly known transducer is the microphone. In terms of function, the microphone is an electro-acoustic transducer which reacts to pressure waves and produces analogous electrical impulses. The accuracy of this conversion is measured by the microphone's sensitivity and frequency response. The sensitivity of a microphone is a technical specification indicating how much of the acoustical energy arriving at a mike's input can be converted to usable electrical impulses. The frequency response refers to the range of frequencies to which the microphone is sensitive and the deviation in sensitivity throughout that range. The ideal microphone will exhibit a flat response, meaning no deviation, over the entire audio spectrum. But this ideal transducer is of course hypothetical; microphones exhibit various combinations of frequency ranges and area of varying sensitivity within those ranges. To say a microphone has a frequency response of from 100 Hz to 10k Hz means only that it responds to frequencies between those extremes. The response at 100 Hz may be "X," the response at 600 Hz may be "2X," and the response at 5k may be "1/2 X." For most purposes the flatness of a microphone's response is more important than its frequency range. If the microphone is used as a transducer for flutes and violins, a smooth response at the higher end of the spectrum is more important than an extended lower range. Conversely, a microphone used for the lower instruments requires a smoother low-frequency response.

Since the quality of an amplified signal can be a very subjective matter, the composer should become familiar with the characteristics of all of the microphones in the studio. It will be found that similar microphones, even those of the same specifications manufactured by the same manufacturer, may actually exhibit quite different characteristics. The composer must also remember that when used in a composing or performing situation, the microphone is the first device to come in contact with the sound and that it will define the quality of the rest of the system.

The least expensive type of air microphone is the carbon mike. (The input transducer on the normal home telephone is essentially a carbon mike.) Its operation is a result of varying sound pressures causing variations in resistance between encapsulated carbon granules. The carbon mike has a very limited frequency response, usually about 80 Hz to 7.5k Hz. Of course, if a carbon mike with the desired frequency range is available, it may be used as a processing filter. *Do It* by composer Robert Erickson specifies the use of a carbon mike precisely because of the desired effect of limited frequency response.

The crystal microphone operates on a basis of mechanical strain. Sound pressure waves move the microphone diaphragm, which in turn places a mechanical strain on a piezoelectric crystal such as quartz or Rochelle salt. In reaction, the crystal produces electrical charges. Crystal microphones are also quite limited in their frequency response. (Contact microphones, which transduce pressure waves transmitted through solid mediums, also operate with piezoelectric elements. The piezoelectric element is connected directly to the output leads and is usually sealed in a rather fragile casing. The composer or performer will find that contact mikes have a longer life if the case is opened and packed with epoxy cement. This will make the unit more stable as well as preventing the output wires from breaking contact with the crystal.)

Operating on a principle similar to the crystal microphone, the ceramic microphone exhibits a wider and smoother response than either the crystal or carbon mike. The disadvantage of a ceramic mike is its high impedance. High-impedance transducers are hard to work with because they are so susceptible to noise and hum. This is especially critical when using cables longer than 15 or 20 feet. Special bridges are available to convert high-impedance lines to balanced low-impedance lines and are well worth their moderate cost.

Dynamic microphones use a small coil which is moved by the pressure of sound waves on a diaphragm. The coil moves back and forth in the field of a permanent magnet which, in turn, generates a current in the coil. The ribbon microphone operates by means of an aluminum alloy foil ribbon suspended in a magnetic field; the ribbon's movement results in an induced AC current. Both the dynamic and ribbon microphones are in the medium price range and are adequate when working with somewhat limited ranges and the human voice. The ribbon microphone contains a powerful horseshoe magnet and is therefore relatively heavy. For this reason, plus the fact that ribbon mikes are very sensitive to wind and over-accented fricatives, the dynamic microphone is often preferred.

The professionally preferred microphone is the condenser or electrostatic microphone. This type of mike generates signals as a result of variations in capacitance between two charged plates, one of which is the diaphragm. The frequency response of these mikes is excellent and if a professional sound is desired they are essential equipment for the electronic music studio. The only provision one must consider is that condenser mikes require an additional amplifier built into or immediately external to the casing to convert the signal to a level suitable for line transmission. Condenser microphones are also quite expensive, but if one considers that the effectiveness of the transducers defines the effectiveness of the whole system, they are well worth their cost.

When working with any microphone one should be aware of its particular field pattern. Often referred to as the directional characteristic or polar pattern, the field pattern defines the area or direction to which the microphone is most sensitive. A cardiod or unidirectional microphone is more sensitive on one side than on the other, as illustrated in figure 12.1A. The null on the back side of the mike should not be taken as absolute since it will be frequency-sensitive to a certain degree. This is especially true of low frequencies. The bidirectional microphone exhibits maximum pick-up in two opposing directions, with the null at a 90° plane between the two lobes (fig. 12.1B). With bidirectional mikes, the distance from the sound source will play a large role in the character of the sound. This is especially noticeable with very close miking. At distances less than about two feet, the bass frequencies are very strongly emphasized. Consequently, the sound source should not move within the field and the use of equalization circuits can be very advantageous. Ribbon mikes, which are bidirectional microphones, are very sensitive to fricatives, so it is advisable to use wind shields and speak across the mike's face.

The rifle, gun, or super-directional microphone is a dynamic mike which incorporates a battery of various length tubes. This type of mike is intensely directional except to frequencies exhibiting wavelengths much longer than the length of the tube. A field pattern falling between the bidirectional and cardiod pattern is the super-cardiod, as illustrated in figure 12.1C. The omnidirectional or nondirectional microphone (fig. 12.1D) ideally is sensitive to all frequencies coming from all directions, but in practical use omnidirectionality is only true for frequencies below 5k Hz.

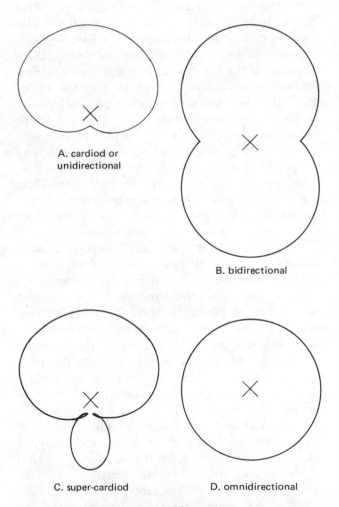

A. cardiod or
unidirectional

B. bidirectional

C. super-cardiod

D. omnidirectional

Fig. 12.1. Microphone field patterns

It is impossible to make any truly objective statements concerning actual microphone placement for the composer or performer. In commercial recording situations there are certain fidelity standards which guide the placement of microphones and in those situations there are definite procedures for microphone location. But the com-

poser is often concerned with using the microphone as a modification device as well as a pressure-to-signal transducer and hi-fi guidelines do not apply in all cases. There are several points that the composer should keep in mind, however, which may save considerable time in his experimentation:

1. Use low-impedance mikes. They are less susceptible to noise and permit the use of longer cables.
2. Consider the signal/noise ratio of the total environment as well as the different locations within the environment.
3. Remember that higher frequencies are more directional than lower frequencies.
4. Consider the inverse-square law: When the sound source's distance from the mike is multiplied by X, the intensity is divided by X^2.
5. When using multiple microphone systems, make sure they are in phase. This may involve turning bidirectional mikes 180° to match the phase of the unidirectional mikes.
6. Close miking cuts down transduction of the room reverberation.
7. Securely tape down all microphone cables. Run the cables away from areas of audience interference.
8. Experiment!

The most common output transducer is the speaker. Since the purpose of an audio system is to produce sound waves in an environment, the signal-to-air pressure transducer is of prime importance. Speakers are dealt with in chapter 13, but the point to be emphasized is that they must be of the highest possible quality for whatever purpose they are to be used. In a performance situation, a minimum of 35 to 40 watts is recommended and the cone size should be considered in relation to the masses of air to be moved in the performance environment. In a studio, speakers will still have the same response requirements but the smaller environment permits the use of a smaller system. In many cases the use of large theater speakers in a small studio situation defeats the whole purpose of a large speaker system, since the speaker-to-space coupling is often very unsatisfactory. Headphones, although excellent for listening to commercial recordings, are often unsatisfactory for monitoring the composition of electronic sound. This is due to the fact that commercial recordings are produced with built-in acoustics and the reproduction through earphones simulates reproduction in a live room.

In electronically-generated sound, the signal goes directly from the system output to the headphones and there is very little acoustical interaction before the sound reaches the ear. Consequently, the sound may take on an entirely different character when reproduced over a speaker system. Another precaution in working with headphones is that they act as compressors. Low-gain signals will seem much softer and high-gain signals will seem much louder over speaker systems than over headphones. Driver units are signal-to-pressure transducers which result in vibrations being produced in solid matter. It is possible to attach a driver to a wall and use the entire wall surface as a giant speaker. In *ABM*, composer Daniel Lentz requires a driver to be attached to the body of a string bass, thus using the instrument as his speaker. In *Senescence Sonorum,* the same composer specifies that drivers be attached to the bodies of the actual performers.

The basic law of electronic music, as stated in the epigraph to this book, is even more applicable to jacks and plugs than it is to the length of patchcords. Unless a composer is limiting himself to working with the modules found on one particular system, he will inevitably be in constant need of adaptors to allow him to make a patch from a particular device with one connection format to another device with a different connection format. The simple task of patching the system output to a tape recorder or an amplifier may call for special adaptors. Even commercially-manufactured electronic music systems cannot decide on a standard connection format and, in addition to the necessity of voltage interfaces, their compatibility depends on the availability of adaptors. This lack of standardization among the audio equipment manufacturers in the United States forces the composer working with a variety of equipment to spend much of his studio time searching for patchcords and adaptors. The composer must also consider that each time an adaptor is added to a signal path it contributes a certain amount of insertion loss and noise.

The most common types of connectors are illustrated in figure 12.2. The RCA, phono, or pin plug is the type most commonly found on home stereo/hi-fi equipment (fig. 12.2A). Although it is one of the more common plugs, some manufacturers avoid using it because the outer ground terminal has a tendency to expand with continued use and must occasionally be re-shaped to make a tight fit. The phone plug (fig. 12.2B-C) is available in either a two- or three-connector format.

The guitarist is familiar with this type of plug since it is commonly used with commercial guitar amplifiers. Various low-impedance microphones also use the two-connection or tip-sleeve format. A microphone requiring a balanced line may use a phone plug with the ring-tip-sleeve format. This type of connector may also be used for transmitting stereo and binaural signals with a single patchcord by sharing the same ground. Many people prefer the use of phone plugs because of their sturdiness. By the same token, many people avoid their use in smaller studio situations because they require thicker cable and are bulkier to handle. The XLP or cannon plug (fig. 12.2D) is a three-terminal connector usually used with balanced-line transmission such as with balanced-line microphones. The XLP or cannon plug is preferred over the ring-tip-sleeve phone plug because of its special locklatch which insures a tight connection and cannot be accidentally pulled out. The mini-phone

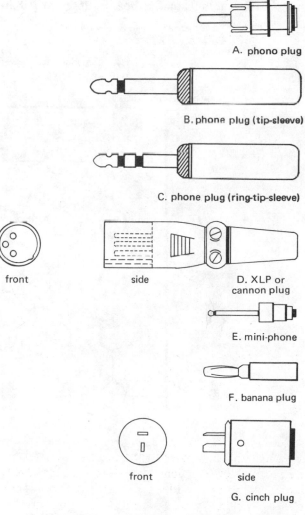

A. phono plug

B. phone plug (tip-sleeve)

C. phone plug (ring-tip-sleeve)

front   side   D. XLP or cannon plug

E. mini-phone

F. banana plug

front   side

G. cinch plug

Fig. 12.2. Common connectors

(fig. 12.2E), as its name implies, is a midget version of the two-connection phone plug. The miniphone format is used by some manufacturers because of the relatively small space required and the fact that they take up very little room on a patching panel. These plugs are less sturdy than some of the others and must be handled with more care. The banana plug (fig. 12.2F) has a single-terminal format and is used for the patching of DC and trigger voltages. The plugs are usually encased in red or black mountings to differentiate between positive and negative lines. Like the phono plug, the banana may begin to lose its shape after prolonged use and will occasionally have to be reshaped to make a tight connection. The cinch plug (fig. 12.2G) is also found in certain systems and is commonly used for DC and trigger voltages.

Some manufacturers of electronic music systems are attempting to solve the patchcord problem by using internal patching manipulated by switches or through matrix boards. Internal patching with switches for routing signals to the various modules does solve the patchcord problem, but it also presents a few of its own. If the designer is not extremely careful to allow for every conceivable patching configuration, he may limit the composer in his approach to that particular system. At the same time, a switching function often does not provide the number of multiple inputs and outputs required by many configurations. While many composers pay very little attention to how a particular module is intended to be used, such a lack of knowledge is often the source of their creative approach. Consequently, the designer is usually at a loss in trying to outguess composers' needs.

A more logical approach to internal patching is the matrix board. The matrix is an array of intersections formed by the placement of the various modules' inputs and outputs on an X-Y axis, as illustrated in figure 12.3. In this simple matrix, patching two oscillators to the ring modulator would involve placing a connection pin at points

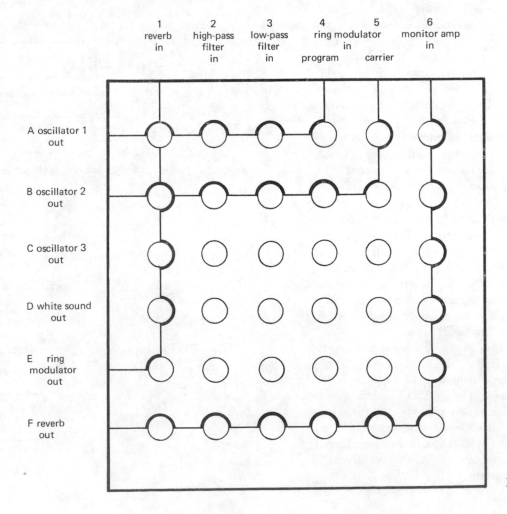

Fig. 12.3.   Matrix

4A and 5B. The modulated product could then be subjected to reverb by placing a pin at intersection 1E. Intersection 6F would then provide the final output. This approach allows multiple inputs and outputs and the composer is not as limited as he is with other types of internal patching. Matrix boards also allow the composer to keep simple and accurate records of particular patching configurations by designating board references. In certain cases the visual aspect of a matrix is also preferred because the signal routing is more readily understood than trying to trace down patchcords. The next logical step in system design may even be voltage-controlled patching configurations.

The often overused technique of varying the playback speed of prerecorded sound is given new possibilities with the "zeitdehner" (time-stretcher), also referred to as information rate changer or pitch and tempo regulator. This device is a special playback arrangement which allows for speed variations without affecting the frequency of the recorded material. Conversely, the frequency of the recorded material may be changed without changing the playback speed. This is accomplished by means of several playback heads mounted on a rotating cylinder. The individual heads are arranged so that only one head at a time comes in contact with the tape. Heads are so spaced that at the exact moment one head leaves the tape sur-

face another head has rotated around to take its place. If the cylinder is rotating in the same direction as the tape is moving, the monitored signal will be at a lower frequency than the recorded signal. If the heads are moving in a direction opposite to the tape motion, the effect will be a rise in the monitored pitch. This frequency change is due to the Doppler effect described in chapter 9 and has no effect on the rate of information. If the speed of the tape is varied in certain relationships to the rotation of the head cylinder, however, the rate of information can be changed without affecting the frequency. Both frequency and rate can be continuously varied from half the original format to almost double. As well as being very useful for adjusting fine tuning, and for sync purposes, the zeitdehner can also be very effective in producing timbre modifications. Since it is possible with it to prolong various transient states without changing the frequency, the zeitdehner is able to capture sounds that would otherwise be impossible to obtain. Due to the physical arrangement of the cylindrical mounting, there is a certain amount of distortion as the heads rotate in and out of position on the tape, but the amount of distortion is quite low and can usually be masked if that particular sequence appears with other tracks of sound. Otherwise the "bumps" may be eliminated by scrupulous editing.

One of the biggest problems facing the electronic music composer is the control of noise in the record and playback systems. Every system has a dynamic range which is defined by the residual noise of the system being the low-level limit and the power handling capacity determining the high-level limit. A noisy system is defined as having a noise level that is insufficiently below the

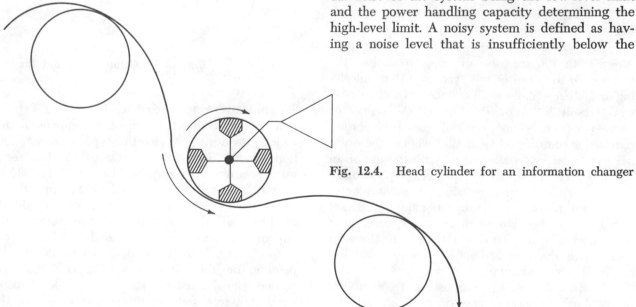

Fig. 12.4.   Head cylinder for an information changer

highest signal level to the degree that it interferes with the intelligibility of the lowest levels of the information signal. The most effective way to deal with noise is to keep the systems in top-quality condition and to exercise great care during the recording process. Due to the unavoidable inherent noise level in some systems, however, several other methods have been devised to deal with this problem. The first method is signal compression. If a particular sequence has a hypothetical dynamic range of from 60 to 70 db, it will require a fairly high gain level to make that amount of variation in gain available. If a system begins to introduce noise at that high a gain setting, then a compressor may be used to compress the 60-70 db range to a more workable range of perhaps 40-45 db. Compression differs from overall manual gain reduction in that while gain reduction results in equal amounts of suppresion to the total envelope, compression is a result of applying most of the gain reduction to the higher amplitude peaks (fig. 12.5C). A limiter is a type of processing device which only affects the peaks of a particular signal. Up to a specific level the output signal is linear with the input signal. The instant the input signal reaches a preset amplitude level, it is maintained at that level and not allowed to go any higher. Limiting differs from compression in that it only reduces amplitude peaks; signals below the predetermined level are not affected (fig. 12.5D). A compressor/limiter applies the combined functions in several different manners. The usual application is to apply compression to the lower portion of the dynamic range and use the limiting function as a safeguard against sudden amplitude surges which may exceed the top level for which the compressor is set to function. Along with the function of noise reduction, the compressor and limiter are used in AM broadcasting and other situations where excessive gain levels could result in overmodulation of the signal. In cases where only one step of signal processing requires a compressed or limited signal, the original gain level may be retrieved with the use of an expander. The expander provides a complementary function to the compressor, since it provides automatic gain increases to a proportionally lower level signal. A combination compressor/expander unit is referred to as a "compander" and is usually used to improve the signal-to-noise ratio in communications and reproduction systems.

While it is not the purpose or responsibility of this book to endorse specific commercial products, the uniqueness of the Dolby Noise Reduction

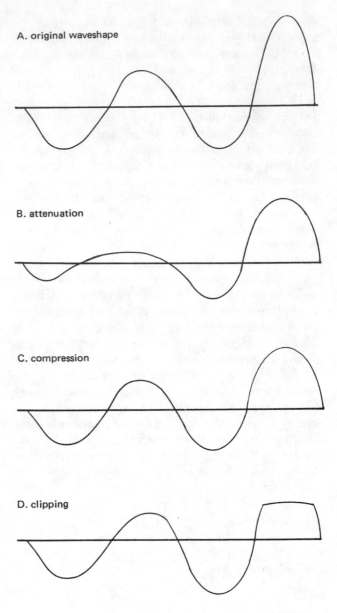

A. original waveshape

B. attenuation

C. compression

D. clipping

Fig. 12.5.   Compression and limiting

System warrants its discussion. The Dolby Type A is a very specialized design of a compander unit which provides a very effective type of noise reduction. The unit divides the input signal into four separate spectrum of frequencies below 80 Hz, 80 to 3k Hz, 3k Hz and above, and 9k Hz and above. Frequency components above a certain amplitude level are passed straight through the system without any further processing. Signals existing below a specific level are boosted by 10 to 15 db, depending on their frequency. The composite recorded signal then contains no low-level components except for the noise introduced by the recording process. During playback the originally boosted signals are compressed back to their original low level and the same amount of compression is applied to the noise contributed by the recording process. The overall result is a very specialized form of equalization which reduces noise by 10 to 15 db. Print-through, cross-talk, and hum are also subjected to about 10 db suppression. Of course any signal processed through a Dolby System must be reproduced through a Dolby System and any further re-dubbing may replace the negative recording effects which were originally suppressed. It is possible to make dubs of the Dolbyized master on regular recording machines and then reproduce the dub through the Dolby System. In building up several generations of tapes, the individual source tapes should not be processed by the Dolby. The final composite dub-down is the generation to be processed or there is a danger of producing varying noise levels. Also, if other treatment—such as modulation, filtering, etc.—are to be done, these processes should not be manipulated while the signal is in the Dolbyized state. Attempts to alter the processed signal can result in low-level amplitude modulation and distortion to the reproduced signal. It is perfectly safe, however, to edit the processed tape without danger of distorting the processed signal. Although the Dolby System is used primarily as a noise reduction system, the processed tapes are often used as a means for detecting low-level distortion and noise. The composer might also consider the possibility of using the processed signal reproduced on a normal deck as a final modification means in itself. Currently available in several home systems, the Dolby is often used with a very low-noise, chromium-dioxide cassette tape, which further reduces the noise problem contributed by the recording/playback process. (For a more detailed description of the function and operation of the Dolby System see R. M. Dolby, "An Audio Noise Reduction System," *Journal of the Acoustical Engineering Society*, Vol. 15, no. 4, Oct., 1967.)

Clipping is a special means of limiting which also limits amplitude peaks to a specific preset level. While limiting usually applies to overall envelopes and their amplitude, clipping is usually applied to either the positive or negative polarity and may be used for a certain amount of timbre modification. In figure 12.6, a sine wave is subjected to various amounts of clipping. As shown, it is possible to clip a sine wave to such a degree that it will exhibit almost the same characteristics as a square wave. Of course this amount of clipping will also result in a very noticeable gain

loss. As well as providing a certain amount of timbre modification, the clipping of various control voltages can result in some very interesting modulation products. Clipping may be executed to the

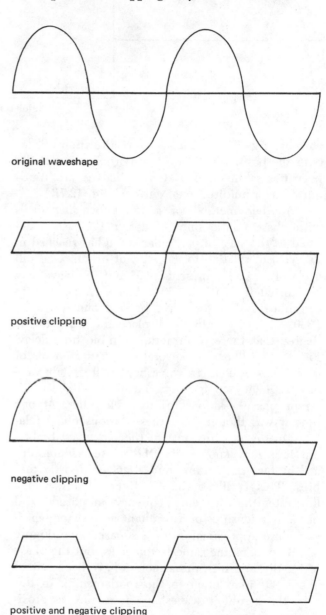

original waveshape

positive clipping

negative clipping

positive and negative clipping

Fig. 12.6. Clipping

degree of completely eliminating either the positive or negative portion of a waveshape. Referred to as rectification, this manner of clipping is used to convert an oscillating or AC current into an unidirectional current or DC. This technique was referred to in chapter 6 as a method for converting AC signals into trigger pulses. Half-wave rectification uses only the positive or negative portions of the wave in the production of the unidirectional

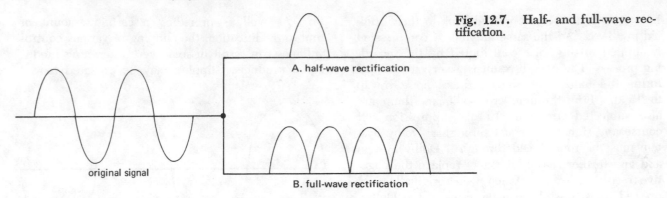

Fig. 12.7. Half- and full-wave rectification.

A. half-wave rectification

original signal

B. full-wave rectification

current (fig. 12.7A). Full-wave rectification utilizes both the positive and negative portions; one of the polarities is inverted and both halves are transmitted as a unidirectional current (fig. 12.7B).

Another method of sound processing deals with phase relationships of a signal. Phase is defined as the stage a particular wave has reached in its cycle in relation to its point of origin. One full cycle of a wave represents 360° and the wave may be shifted from 0° to 360°. It is even possible to continue to shift the wave beyond one full cycle (360° +) and eventually displace the wave to the degree that there is an actual audible time delay. Figure 12.8 illustrates several different amounts of phase shift. A complex waveshape will contain various frequency components, all of which bear different phase relationships to each other. At one time it was thought that these various phase relations made no difference to the perceived timbre, but it is now known that the phase relationships are in fact quite important to characteristic timbres. This is illustrated by figure 12.9A, which illustrates the different frequency, amplitude, and phase relationships of a resultant waveshape which is a close approximation of a square wave. Figure 12.9B contains the same frequencies, but the phase of the 3rd and the 5th harmonics have been shifted about 90° in relation to the fundamental. In this case the resultant waveshape is a close approximation of a sawtooth wave.

If two waveshapes are equal in amplitude and frequency and are being transmitted through the same medium 180° out of phase with each other, the result will be complete cancellation of both waves (fig. 12.10). This can be demonstrated by showing that their combined instantaneous voltages, will equal zero—(+3 volts) + (−3 volts) = 0 volts. Even similar waveshapes with less critical phase relationships will still produce a certain amount of cancellation. Although cancellation can be a very annoying problem in high-fidelity re-

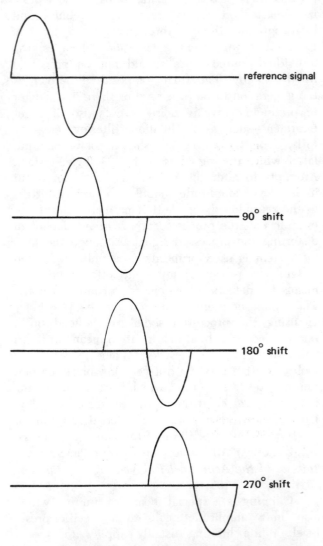

reference signal

90° shift

180° shift

270° shift

Fig. 12.8. Various amounts of phase shift

production, the composer may use it to achieve very desirable effects. One example is the use of phase cancellation to produce band-reject effects using a band-pass filter. This calls for the signal to be split and one leg taken to the band-pass

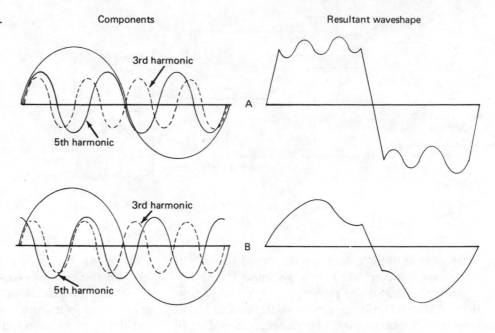

Fig. 12.9. Phase relationships in a complex signal.

Components

Resultant waveshape

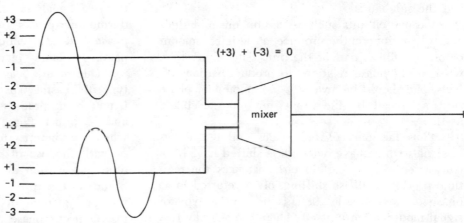

Fig. 12.10. Additive phase cancellation.

$(+3) + (-3) = 0$

mixer

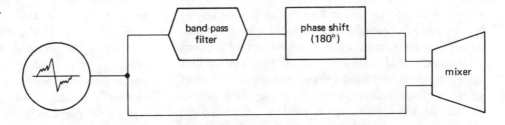

Fig. 12.11. Patching configuration for using phase shift for converting a band-pass filter to a band-reject filter.

band pass filter

phase shift (180°)

mixer

filter and at the same time subjected to a 180° phase shift. Then, in combining the processed signal with the direct signal, the band-pass frequencies will cancel out of the composite signal, simulating the effect of a band-reject filter (fig. 12.11).

Cancellation may also be used to simulate ring modulation with VCAs. In chapter 3 it was

explained that ring modulation produced the same sideband structure as amplitude modulation but without the presence of either the carrier or the program frequencies. Therefore, by producing amplitude modulation and using phase cancellation to eliminate the carrier and program signals, the result will be the same as ring modulation. This technique requires VCAs with separate positive

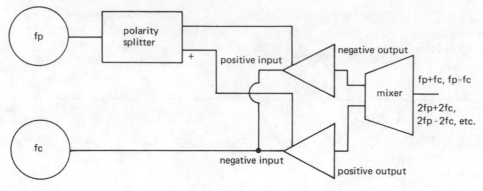

Fig. 12.12. Rectification method for simulating ring modulation

and negative inputs, such as are found on certain commercial electronic music systems. Using opposite polarities of the program and carrier to produce AM sidebands, as shown in figure 12.12, will eliminate the carrier and program signals and leave just the sidebands.

Various circuits such as certain mixer designs and filters inherently produce a definite amount of phase shift as part of the processing. Therefore, when using phase relations to produce various effects, one should be aware of the amount of phase shift produced by the processing modules being used.

Thus far, only characteristics and techniques of signals which have been phase shifted have been considered. Under certain circumstances the real-time process of phase shifting, often referred to as phase or angle modulation, is used as a type of signal modification in itself. There are actually two different approaches to phase modulation, both of which can be used very effectively by the composer. Probably the most familiar to the composer is the "swoosh" or "churning" sound which is characteristic of a narrow noise band sweeping through a complex signal. This effect is the result of various components of a complex wave going in and out of phase with each other, producing varying amounts of cancellation. The classic method of producing this effect is to record the same information on two separate tape recorders and varying the synchronization during playback. This requires a variable-speed tape recorder which will allow minute variations in speed. The sync difference should not be so critical as to produce an echo but just enough to produce definite phase variations. As the two playback machines are brought in and out of phase with each other, the characteristic churning phase distortion will be produced. The same effect may be simulated in quite a different manner without

attempting to produce out-of-phase reproduction. If two tracks of stereophonic or binaural information are simultaneously panned to opposite channels, there is a certain amount of phase distortion at the point in the middle of the stereo field where the two signals cross. If both channels are mixed during this process with a non-linear device, the phase distortion will occur for the entire period the panning is taking place.

Due to the beautiful effects produced by this type of phasing, special phase-shifting equipment is now being produced especially for the composer and performer. Phase-shifting circuits are available which may be operated either manually with a pot or with the use of control voltages. As with all other modulation devices, the frequency and amplitude of the applied control signal determines the rate and amount of modulation—in this case the instantaneous phase of a given signal is varied in accordance with the applied control voltage. The amplitude of the control signal determines the amount of phase shift, and the frequency determines the rate. If the control signal is a subaudio frequency, the phase will be modulated to produce churning phase distortion. As the control frequency approaches the audio range, the modulation process will produce resultant sidebands which are similar to the sideband frequencies produced by frequency modulation (see chap. 4, p. 12). Since varying the phase is an indirect way of varying the frequency, phase modulation is sometimes referred to as "equivalent FM." In broadcasting, phase modulation is sometimes substituted for frequency modulation, since it is transmitted, received, and demodulated in the same manner. The advantage of phase modulation is that it produces a more stable center frequency. To the composer this means that the modulation index is determined both by the amplitude and by the frequency of the control signal. Consequently, higher frequencies along with greater amplitudes produce proportionally higher phase-modulation indices.

One of the most misused words in the field of electronic music is the term "stereophonic." How often do we see ". . . for stereophonic tape"? It may be a bit academic to draw attention to this misuse but clarification of terms may lead the composer to a more careful consideration of the final mixing of multi-track sources. Stereophonic reproduction is the result of recording a single sound or composite group of sounds from at least two different locations. If a symphony orchestra is recorded by placing microphone A at the left of the ensemble and microphone B at the right, the reproduction of both tracks simultaneously will be true stereophony. Although the left side of the orchestra will be most apparent on channel A, the sounds produced by the instruments on the right side of the orchestra will also be heard, to a lesser degree, on channel A. At the same time, the microphone for channel B will pick up sounds from both sides of the orchestra, with the instruments situated nearest the microphone being the loudest. Because of the relative amplitude relationships produced during playback, each instrument will seem to be located at its appropriate spot within the stereophonic field. Even a single sound source recorded and reproduced with a stereo system will not be heard just from the areas of the speakers but will encompass the entire stereo field. If the two speakers are spread too far apart, the characteristic hole-in-the-middle effect is very evident. This is often compensated for by mixing parts of both channels A and B and routing the composite signal to a third speaker located midway between the other two. An even more effective method would be to make the mixture during the recording process or, if possible, to make a three-channel recording. The more individual recording and reproduction channels that are available, the more precise will be the directionality of the individual instruments.

A binaural system is one in which there are two independent channels of sound with no attempt made to re-create an acoustical stereophonic field. A binaural recording would be one in which a clarinet is recorded only on channel A and then the tape is rewound and a trumpet is recorded in sync on channel B. During reproduction each instrument would be heard only from its respective speaker location and the only interaction between the channels would take place in the acoustical space between the speakers and the listener. In electronic music, unless the source tapes were true

stereo recordings, most generated sequences are binaural. Splitting a signal and patching it to the two different inputs of a stereo recorder will still lack the spatial characteristics of a true stereo recording in reproduction. If a monophonic signal is split and mixed with two channels of true stereophonic sound, the binaural signals produce the illusion of having more stereophonic characteristics.

The true stereophonic effect is due to many different factors, including amplitude and phase, and the directional stereo array is created by reproducing the exact intensity and phase characteristics as they were in the real acoustical environment. Taking advantage of the phase phenomenon, commercial systems are now available which can create a pseudo-stereophonic field from a monophonic recording. This is usually accomplished by phase-shifting various components of the composite signal on different tracks so that one signal reaches the listeners' ears before the other. While they are actually much more complicated than the last statement would imply, pseudo-stereo systems or "stereo-synthesizers" work very well in creating stereophonic arrays. (A detailed explanation of one approach to pseudo-stereo is Robert Orban, "A *Rational Technique for Synthesizing Pseudo-Stereo from Monophonic Sources*," *Journal of the Audio Engineering Society*, vol. 18, no. 2, April, 1970.) In addition to the obvious application of creating stereo images from monophonic sources, these systems can also provide other functions. Since the effects of directionality are largely cued by phase differences, a monophonic mix of the pseudo-stereo channels will not result in the "center build-up" caused by other dub-downs of stereo channels. Another application is the use of only a single output from the system. Since the spread and location of the images in the stereo field are a result of phase variation, the use of one output channel can result in various phasing effects. Units are also available which provide for the voltage control of the stereo image which is very similar to voltage-controlled panning. In this case the actual controlled parameter is the phase.

Stereophonic playback systems require that special care be given to speaker phasing and location. The ambience, or characteristic acoustics, of the environment will also have a great influence on the directionality of the individual signals and the separation between the channels. The composer will also find that minute intensity changes are more noticeable in a stereophonic field than with binaural reproduction. While technical considerations should be of concern to the composer, the use of a stereophonic, monophonic, or binaural system has no aesthetic implications in itself. As with any technique associated with any art, success depends on the manner of application.

Despite the many changes brought about by voltage control, the tape loop has held its place as one of the prime techniques used by the composer of electronic music. One of its most imaginative uses has been in the music of Steve Reich (discussed in relation to gating, p. 47). Loops may provide ostinato rhythmic patterns or may be used to indefinitely sustain various recorded timbres. In *Rice, Wax and Narrative,* composer Daniel Lentz calls for a large tape loop to enclose two on-stage performers, thus taking advantage of its visual as well as sonic possibilities.

The most important consideration in working with tape loops is the splice. When subjected to several repetitions, a noisy splice becomes even more noticeable and can ruin whatever function the loop is to serve. If the event on the tape is made up of several attacks and decays, the ideal spot to make the cut is at the very beginning of an attack. As explained in chapter 11, attack transients can be used to mask any noise caused by the splice. If the loop consists of a single continuous event with no attack or decay, very special care will have to be taken with the splice, but if the tips given in chapter 11 are followed, an effective splice is possible.

The second consideration when using loops is the tape tension. If a tape is not kept flush against the playback head at a constant tension, there will be constant fluctuations in the output gain, and speed variations caused by the changes in tension. If the tape decks use only pressure pads and a capstan drive, there is usually no problem and the size of the loop is of no consequence; the interaction between the pressure pads and the capstan keep the tape flush against the head at a constant tension. A tape deck with tension arms, however, is designed to work in conjunction with the torque supplied by the feed and take-up reels. Unless the tape loop is the exact size to supply the necessary torque, the tension will not be regulated and the playback will be very erratic. One solution to this problem is a variable-length tape guide, as illustrated in figure 12.13. The guide is adjusted to the exact size of the loop so that the tape is under constant tension at all times.

An approach to providing tape tension which allows more applications is a loop board. Illustrated in figure 12.14, the loop board is an alumi-

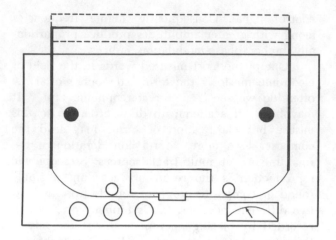

Fig. 12.13. Variable-length loop guide

num plate with provisions for placing tape guides or additional playback heads at almost any point on its surface. If the board is to be used only to provide tension for a tape loop, then the placement of two or three tape guides forming a triangle will suffice. The composer also has the possibility of inserting playback heads in the board, making it possible to monitor the tape at multiple points along its path, these to be mixed with the other playback points or taken to an individual channel. One advantage of the board is that the tape is not necessarily spliced end to end in a loop. Reel-to-reel formats are applicable to loop boards.

Some studios oriented to the more classical methods of electronic music production have a bank of several playback decks especially intended for use with loops. These machines differ from the normal tape deck in several ways. They are usually full-track formats, since most loop material is monophonic. Since their only function is to reproduce recorded material, they only contain a single playback head. The playback circuits are usually external to the actual deck chassis and it is a very simple matter to have variable-speed playback provisions. This is especially useful when the loops are to be used for precise rhythmic effects, since they can be finely adjusted to exact playback tempi. Another feature often found on a loop deck is a provision for reversing the motors in order to play the tapes backward without turning them over. This is also possible on capstan drive machines which have three separate motors for forward play and record, rewind, and fast forward. Threading the tape on the back side of the capstan roller will feed it backwards past the playback head. In order to keep the tape in constant contact with the head, it is sometimes necessary to bypass the left-hand

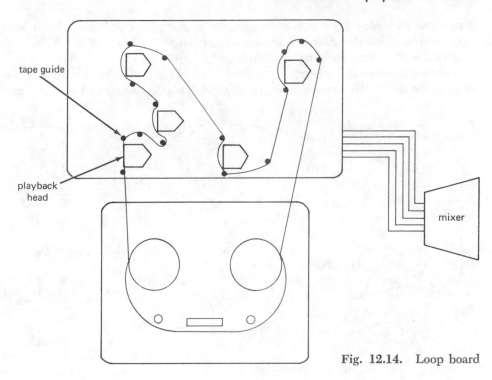

tape guide

playback
head

mixer

Fig. 12.14. Loop board

tension arm and thread the tape directly to the
left-hand reel. This is rather a make-shift technique
and most machines are not intended for it. It
should only be used when there is no chance of
damage to the machine and where time does not
permit reversing the tape, such as in a live performance situation. With a bank of loop machines,
each head should have its own separate preamplifier with all of the output jacks located at a single
patch panel. This panel would be even more practical if it also contained at least two mixers for
combining the loop outputs into various channels.

It is essential that a studio have a minimum
of electronic test equipment, but the use to which
a composer puts this equipment depends on his
training. Many successful composers have never
once felt the need to refer to an oscilloscope or a
waveform analyzer. (If one is dealing with a primarily sonic art, then that which cannot be judged
by the ear is of no real consequence.) But there
are also composers who would not think of making
a patch without first double-checking the impedance or monitoring the output on an oscilloscope.
Some of the more technically-oriented composers
are even so familiar with the visual representation
of sounds that they often produce compositions
relying entirely on scopes and meters and do not
use audio monitoring at all. (Many things show up
with test equipment which may illustrate the cause
of a certain effect or manner of processing not re-

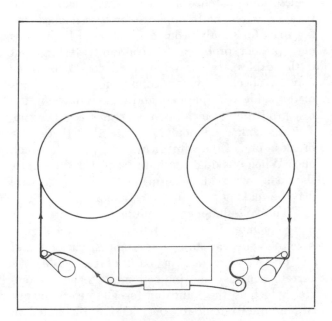

Fig. 12.15 Tape path for reversing tape play direction.

sulting in the desired outcome.) Perhaps the realistic approach is to rely on the sonic properties of the
processing but have the test equipment available
in the event of any malfunction or situation in
which it could eliminate the need for guesswork.

The simplest and often most-used test device
is the continuity tester. This is simply a DC bat-

tery in series with a light bulb with an open circuit and two test prods attached at each end (fig. 12.16). By attaching the prods to each end of any transmission line, the circuit is closed and the light activated if the transmission line is good. This

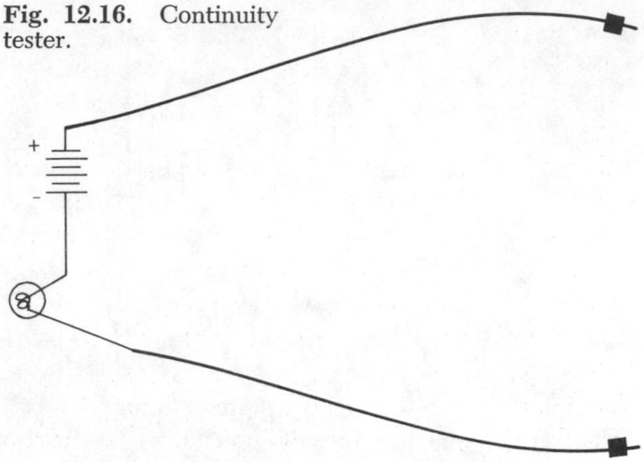

Fig. 12.16. Continuity tester.

device is especially useful in checking for broken cables and patchcords. Very long cables and speaker wires with opposite ends stretched too far apart for simultaneous connection of both prods may present problems for continuity testing, but if the cables are coaxial or twin conductor, they may be checked by connecting the common ends of the cable with jumpers and then connecting the test prods between the two wires at the other end. This of course can only indicate that there is a break in one of the wires; it will not indicate which one. When making continuity checks, the cables should be wiggled, since many breaks in the wire may be making momentary contact.

The volt-ohm-meter, multimeter, multitester or more commonly the "VOM" provides meter indications of wide varieties of resistances, currents and AC or DC voltages. The basis of the VOM is a current sensitive moving-coil meter or galvanometer which is the indicator for all measurements. A simplified circuit for the VOM is illustrated in figure 12.17. The battery is used only when resistance is being measured. Before any measurements are taken, the test prods must be shorted together and the zero-set potentiometer adjusted so that the pointer is exactly on the far right division or "O" on the scale. If at any time the pointer cannot reach the "O" mark, this may be an indication that the meter's battery needs replacement. Because the VOM is a multipurpose instrument it requires different scales and switching arrangements for different modes of operation. A typical

VOM may have four scales for measuring AC, four scales for measuring DC, one scale for measuring ohms (resistance), and one scale for making decibel measurements. To aid in reading, the DC, ohm, and decibel scales are often printed in black,

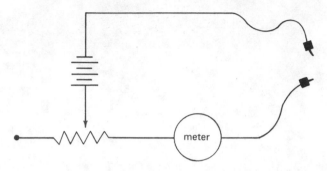

Fig. 12.17. Simplified VOM circuit

while the AC scale is printed in red. Besides having different scales for different measurements, the scales also have different formats. The AC and DC scales are linear, which means that all of the divisions are equidistant from each other throughout that particular scale's total range (fig. 12.18A). In some cases it may be found that the lower end of the AC scale is slightly non-linear. To provide for accurate reading, the voltage scales are provided with a switch with indications such as 10x, 100x, etc. The ohm scale is non-linear (fig. 12.18B). The ohm scale is also affected by the resistance range switch. This switch increases or decreases the total resistance of the VOM; it acts much like the range multiplier on an oscillator. If while measuring the value of a resistor the meter gives a reading of 150 ohms with the range in the Rx10 position, the value of the resistor would be 1500 ohms. If the same resistor were measured with the switch in the Rx100 position, the reading on the scale would be 15 ohms. Due to the non-linearity of the scale, the range switch is very useful for adjusting the meter to give a more accurate reading and provide for easier interpolation. The logarithmic scale (fig. 12.18C) has the "O" indication toward the center, with plus and minus signs to either side. This scale is in terms of decibels and, like the ohms scale, becomes slightly more crowded toward the left. Unlike the ohms or voltage scales, the logarithmic scale has no range multiplier.

The value of a VOM, as with any other piece of equipment, can only be measured by the amount of useful information the instrument provides. The amount and accuracy of this information, in turn,

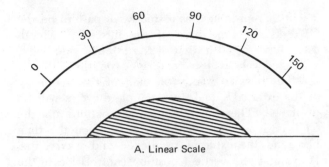

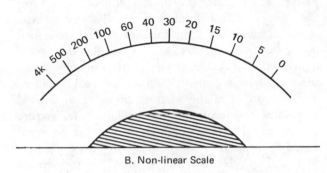

A. Linear Scale

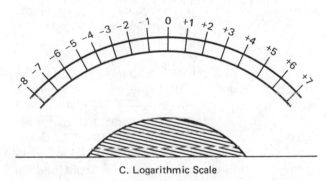

B. Non-linear Scale

C. Logarithmic Scale

Fig. 12.18. VOM scales

depends on how well the user understands the operation, application, and limitations of the device. A very basic list of VOM applications would include:

1. resistance checks,
   a. power resistors,
   b. variable resistors,
   c. insertion loss,
   d. attenuation,
2. continuity checks,
3. checking tubes and transistors,
4. checking switches,
5. checking relays,
6. checking variable capacitors for shorts,
7. tests for leaky capacitors,
8. checking diodes,
9. checking speakers,
10. checking AC and DC voltages,
11. measuring tube voltages,
    a. line,
    b. battery,
    c. power supply,
12. taking in-line decibel readings.

Instructions concerning each of the above applications would comprise a separate volume in itself and the above list is by no means exhaustive. No attempt should be made to use the VOM or any other test equipment without thoroughly reading the manufacturer's instruction manual, which will provide complete instructions for each type of test. Through a wrong connection or by improper usage, the VOM could very easily be permanently damaged. One of the best methods to familiarize one's self with test equipment is to purchase it in kit form and to personally do the assembling. The kits usually use printed circuits and the instructions are very clear. If the instructions are carefully followed, even a novice will have no trouble. There is a definite mystique about personally-assembled devices—they seem to have more usage and find more applications.

The vacuum tube voltmeter or VTVM is similar in many ways to the VOM in that it provides measurement of AC and DC voltages and currents along with resistance measurements. The difference is that the VTVM utilizes the amplifying properties of a vacuum tube, or in some cases a transistor. Consequently, the VTVM has a much wider and finer range than the VOM. The voltage scale, with the use of a multiplier switch, has a range from zero to as high as 1,500 volts AC or DC, and the resistance scale may range from .1 ohm to 1,000 megohms or higher. Because of the higher voltage requirements of the vacuum tube, the VTVM must operate from a 120- or 240-volt supply, and thus the VTVM is not as portable as the battery-powered VOM and is usually used more in studio rather than field applications. Transistorized VTVMs however, require only battery voltage and can be very light and compact.

Along with most of the applications listed for the VOM, the VTVM can also determine and measure the characteristics and response of equalizer and filter networks. Basically this is accomplished by putting an oscillator in series with a VTVM, a filter or equalizer, and a second VTVM and measuring comparative input and output voltages or decibels. In this manner the characteristics and roll-off of any equalizer or filter may be plotted very accurately. This technique is thoroughly described by Howard M. Tremaine in *Passive Audio Network Design* (New York: Howard W. Sams, 1964).

One of the most familiar pieces of equipment in a studio is the oscilloscope. This device operates by means of two sets of deflection plates, one horizontal and one vertical, controlling the movement of an electron beam focused on a cathode ray tube (CRT). Horizontal deflection is usually controlled by the oscilloscope's internal time base oscillator which produces a sawtooth waveform. The sawtooth waveshape is used because its steady rise in voltage moves the beam horizontally across the CRT at a uniform rate and its rapid change in polarity deflects the beam back to its starting position in a minimum amount of time (fig. 12.19).

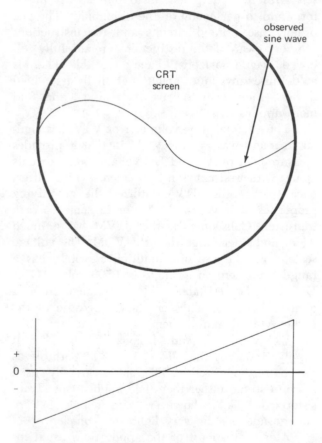

Fig. 12.19. Sawtooth wave used to control the horizontal sweep of an oscilloscope.

The amplitude and frequency of the sawtooth wave determine the length of the sweep, which is referred to as the "time base."

The vertical direction of the beam is determined by application of an external signal. If a sine-wave voltage is applied to the vertical sweep it will be reproduced as a sine-wave pattern on the CRT. If the time base of the internal sawtooth oscillator is equal to that of the external sine wave, a single cycle will be displayed on the CRT. If the time base is exactly one-half of the frequency of the external signal, two complete cycles will be displayed. Therefore the display pattern on the CRT is dependent on the ratio between the time base and the external frequency and waveshape. Horizontal and vertical position controls locate the pattern at any point on the screen. The stability of the time base oscillator is controlled by a sync signal in much the same manner as that described on page 19 in chapter 4. A sync signal selector allows internal, external, or line frequencies to be used as sync signals. When in internal position, a small portion of the vertical input signal is used to control the frequency of the horizontal sweep. The external position allows any other external signal to be used. The line position taps off a portion of the 60 Hz line voltage used for the scope's power supply. The amplitude of the sync signal, controlled by a potentiometer on the front of the scope, should be set at the lowest effective point. Excessive sync voltage may result in distortion in the displayed patterns.

It is possible to use external signals for the time base frequency. If a sine wave is used, the return trace is visible because of the equal rise and fall time of the sine wave voltage. External sine-wave sweep frequencies are very useful in determining unknown frequencies. If a known frequency is applied to the horizontal input and an unknown frequency is applied to the vertical input, the combined effects on the deflection plates will result in what are referred to as Lissajous figures. If the two input signals are of equal frequency, amplitude, and phase, the CRT display will be a perfect circle. By varying any one of the signals' parameters, the pattern can be transformed into an unlimited number of fascinating figures. Many composers and artists are involved with the production of oscilloscopic art—the production and control of Lissajous figures as an artistic medium in itself.

Although the ear should be the final judge of the desired sound, the scope is useful in designing a very precise control envelope. As well as the normal applications of frequency measurement, determination of phase relationships, measurement of AC and DC voltages, etc., the oscilloscope may be used as a very unusual source of complex waveshapes. If a photo-cell is placed directly in front of the CRT display screen, the illumination caused by the beam will supply varying amounts of light to the cell, which in turn will couple signals to the input of an operational amplifier. The "op-amp" output is then used to control the scope's vertical amplifier in such a manner that gain from the amplifier causes the beam to move downward on the CRT. An opaque mask is cut from some material to match the shape of the desired wave and this mask is placed on the face of the CRT screen in front of the photo-cell. As the photo-cell sees less light the beam begins to drop below the mask, the signal to the amplifier begins to decrease and the beam is then deflected back above the mask. Therefore, as the beam is swept across the screen at a frequency determined by the time base oscillator, a voltage is produced by the op-amp which exhibits an envelope similar to that of the opaque mask. This technique, which has certain limitations, is discussed in detail by M. L. Eaton in *Electronic Music: A Handbook of Sound Synthesis and Control* (Kansas City; Orcus Research Company, TP-3003, 1969).

In *Night Music* (Odyssey record no. 32 16 0160) by composer Richard Maxfield, the oscilloscope is used as a sound source in quite a different manner. The synchronizing input signal for the time base oscillator is fed by two external oscillators, one producing variable frequency subaudio pulses and the other producing a supersonic sawtooth wave. The result is that the subaudio pulses continually modulate the tapped oscilloscope output through multiples and submultiples of the supersonic sync signal. This output is then heterodyned with the bias frequency of a tape recorder (40k to 80k Hz) to produce a variety of resultant frequencies.

The disadvantage of using an oscilloscope for frequency measurements is that it requires a visual comparison between a known and unknown frequency. A device that requires much less computation is the digital frequency counter. On it the frequency of any input signal is displayed numerically, usually with five sets of numbers from 0 to 9. The readout digits must be interpreted in terms of the gate or counting time. A representative frequency meter may have four possible gate times, selected by a switch on the front of the instrument. Common gate times are .1 second, 1 second,

10 seconds and manual timing control. With the gate time in the .1 position, the meter will register however many cycles occur in .1 second. If the digital display were 00064 with the gate in the .1 position, it would indicate that the test frequency is 640 Hz. The same frequency readout with a .1 gate time would be 00640, and a 10 gate time would result in a 06400 readout. It can be seen that the most often used time would be 1. When very accurate readings are required, however, a higher gate time may be more practical. The frequency counter is extremely useful in setting oscillators at exact frequencies. If a composer is attempting to create an exact predetermined side-band structure, the carrier and program frequencies must be exact and a frequency readout can save a considerable amount of time. It should be kept in mind that some oscillators have tendencies to drift from their settings and a frequency readout at one moment will not necessarily coincide with the readout of the same oscillator setting at another moment. The amount of oscillator drift can easily be determined by taking frequency readings at regular intervals and plotting the figures on a graph.

The VOM, VTVM, oscilloscope, and frequency counter are by no means the only test apparatus which may be used by the composer. A more complete list of applicable test equipment would include distortion meters, intermodulation analyzers, resistance and capacitance substitution boxes, RF generators, signal tracers, tube checkers, transistor testers, and on and on. One can see by the length of this list that an adequate discussion of all available test apparatus could comprise several volumes in itself. After one has had considerable experience with the VOM, VTVM, scope and frequency counter, however, and understands all of their applications, he will find that these four instruments will usually be adequate for most compositional applications. The composer or performer should not attempt to operate any test equipment with only the information presented here. Thoroughly read an instrument's instruction manual before any tests are made. Unlike most commercial electronic music systems, test equipment is not novice proof and misuse could result in permanent damage.

live electronic music

For many years the anti-audiences of electronic music objected to the lack of visual activity during concerts. Up to the middle of this century musical performance involved the participation of a live performer. Because of this apparent tradition, and partly due to the visual-aural reinforcement involved, contemporary audiences have often expressed dissatisfaction with having to rely on speaker baffles for visual stimulation. It is true that in some cases there may be a definite need for visual reinforcement of sonic events, but in other circumstances the ideal environment for listening to music is on a soft rug in a completely darkened room. If a work is composed purely as an audio event, the composer should carefully examine the aesthetic precepts of his composition before being persuaded to add visual accompaniment. The popularity of inter-media and mixed theatre, however, has made it possible for many composers to expand their creativities to incorporate both sonic and visual activities into a very successful single art form which would not be as effective as it is without the contributions of both disciplines. The light shows and color organs of the discotheques of the late 1960s have now been developed to the state that interfaces are available for producing very complex light patterns using audio and control signals from commercially available electronic music systems. Many composers are also using ordinary oscilloscopic patterns incorporated as visual counterparts to the sound patterns controlling the scopes, and studios are now being designed with interfaces to provide visual patterns for every audio event produced.

Some of the more successful expeditions into the realm of oscilloscopic art have been carried out by composer Lowell Cross since the mid 1960s. Using a television set in a manner similar to an oscilloscope, he creates and manipulates Lissajous figures as a result of his composed audio tracks. Due to the interaction of the audio and video parameters, Cross composes in consideration of both the emotive and visual results of the sounds being produced.

Audio-visual art, while it does present an audience with visually stimulating events, may or may not involve a live performer. In observing a performing musician, the audience is of course affected by the sonic events being produced, but at the same time it is also influenced by the theatrical consequences of an artist displaying his craft. Although live electronic music was not specifically created to satisfy the demands of this particular tradition, it is certainly a result of that tradition. There is a great amount of existing literature for various ensembles to perform with pre-recorded tape which requires a performer to manipulate the playback deck on cue from a conductor or a score. In this case the electronic processing of the sounds have taken place at a time and place external to the performance. In the true sense of the term, "live" electronic music requires sound manipulation as part of the actual performance. This may call for one or more performers to produce signals via acoustical or electronic instruments and for performers to control the real-time processing of those signals. A live electronic situation may be as simple as the normal methods of amplifying an acoustic instrument or as complex as the patching network illustrated in figure 14.2 in chapter 14. Some situations call for purely acoustical sound sources, while other compositions require the addition of electronic sound sources. Still other compositions, such as *Sine Screen* by David Behrman call for the exclusive use of electronically-generated signals in a live performance. In addition to its aesthetic consequences and technical implications, live electronic music has also placed the audio engineer in the role of a performing musician.

A distinctive example of live electronic music literature is *Bert Bows, Bells and Balls His Bass* by Frank McCarty. This composition, written for bassist Bertram Turetzky, together with requiring the bassist to perform very virtuosic passages, a running monologue, and some very comic theatrics, utilizes a tape recorder as an additional performing instrument. This piece puts itself together as part of the live performance. The completed composition is a mixture of two pre-recorded tracks along with live performance utilizing various degrees of tape echo and feedback. The electronic patching diagram for it is shown in figure 13.1.

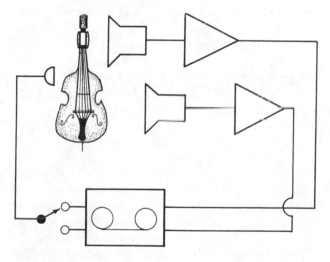

Fig. 13.1. Patching diagram for *Bert Bows, Bells and Balls His Bass.*

The bass is transduced by an air microphone, with the gain controlled by a foot-pedal attenuator. The output of the attenuator is dependent on the amount of depression applied to the pedal by the performer. The output is then patched to a switching unit which will allow it to be switched to microphone input A or B of a three-head, two-channel stereophonic tape recorder. Output channels A and B are then taken to a stereophonic amplifier whose output is patched to monitor speakers behind the performer.

A brief description of the performance is as follows: As the performance begins the microphone is patched to channel A of the tape recorder which is running in the record mode with the monitor output gain level set at zero. The performer is involved with a monologue about the history and development of, and contemporary interest in the string bass. At various intervals the performer interrupts his monologue to perform single events on the bass and at the same time raises the output gain of the foot-pedal attenuator so that only those events are recorded on channel A of the tape. After each event the performer must raise the pedal so that no other sounds are recorded other than those indicated on the score. This sequence of monologue and isolated events is continued for about five minutes. What now appears recorded on channel A of the tape is a series of single events separated by varying periods of silence. Continuing with the monologue, the performer rewinds the tape, raises the output gain of channel A and switches it to "tape monitor," and switches the microphone to channel B input. Channel B is set in the "record" mode, with the output gain level at zero, and channel A is set in the playback mode. The performer and audience will now hear the first recorded sequence of events from the channel A monitor speaker while channel B re-records the playback of that sequence along with the live sounds being produced by the performer. At this point the performer must remember to depress the foot pedal so that the composite signal of the playback and the live performance reaches channel B input. The performer continues his monologue until he hears the playback of the first event recorded on channel A. From this point on, each event monitored from channel A serves as an audio cue to perform an extended event notated in "Part: The Second" of the score.

After this second sequence is recorded, the tape is again rewound and channel B, containing a mixture of the channel A sequence and the previous live sequence, is played back over the monitor speaker for that particular channel. At the same time, channel A is again set to record, with the monitor switch left in the "tape monitor" position, and the output gain is slightly raised. The performer then plays a series of semi-improvised events along with the two previously recorded sequences, which are also used as cues. At various times during this final sequence, the foot pedal is used to raise the input level to channel A to produce tape echo and acoustical feedback. This is possible because the air microphone will pick up the delayed playback of each performed event, resulting in a sustained repetition (as described in chap. 10). During the performance the performer is also occupied with attaching objects such as bells, string clamps, and ping pong balls to his bow and bass and to his own body. As well as serving to distort both the visual and sonic parameters of the performance, these theatrics also qualify the composition as being for "prepared bass." The overall result is the construction of audio-visual events and situations which, with the aid of a tape recorder, is witnessed from beginning to end as part of the total performance.

The use of electronics in *Bert Bows, Bells and Balls His Bass* seems quite simple when reading the score or observing a performance, but there are many things which had to be considered in its planning and in the organization of a performance. Perhaps the most critical point of the entire piece is the control of volume levels and location of the speakers. The playback level of the first recorded sequence must match as closely as possible the level of the live performer. Consequently, the piece is easier to perform if a second person is used to ride gain on the levels. The theatrics of the piece are more effective, however, if a single performer can manage all of the manipulation himself. So the first consideration is to experiment with many different tape-recorder and amplifier levels. If possible, this should be done in the same environment in which the performance will take place. One level setting may work quite well for one situation and will be completely wrong for another. The performer must also put in considerable practice with the foot pedal, so that the input gain to the tape recorder is neither too high nor too low. For the first two recorded sequences, the microphone input gain should be set so that complete depression of the pedal results in the desired recording level. This precaution frees the performer from having to be concerned with precise pedal positions at this point. The third sequence, however, does require different pedal settings. The recorder input and output levels must be set so that various amounts of gain to the recorder result in various amounts of echo and sustained feedback as a result of interaction between the microphone and speaker fields. Then the number and intensity of the repetitions and amount of feedback is completely controlled by the performer. Since the tape echo is used only in conjunction with channel A, only that monitor speaker should be within the immediate microphone field. If the speaker for channel B is too close to the microphone, the playback from channel B could interfere with feedback effects. The placement of monitor speaker

A is also critical for the acoustical mixing of the first two sequences, and to get desired results will usually require a bit of experimentation. This brings up one of the basic considerations of live electronic music performance: Always plan to have as much time as possible before the concert to acquaint yourself with the performance environment. With this particular composition, remote control provisions are really unnecessary because the performer should also have immediate access to the deck and amplifier to control the gain levels. If it is impossible to have a switching unit to redirect the microphone input, this may be done manually by the performer. A final consideration is to provide the performer with exactly five minutes of recording tape with a great deal of leader at each end. By using a timed reel of tape, it will be easier for the performer to keep track of the timing —and the extended leader will serve as insurance that the tape doesn't accidentally run off one of the reels during the record, rewind, or playback process.

Another example of live electronic performance which requires a more complex set-up is *Vanity Faire*, composed by the present writer of this manual (Allen Strange, *Vanity Faire*, Champaign, Ill.: Media Press, 1969). The sound sources for this composition are three music boxes resonated and transduced through tympani shells, a female narrator, and a pre-recorded tape. The score for the patching of *Vanity Faire* is reproduced in figure 13.2. The audio portion of the performance is produced in the following manner: A small contact microphone is attached to the head or shell of each tympani, on top of which is placed a music box. The performers then use the tympani as resonant filters by varying the tension of the head. The three signals from the music boxes are mixed to a composite signal and patched to channel A microphone input of a stereo tape recorder. The monitored output is split and one leg is monitored through one channel of a stereophonic amplifier. The other leg is routed back to the line input of channel B, resulting in a delay between the two channels. The take-up reel for the recorded tape is on a playback machine located at least three feet from the recording deck. This will result in about a 4- to 5-second delay between the two monitored decks.

The output of playback channel A is taken to the other channel of the stereo amplifier and channel B is patched to the carrier input of a ring modulator. The narrator is transduced with an air microphone provided with its own separate pre-

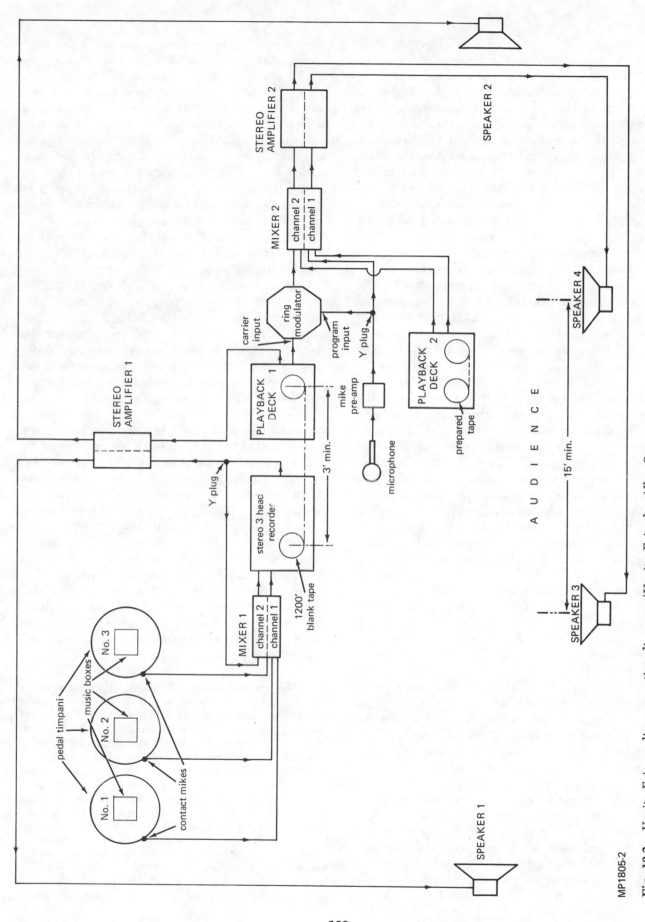

Fig. 13.2. *Vanity Faire* audio preparation diagram. (*Vanity Faire* by Allen Strange, Media Press, 1969. Used by permission of the publisher.)

MP1805-2

amplification. The mike pre-amp output is split, with one leg patched to the program input of the ring modulator, the other leg to channel B of a stereo mixer. The output of the ring modulator is patched to channel A of the same stereo mixer. The prepared tape is played on a third deck, with its respective outputs also patched to channels A and B of the stereo mixer. Channel A of the mixer then contains the ring-modulated product of the narrator's voice and the delayed music box playback, along with track A of the pre-recorded tape. Channel B contains the unmodulated amplified voice and track B of the pre-recorded tape. Both output channels of this mixer are then amplified and taken to two separate speakers. This system then provides four separate but interrelated audio outputs. From speaker 1 is heard the amplified music boxes; from speaker 2, a delayed repetition of what was heard on speaker 1, giving the impression of twice the number of music boxes; from speaker 3, the modulated voice and track A of the tape; and from speaker 4, the unmodified voice and track B of the tape. During the course of the performance, along with various rituals executed by the music box performers, the normal amplified voice of the narrator is slowly faded out while the level of the modulated voice is slowly raised. The effect is a smooth transition from intelligibility to total distortion, along with a simultaneous change in the monitored location of the voice.

In this composition the prime performer is the engineer, whose job it is to keep the levels at a constant relationship and to guard against acoustical howl, which is likely to occur when working with high microphone levels. With this composition the performers must be aware of the "precedence effect." That is, in most locations in the hall the amplified voice will take precedence over the unamplified voice. This is because location is largely determined by what sounds reach the ear first. Since signals travel along wire faster than through air, the speaker will usually appear to be the direct source of the sound. In this case the precedence effect is desired and adds to the transitory passage between the normal and modulated voice.

An example of a combination of audio and visual technology in a live performance situation is *Photo-Oscillations* by composer John Mizelle. Seven oscillators are controlled in different manners by seven individual photo-cells. One cell may control the output waveform of one oscillator and another cell may act as a make or break (on or off) switch for another oscillator. Figure 13.3 is a patch-

ing diagram for the various components. (The complete score for *Photo-Oscillations* appears in *Source-Music of the Avant-Garde*, no. 6, July, 1969.) In one of the three performance versions, one or more 6-milliwatt lasers are used as light sources and the performers are instructed to walk about in the light display, stopping the laser beams and thereby controlling the various photo-cell-controlled functions. The performers also supply light sources by carrying fluorescent lamps. Other performance versions call for street construction flashers and television sets as controls.

Many composers and performers interested in improvisation and free form situations are also incorporating the use of live electronic sound production and modification. This, of course, calls for the performer to have a very thorough understanding of the different devices being used. An improvised situation may involve the performer in several different ways. The performer may have total control over all of the parameters of the sounds or he may control only one of the processing steps while other performers control and modify the same signal in other manners. Another approach may be to have two or more performers supply each other with signals for processing in a live improvised situation. Some events may be monitored only by the performers through earphones and they, in turn, select what material will be heard by the audience. Other situations require that all of the processing be heard without the censorship of the performers. An example of a composition using the electronic medium in a somewhat improvised manner is *x g 794 −3+/vii ac F o⁻8.A 699k4 7/28zw ÷ Ba csf L⁹⁸ᵐ £ La Cathedral des Escargots (6 spodes and an injunction for plutocrat)* by British composer Ranulph Glanville, assisted by and in collaboration with John Cassidy. The following is from the score:

The whole concert will consist of a performance of the above work, which constructs together sounds of varying degrees of predictability and of different sources, and which distorts, combines and amplifies them into a structure within which improvisation and freedom are subjected to partial control, and which produces continuing movement through many sound worlds. These interact and are placed in differing perspectives by the performers, all of whom use the same score. The performers are very important in the realization of this piece, because they are constructing it in detail (as well as playing it) from the system to which they react in their own ways. They have to be prepared to catch the scrapes thrown up by others, and to control them all. They also produce from the various groups of controls their own performing order.

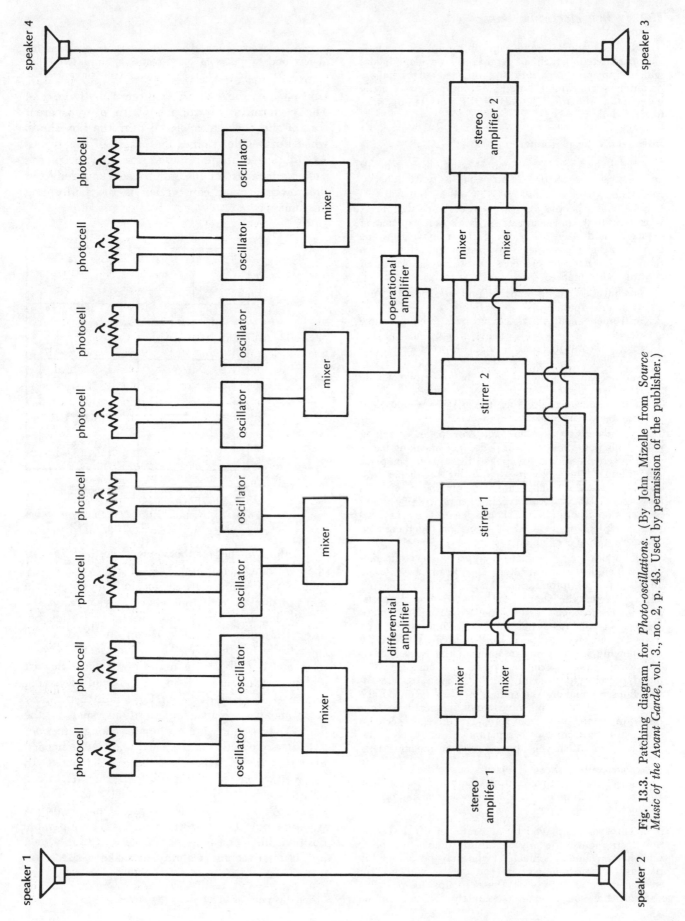

Fig. 13.3. Patching diagram for *Photo-oscillations*. (By John Mizelle from *Source Music of the Avant Garde*, vol. 3., no. 2, p. 43. Used by permission of the publisher.)

The skeleton is made up of groups of controls and parameters which are constantly developed, and which transform one into the other. Some of these parameters are sound based, and others are visually based (the "theatrical" aspect of the work is important to the whole piece).

Instructions for performers:

Read the keys: check against score: learn symbols and positions, etc. then learn what is written here—this is not a conventional piece of music, but is a system in which people may improvise their own music. It is a catalyst, and a unifier. It is also an explanation of itself, and a justification of it. It may, thus, be played using techniques and instruments for which there is no notation. It consists of various levels of control, performance, etc:

1. uncontrolled continuous sound (accidental unavoidable sound)
2. instruments-controlled sound-performers (make sound)
3. selection-control (control and distort sound)

1. is obviously the laughs, etc. that are unavoidable
2. is the performers' reactions to the score
3. is the controller affecting the player's sounds and the sounds he makes.

The piece consists of title page, key pages, speaking pages, box pages and control page. The speaking pages provide sentences that are spoken throughout the piece (if wished). They may be shared out, or all performers may have a set. They are not only the words that may appear: they are an explanation of the piece, and the reactions the audience should have. They may appear complete or incomplete, alone or together, anywhere in the piece, in any order.

The box pages are an analysis and classification of the factors that constitute a sound, and have basically 3 types of information. The diagram at the top left represents the shape of the interaction of parts, and hence to some extent the length of the piece (time-span). It need not be followed at all, if you have a good enough reason, and you can be selective in following it (as you can with all the instructions). The word at the top right is the musical characteristic/mood/polarity to be emphasized. The boxes are instructions for making the sounds in each section. Each is given a specific meaning, and subjected to four types of control: a free sign, an increase/decrease scale, a specific meaning sign and a set of changing symbols (to which you apply your own meanings).

The control sheet is placed over the box sheets and selects and further controls the possibles listed on the box sheet, giving a complete set of performing instructions.

The score is played by any number of players on any instruments, for any length of time (the sheets may be repeated). Someone (who may be one of the players, or someone else or one of the audience, or may come out of one of these groups temporarily) controls the sound made separately by each sound source and combines them, as well as making his own sounds (e.g., someone operating amplifiers, ring modulators, filters, etc., or a conductor/singer).*

One page of the score is illustrated in figure 13.4 The performers are supplied with a transparent control sheet which is placed over the box sheets which further determines the nature of the events. As with any other improvised situation, the piece's success depends on the performers' knowledge of the resources and capabilities of the performing instruments.

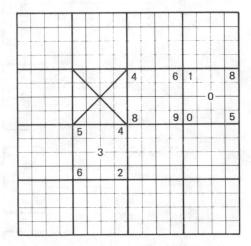

Fig. 13.4. Excerpt from score and performance instructions for *x g* —3+. . . (Used by permission of the composer)

Although the compositions described in this chapter cannot represent all of the various approaches to live electronic music, they present a point of departure. It took about 15 years after the art of electronic music was put into practice before electronic equipment began to be designed specifically for the composer. Live electronic performance is still a very new approach to the art and performers are still in the position of having to use equipment designed for studio use. Many electronic performance organizations, such as the Sonic Arts Group, are fortunate enough to consist of people with the technical knowledge needed to design special equipment for special needs. In other situations the composer/performer is forced to use only the equipment normally found in a studio. Working with this equipment in a real-time situation puts the performer in a very vulnerable position. In the past the performer had to rely only on his own technical ability to make a successful

*Used by permission of the composer.

performance, but with live electronic music performance he must also rely on the reliability of the equipment. If any part of an electronic network should suddenly not work up to the standard expected by the performer, the success of the entire performance is in jeopardy. For fear of suddenly being "unplugged," many composers and performers have avoided the electronic medium as a means of expression. Murphy's Law, "If anything can go wrong, it will," is especially applicable in electronic performance situations. For just this reason, performers must have a thorough knowledge of the equipment, an almost over-organized approach to the concert ritual, and must anticipate problems which could interfere with the performance.

The first consideration of any performance situation is the performance space itself. The performer should sit silently in the audience area and listen, in order to acquaint himself with ambient sound levels. Just as recording tape has a certain signal/noise ratio, so does any environment. This consideration is very important when setting amplification levels and getting correct balances. The performer should next check the liveness and reverberation of the area. Any excessively reverberant area should be avoided when placing speakers, since a very live hall will often destroy the effects of amplified sounds, especially when spatial parameters are important. Very reverberant environments may be dealt with by placing the speakers as close to the audience as possible. In placing the speakers, one should also refer to any special instructions in the scores. If the score calls for monophonic amplification, should more than one speaker be used? Should the audience be totally surrounded by speakers? If the amplification is stereophonic, binaural, or multi-channel, how should the speakers be located? Should there be more than one speaker per channel? All of these questions involve speaker-to-space coupling and depend on the particular environment and the intentions of the composer. In consideration of this, the guiding principle is that all of the sound should be distributed equally throughout the environment so it is properly perceived by all of the audience. This may involve a certain amount of experimentation before the correct combination of speakers and their location is found. As a general rule, the best listening area for true stereophonic amplification begins at a distance in front of the speakers which is equal to the distance of their separation. This ideal listening field extends to a distance twice the distance between the speakers. If the audience

area extends back 24 feet, the two speakers should be placed about 12 feet apart and 12 feet from the first row of the audience. The addition of a third middle speaker which produces a mix of both outside channels will allow for a wider separation of the speakers and will produce a wider sound field. With many of the contemporary audience/performer relationships, the seating area is not always predictable and again the performer is required to rely on his judgment of the environment and the intended results of the performance for correct speaker formats. There are two basic rules which should be followed in any type of speaker configuration, however. First: *Be sure all speakers are in phase.* This means that the amplifier output terminals must all be in the same relationship to all of the speaker terminals. Amplifier terminals are usually labeled "ground" and 4, 8, or 16 ohms. It doesn't matter what side of the speaker the ground is connected to as long as it is consistent with each speaker in the system. Figure 13.5 illustrates correct and incorrect phasing for a single stereo system. Phasing is very critical, since its neglect could result in phase distortion or cancellation of the signal. This is especially important when working with monophonic sources. Many times a very long speaker cable is required and it

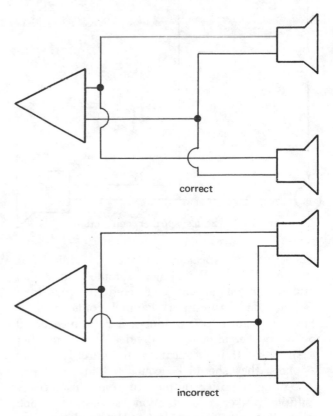

correct

incorrect

Fig. 13.5. Phasing for stereo speaker systems

is difficult to keep track of which side of the twin-conductor wire is to be connected to which side of the speaker. Most speaker cable, the preferred being #18 zip cord, has a small ridge running the entire length of one of the wires. In trying to remember which side of the wire goes to what side of the speaker and amplifier, the neumonic device "ridge right" will serve as a reminder that the side with the ridge always connects to the right amplifier terminal and the right speaker terminal.

The second basic rule in consideration of speaker connections is concerned with multiple speakers. Two or more speakers may be connected to reproduce the same signal in one of three manners: series, parallel, and series-parallel. Series connection can be thought of as sort of a loop between the amplifier outputs and the speakers. As shown in figure 13.6, the speakers are connected with the terminal for one speaker providing the input to the next successive speaker. With series

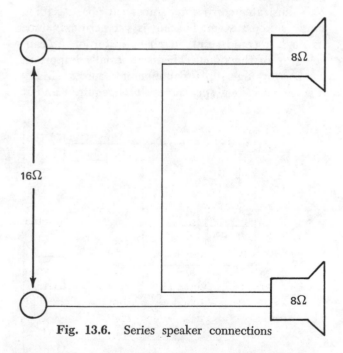

Fig. 13.6. Series speaker connections

connection, the speaker resistance is additive. If both speakers in the above example had 8-ohm ratings, they should be connected in series to a 16-ohm amplifier output. Parallel connection, as shown in figure 13.7, produces a resistance equal to the speaker impedances divided by the number of speakers. If both speakers in figure 13.7 were 16 ohms, they should be connected in parallel to an 8-ohm amplifier output. In some instances a multiple-speaker configuration is desired which will maintain the original rating of a single speaker.

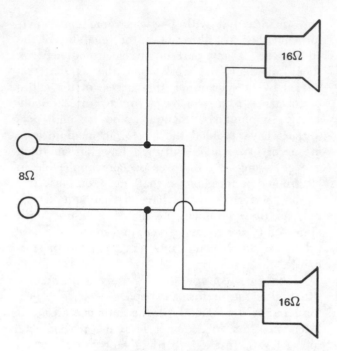

Fig. 13.7. Parallel speaker connections

In this case a series-parallel connection is used as illustrated in figure 13.8. If all the speakers in the configuration were rated at 8 ohms, the leads would be connected to an 8-ohm amplifier output. When working with transformerless transistor amplifiers, series or parallel speaker connections are not quite as critical but the performer might consider the economics involved—series connections usually requires less wire.

A final consideration in relation to speakers is how much power they can be expected to handle. Since much electronic music utilizes extremes of loudness, amplifiers for it must be able to supply a minimum of 40 watts per channel (rms) and the speaker system must be able to handle this load with minimum distortion at both ends of the audio spectrum. When loudness begins to distort the speaker response and cause phase variations, the gain should be reduced to a more efficient level, or more efficient speakers must be used. Loudness is only effective if it also involves faithful signal reproduction. Many times higher gain levels may be simulated by using multiple-speaker systems. In this event speaker placement plays an important role in achieving the desired effects.

The location of the speakers should also be considered for *all* of the works to be presented in a particular concert. Attempting to re-patch speaker connections often results in tremendous confusion and adds one more thing for the performer to be concerned with during the course of a per-

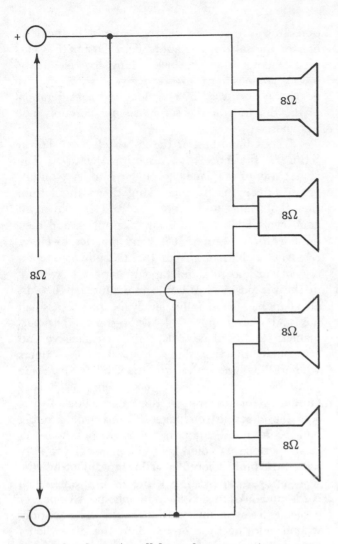

Fig. 13.8. Series/parallel speaker connection

formance. If it is absolutely necessary to re-wire speaker connections during a concert, try to plan the concert so this may be done during intermission. If this is not possible, make use of a speaker selector switch. Nothing can destroy the mood of a concert faster than someone running about between pieces armed with a screwdriver.

After all of the speakers are properly located begins the actual setting up of the various components used for each composition. Experience has revealed one very important rule for live presentations: *Have one, and only one, person responsible for the set-up of each composition.* Just as too many cooks spoil the broth, too many audio technicians unplug the connections. With one person in charge, organization will be his own and things will run much more smoothly than if two people are trying to plug into the same jack. This

person responsible should thoroughly know the workings of the composition and have previously drawn a patching diagram of it from which to work. If at all possible, each composition should have its own set of components which are separate from the other components used in the other pieces on the same concert. If this procedure is followed, the only patching necessary between pieces is to change the power amplifier inputs from one system to the next. If it is absolutely necessary to interchange components from piece to piece, the concert coordinator should make an exact plan for what is needed for each separate piece and how and when and from where the exchange is to be manipulated, and to plan the concert so that most of the re-patching is done during an intermission.

When the actual set-up begins, the first thing to do is *Connect the speakers to the amplifier outputs.* This safeguards against damage to the amplifiers. If the amplifiers are switched on without having a load on the output, there is great danger of burning out the output transformers. When laying the cable for the speakers, do not spare the masking tape. Tape all speaker and AC cable to the floor and to the legs of the table holding the equipment. If there is even the remote possibility of someone tripping over a wire, it will certainly happen. When laying speaker cable and AC cable, consider audience interference. Avoid running wire through any area where people may congregate. Also take care that an AC line does not cross over or run parallel to or come in direct contact with a speaker cable. This is often the cause of a very annoying 60 Hz hum in the speakers. Once all of the components are in place, it is a wise practice to tape them to the table so they won't be moved or accidentally unplugged.

Do not plug in the AC cords until all components are connected. This will ensure that no components are switched on without a load. This also applies to devices which contain their own DC batteries. If some mixers are turned on without a load, there is danger of causing resultant noise in the transistors. Some performers prefer to set up concerts with all the components switched on so it is possible to check the continuity of all the connections during the patching process, their reasoning being that it is thus easier to locate a bad connection or broken patchcord if each component is checked as it is being patched into the network. It is this writer's opinion that the time saved by this approach is usually less than the additional time required in turning the amplifier gain up and down and switching components on and off while connecting the various patchcords. If the performer has provided himself with a diagram of the network, there will usually be very few problems encountered in tracing down bad connections. As for component failure, it is good practice to use fresh batteries for every concert and to check all patchcords before they are used. This can be done with a continuity tester or a VOM.

After all of the components are patched together, the performer should again refer to his check list and double-check all connections. No matter how experienced he is, there is always the possibility he has forgotten something. Even after he has set up a particular performance situation so many times that it is done almost automatically, the wise performer will still refer to a check list.

After all components have been checked and double-checked, plug in the AC and turn on the power switches and turn up the gain to check for noise. The five main causes of noise in a network are—

1. Faulty patchcord: or loose connections. First make sure all plugs are securely set in their sockets. If noise persists use the VOM or continuity tester and re-check all patchcords and speaker connections.

2. Impedance mismatch. Double-check to see that all input transducers are correctly pre-amplified and are terminated in the correct power amplifier input. Check that speakers are terminated correctly.

3. Grounding. If nothing else helps, use jumper cables to interconnect the ground potentials of the various components. Also try reversing the polarity of the AC supply (reverse the plug).

4. AC cables over speaker cables.

5. Audio being powered from the same circuit as the lights or other video circuits. Neon lights are one of the biggest causes of a noisy network as well as adding considerable ambient noise to the room.

Once the performer is satisfied with the audio portion of the set-up, he should be concerned with the visual aspects. Go out into the audience area and quietly concentrate on how the set appears. Is it visually coherent with the composition? Many times a sloppy nest of wires and stack of components can be so distracting to the audience that it interferes with the presentation of the performance. On the other hand, a visually complex network can add a certain degree of mystery to the situa-

tion. In any case, the network should be neat, if not for the sake of the audience, then for the sake of a smoother performance. Many live electronic music compositions are conceived with various degrees of theatrical involvement and consideration of the theatrics of the set-up should certainly not be ignored.

Just as important as the approach one takes in setting up the concert is a disciplined wrap-up. The fastest way to misplace equipment is to have an unorganized approach to breaking down the set-up. The first thing to be done is to turn down all gain levels, switch off all power supplies, and then unplug the AC cables. It is good practice to either remove the batteries from the DC-powered components or use masking tape to tape all switches in the off position. When unplugging patchcords, all adaptors should immediately be put in a small box and placed in a tool kit or some other permanent storage place. Adaptors are expensive and are usually the first things to be lost. Performers who are involved with a great many live electronic performances usually carry their own tool kit containing all of the things listed in sections 2 and 3 of the check list on page 137. To avoid getting tools, cords, and adaptors in the wrong tool kit, many performers color code all personal property with strips of colored plastic tape. During the wrap-up, this will also expedite finding out which cords and adaptors belong to whom. All speaker cable and extension cords should be carefully wound and neatly stored. Many needless hours have been spent before concerts untangling nests of wires and cords.

The traveling performer must be even more conscientious about the wrap-up. All components must be carefully stored in a trunk so they can't be damaged while being moved. Large pieces of poly-form material and blankets are useful for this. Some performers even have special bags and boxes for individual components which protect them from scratches caused by the treatment they receive during shipment. One very important word to the traveling performer is to expect nothing in way of equipment from your concert host. Call ahead to confirm what equipment is available, but even then plan to use your own amplifiers and other components, since they are more familiar to you. The only thing you should really expect to find is an adequate speaker system. If one isn't available, have the host rent one for you. A concert pianist is not expected to perform on a studio upright and, by the same token, the electronic music performer has the right to adequate facilities.

The following checklist was developed by Pauline Oliveros for students in the electronic music performance classes at the University of California at San Diego. This approach has served to simplify many concerts and is well worth referring to every time any type of electronic music network is being set up.

Checklist for Performance Electronics

1. POWER SOURCE—AC or DC?
   a. Number of circuits needed? Separate audio from video
   b. Load? Allow 1 amp for 100 watts.
   c. Number of AC receptacles needed?
   d. Number and length extension cords needed?
   e. Number of 2- to 3-prong AC adaptors or vice versa needed?
   f. Spare fuses
   g. Fresh batteries

2. TOOLS AND SUPPLIES
   a. Set of screwdrivers—ordinary and phillips head, small to large
   b. Soldering iron and solder
   c. Long-nose pliers
   d. Regular pliers
   e. Awl
   f. Scout knife
   g. Wire strippers and cutters
   h. Flashlight
   i. Scissors
   j. Electrical tape
   k. Masking tape
   l. Continuity tester or VOM

3. CABLES, CONNECTORS, AND ADAPTORS
   a. Set of alligator clip leads
   b. Assorted length phono to phono cables
   c. Complete set of adaptors
   d. Zip cord #16 or #18

4. BASIC SOUND SYSTEM COMPONENTS

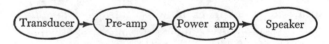

   a. TRANSDUCER (i.e., microphone, tapehead, phonograph, cartridge, etc.)
      (1) High-level or low-level? Impedance? Is transformer necessary?
      (2) Output power? Does it match input of pre-amp?
      (3) What kind of connector does it have? Is an adaptor necessary?
      (4) Power supply?
   b. PRE-AMP
      (1) Impedance at output?
      (2) Output? Does it match input of power amp?
      (3) Input and output connectors? (usually phono)
      (4) Power supply
      (5) Gain controls?
      (6) Equalization controls?
   c. POWER AMP
      (1) Impedance?
      (2) Output power? Will it drive speakers efficiently?
      (3) Tube or transistor? What cautions to be observed in loading the amp?
      (4) Cables and connectors needed?
      (5) Power supply?
   d. SPEAKERS
      (1) Impedance?
      (2) Efficiency?
      (3) Frequency response?

The rituals involved with electronic performance are still quite new, the instrumentation is still somewhat limited, and the techniques are still very primitive compared to what contemporary technology suggests will come in the future. The composers and performers are forced to work in unfamiliar areas, often with unfamiliar equipment and with new approaches to the concert ritual. Consequently, their approach must be with as much technical knowledge, organization, and professionalism as possible. Performers can no longer shun electronic music because they feel it is attempting to eliminate the performer. Live electronic performance is a logical and unavoidable development in the art of manipulating sound, and performers must learn to work with it on a professional level. The tape recorder and oscillator are real-time performance instruments in the same tradition as the piano and flute and must be treated with just as much artistry and understanding. The contemporary music instrument repairman must know as much about circuit design and troubleshooting as he does about replacing saxophone pads or re-hairing a violin bow. To paraphrase some statements of Marshall McLuhan: The true artist, no matter what his field or area of interest, is the person who can realize and utilize the implications of his art and its relationship to the new knowledge of his own time and environment.

14

real-time networks

Most of the devices discussed in this book, with the exception of the recording/reproduction chain and some of the equipment dealt with in chapter 12, can be found as separate modules which comprise a larger electronic music system. Although all of these devices may not be found on any single system, they will usually be found in the studio on separate systems or even as a separate piece of equipment. One advantage of the modular design is that modules are compatible and are powered from the same voltage supply. As this modular approach to design has become more popular, the entire system has come to be considered as a single instrument which can be composed for in itself. Just as all of the various instruments of an orchestra are manipulated to contribute their characteristic timbres and provide various functions to reproduce the thoughts of the composer, the various modules of an electronic music system also provide digital and analogue functions to produce and reproduce the composer's intent. Due to the varying characteristics of certain systems, a composer will often specify that the composition was conceived especially for a particular system. This may be done either to convey some extramusical information, perhaps, or, in the event the composition is to be reconstructed, to aid the performer in his patching configurations. Examples of such compositions include Michael Czajkowski's *People the Sky,* created on the Buchla Modular Electronic Music System (Vanguard Records no. VCS-100069), John Eaton's *Concert Piece for Synket and Orchestra,* and Toshi Ichiyanagi's *Extended Voices* for voices with Moog Synthesizer and Buchla Modular Electronic Music System (Odyssey Records no. 32 16 156).

Many composers apply techniques similar to musique concrete to their work with electronic music systems. Their compositions are the result of several generations of sounds which are finally mixed down to a limited number of channels. This process involves making a patch for one sequence of events and recording it, re-patching the system for a different event and recording that, and repeating this procedure until all of the desired layers are realized. Another application of the electronic music system is the real-time approach. This technique utilizes the system as a concert instrument in which all of the sound events are the result of a single patching network which may or may not involve a performer. Some real-time compositions do require a performer to manipulate switching and analogue functions, or he may be instructed to execute minor patching changes during the course of the performance. Because of the time factor and the nature of real-time electronic music compositions, such patches are usually kept to a minimum. An example is *Entropical Paradise with Bird Call* by Douglas Leedy (Seraphim Records no. SIC 6060). Although this composition was conceived on a Buchla System, it is scored in such a way that it could conceivably be programmed on any system with the required function modules. The composer notates the patching of the various modules with simple, written instructions, first indicating the patches which carry the audio information and then the patches for the control voltages. The pot settings are graphically indicated by providing a diagram for their individual positions. Since the performance instructions allow the control setting to be varied at will, precise notations for the pot settings are not required. The in-

ENTROPICAL PARADISE   with bird call

for Buchla Synthesizer

AUDIO PATCHES

Mix	Output to amplifier 1-3 left channel (A)
	4-6 right channel (B)
	Inputs to left channel (A)—1 from Voltage Controlled Mixer 1-5 out (Gate C)
	2 from Reverb A out
	Inputs to right channel (B)—1 from Reverb B out
	2 from Voltage Controlled Mixer 6-10 out (Gate D)
Reverb	Inputs A from Voltage Controlled Gate A out
	B from Voltage Controlled Gate B out
Voltage Controlled Mixer (Gates C and D)	Inputs 1 (C) from Sine-Sawtooth Generator 1 out
	Inputs 6 (D) from Sine-Sawtooth Generator 1 out
Voltage Controlled Gates	Inputs A from Sine-Sawtooth Generator II out
	B from Sine-Sawtooth Generator III out
Envelope Detector	Input A from Pink Noise Generator out

Optional: White Noise Generator to Sine-Sawtooth Generator f-m input; Pink Noise Generator
to Sine-Sawtooth Generator III f-m input. Vary percent modulation

CONTROL VOLTAGE PATCHES

Sine-Sawtooth Generator I	Input from Envelope Detector output—*ext*
Sine-Sawtooth Generator II	Input from Control Voltage Processor IA output—*ext*
Sine-Sawtooth III	Input from Control Voltage Processor IIA output—*ext*
Control Voltage Processor IA	Input L from Random Voltage Source B out
	Input R from Sequential Voltage Source IA out
Control Voltage Processor IB	Input R (inverting) from Random Voltage Source A out
Control Voltage Processor IIA	Input L from Control Voltage Processor IB out
	Input R from Sequential Voltage Source IIA out
Random Voltage Source	Input A from Timing Pulse Generator I *alternate* out
	Input B from Timing Pulse Generator II *all* out
Voltage Controlled Gates	Input A from Attack Generator output A
	Input B from Attack Generator output B
Attack Generator	Trigger A from Timing Pulse Generator II *all* out
	Trigger B from Timing Pulse Generator I *all* out
Timing Pulse Generator I	Period in from Random Voltage Source B out
Timing Pulse Generator II	Period in from Control Voltage Processor IB out
Sequential Voltage Source I	Pulse input from Timing Pulse Generator I *all* out
Sequential Voltage Source II	Pulse input from Timing Pulse Generator II *all* out
Voltage Controlled Mixer (Gate C & D)	Input 1 (C) from Sequential Voltage Source 1C out
	Input 6 (D) from Sequential Voltage Source 1B out

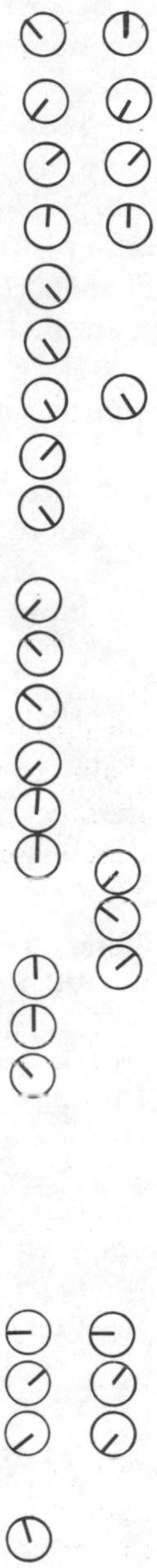

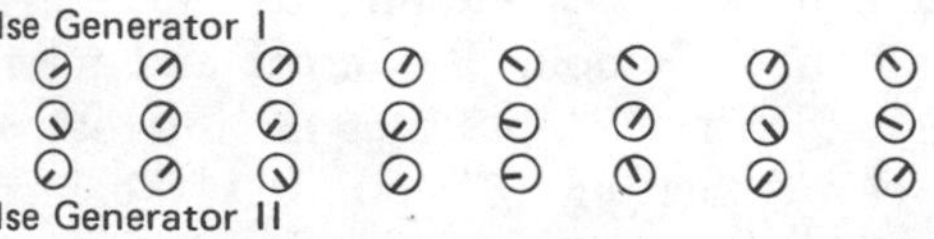

(bracket for Timing Pulse Generators I and II marked: *rep int ext*)

Note: Any control setting may be varied at will. The Control Voltage Processor and Sequential Voltage
Source settings given here will result in a randomly self-programming program which, once initiated, seems to require no further attention.

Douglas Leedy
Santa Monica
March 1969

Fig. 14.1.   Performance instructions for *Entropical Paradise* by Douglas Leedy (1969)

139

dications on the score may be used just as a point of departure. As an aid in tracing the interrelated functions of all of the modules, figure 14.2 is provided as a flow-chart or graphic representation of the score. The only deviation from the original score is the voltage-controlled mixers (1-5 and 6-10). They are actually not used as mixers but rather provide a gating function. Therefore the flow-chart does indicate them as gates (voltage-controlled amplifiers).

Here are the numerical approximations of the control settings indicated in the score:

Channel A output mixer
    input 1—30 percent gain
    input 2—60 percent gain

Channel B output mixer
    input 1—50 percent gain
    input 2—60 percent gain

Reverberation A and B—50 per cent

Voltage-controlled mixer (indicated as VCAs)
    VCA C—100 percent gain
    VCA D—100 percent gain

Voltage-controlled amplifiers
    VCA A—100 percent gain
    VCA B—100 percent gain

Envelope detector
    Sensitivity—60 percent
    Decay Time—1 second

Sine-sawtooth oscillators (externally voltage-controlled)
    VCO 1 waveshape—0 percent harmonic distortion
    VCO 2 waveshape—30 percent harmonic distortion
    VCD 3 waveshape—30 percent harmonic distortion

Control voltage processor—Setting "1" indicates the proportion of combined external and internal voltages. Setting "2" indicates the internal voltage setting. Setting "3" indicates the mixing proportion of the two external voltages.

CVP 1A
    (1) 9/10
    (2) 7.5 volts DC
    (3) 1/1

CVP 1B
    (1) 4/5
    (2) 5 volts DC
    (3) 3/2

CVP 2A
    (1) 1/2
    (2) 7 volts DC
    (3) 3/2

Attack generators I and II
    Attack time—0.05 seconds, decay time—2.0 seconds, sustain time—0.01 second

Timing pulse generators I and II
    repeat mode   pulse length—50 percent
    firing rate—external control

Sequencer I: DC voltage setting for each increment—indicated in DC voltage
    Bank A—9/9/10/10/9/8/8/8/7/8/9/7/8
    /8.5/8/8.5

Sequencer II:
    Bank A—3/5/7/7/3/2/9/5
    Bank B—15/5/.05/.05/3/7/15/5
    Bank C—.05/7/15/.05/3/7/.05/8

Output channel A consists of information supplied by VCO 1 and 2. The frequency of VCO 1 is determined by the DC envelope supplied by the envelope detector. The particular envelope shapes will be quite random, since they are the result of detecting "pink" sound (low-frequency component white sound). This is the part of the system which contributes the "bird call" effects. The amount of frequency activity can be varied by manipulating the sensitivity and decay-time controls on the envelope detector. If a pink sound source is not available, it would be possible to use a white sound generator in conjunction with a low-pass filter. The amplitude of VCO 1 is continually varied by processing the output signal through VCA C. The control voltages for this gate are derived from the third increment bank of sequencer 1. The firing speed of this sequencer is controlled by the trigger output of timing pulse generator 1 (TPG 1). In turn, the firing speed of the trigger pulses is randomly varied by the DC output of random voltage source B (RVS B). Since the random voltage source will not produce an output voltage unless cued by a trigger pulse, another timing pulse generator (TPG 2) is used to provide the needed triggers. The firing rate of TPG 2 is externally determined by another voltage which originates with TPG 1. TPG 1 provides alternate trigger pulses for random voltage source A, which produces random envelopes of DC voltage. These envelopes are then inverted and mixed with the internal voltage of control voltage processor (CVP 1B) and then patched to the external "period" input of TPG 2, thereby determining its firing speed.

The frequency of VCO 2 is controlled by a mixture of DC voltages. A continuous sequence of voltages are provided by bank A of sequencer 1.

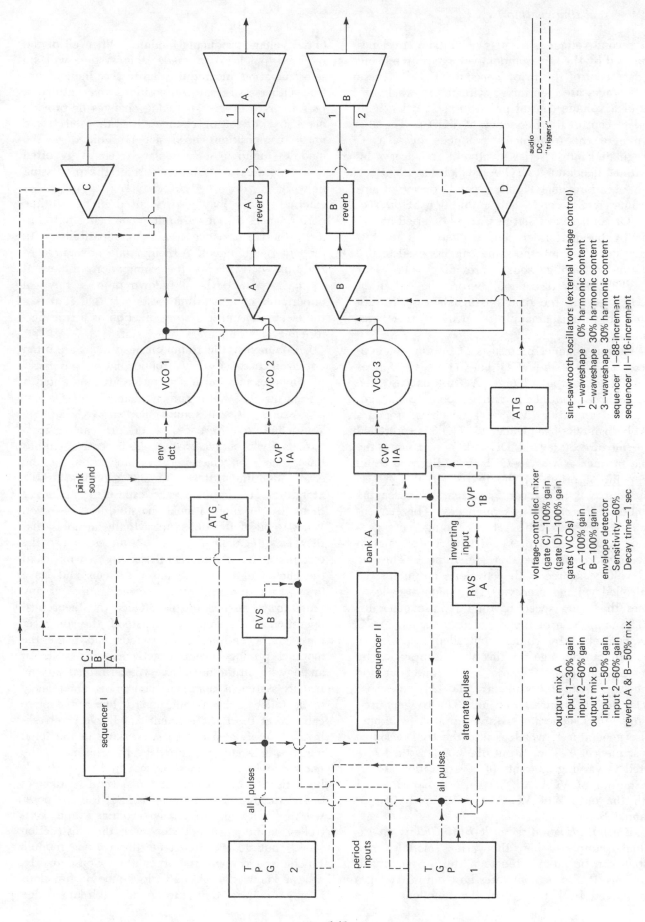

Fig. 14.2. Diagram for *Entropical Paradise*

141

The second voltage is a series of random envelopes produced by the same random voltage source being used to control the firing speed of TPG 1. These two voltages are then mixed with the internal voltage of a voltage control processor (CVP 1A) and used to control the frequency of VCO 2. The amplitude of the frequencies produced by VCO 2 is regulated into a series of attacks and decays by an attack generator (ATG A) which has an attack time of approximately .05 second, decay of approximately 2 seconds, and a duration of .01 second. Of course these settings may be varied at any time by the performer. The trigger cues for this attack generator are the same triggers used to fire the random voltage source providing voltage for the VCO under discussion. Before the output of VCO 2 reaches the final mixing stage, it is subjected to various amounts of artificial reverberation.

Output channel B consists of information supplied by VCO 1 and VCO 3. VCO 1 also supplies a signal for output channel A. In this case, the amplitude is controlled with a separate voltage-controlled amplifier (VCA D) which is programmed by bank C of sequencer 1. VCO 3 is controlled by a mixture of several DC voltages in much the same manner as was VCO 2, the difference being the point of origin of the two external voltages. One source is sequencer 2, which has twice the number of increments as sequencer 1. This sequencer is triggered by pulses from timing pulse generator 2, which also provided triggers for random voltage source B and attack generator A. The second voltage source is the envelope output of the controlled voltage processor 1B, which also determines the firing speed of timing pulse generator 2. The amplitude of the signal produced by VCO 3 is controlled by voltage-controlled amplifier B. The program voltage for this VCA is provided by attack generator B, whose attack and duration times are about the same as ATG A, but whose decay time is about 2.5 seconds. The triggers used to fire attack generator B are supplied by timing pulse generator 1, which is also the trigger source for sequencer 1. The output of VCA B is then subjected to varying amounts of reverberation as was the output of VCA A. The final signal is mixed with the output of VCA D to comprise output channel B.

Entropical Paradise with Bird Call is an excellent example of how the various modules in a system can be interrelated to perform a variety of functions. It also demonstrates how output voltages can be fed back to control the functions of the initial voltage-producing modules. When all of the required patches are made, this system will be self-generating and requires no further human control. Other real-time compositions may utilize a performer to execute patching changes or provide necessary pot setting changes. Real-time electronic music compositions need not be limited to the modules found in a particular system. Very often tape recorders are used as part of the processing network, as described in chapter 10. Any other external device may also be used in a real-time performance, the only requirement being portability to the performance area and compatibility with the other equipment. Although one advantage of real-time networks is the elimination of several source tapes and the dub-down process, the real importance of a real-time system is that it makes the electronic music system function as a true performance instrument.

Commercial electronic music systems are often criticized because they "sound like themselves." A composer may form a negative attitude about a system and use the argument that whatever event is executed, it still sounds like an XXX system. True, due to differences in design, each system has its own characteristics. Even entire studios have their own characteristics, and these can be easily identified after minimum exposure to the literature. This is not a valid excuse for excluding them from compositional possibilities, however. What some of the objectors actually mean is that they lack the knowledge or resources to use the system. A truly resourceful composer will avoid the clichés of electronic music systems and learn to work around and even take advantage of any faults a system may display. Once the theoretical operation of a system is understood, the composer must go beyond its usual sounds and make the modules produce events exactly as conceived. An analogy lies in the use of the Western tonal system. In this system a dominant chord has a tendency to be followed by a tonic chord, but a deceptive cadence at the right moment can be very refreshing. The craft of a composer working in the tonal medium is usually measured by how he makes the notes do what he wishes and not by how he bends his artistic endeavors to fit the natural tendencies of the tonal system. In like manner, the composer working with electronically produced and controlled sound must not stop with the "instruction book," but go on to extend the various module functions and manners of control. Consequently, a basic knowledge of the various module functions is only a point of departure. A thorough knowledge of the medium requires the composer to have enough understanding of electronic theory to allow him to take part in the design, construction, and modification of equipment. This understanding will also serve as an excellent guide to finding new methods of application.

Although this book has purposely tried to avoid aesthetic implications, perhaps a word about experimentation may be appropriate. No matter how experienced a composer is with the equipment in a studio, many events and sequences may still require hours of work and experimentation to realize. A single momentary sound may be the result of three or four hours of re-patching and re-recording. When the final tape is produced, the composer will naturally have a tendency to be more attentive to those events which were the most time-consuming to create. He must not confuse this with aesthetic content, however. The perceiver cannot hear the amount of time and plan-ning spent on the production of an event. As listeners we don't judge the aesthetic content of a composition by the time spent on its creation, but rather by its sonic information.

The preface to this book contained the statement that an art so closely related to technology as electronic music is in part dependent on the development of that technology. This statement should be accompanied by a final word of advice to the composer just embarking on the field of electronic music. Beware the temptations of super-utilization. The fact that a studio or system makes available a multitude of signal sources and processing devices does not mean that each and every module must be utilized in the creation of a single composition. A duet can convey just as much aesthetic information as an ensemble of symphonic proportions. The art is not in the assemblage of sources and control, but is rather a result of their application.

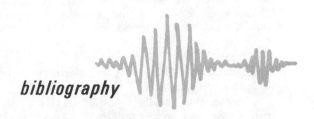

bibliography

This bibliography was compiled in consideration of three factors: *practical knowledge*—all listings supply information which is applicable to practical situations; *comprehension*—the more technical listings are so organized that they may be used by persons with minimal experience in physics and electronics; *cost*—most of the listings are available at a moderate cost. Although the technical publications are often more expensive, such listings are considered very useful, if not essential, as basic reference material.

Due to the bibliographic material available in many of the other writings on electronic music, this listing is not concerned with individual articles appearing in various periodicals. Certain periodical publication titles are, however, listed in the appropriate sections.

This bibliography is by no means comprehensive, and the omission of any publication is not an implication of devaluation or lack of applicability. The listings are a result of practical usage by the author and his colleagues in the field of electronic music.

Special acknowledgment goes to Frank McCarty, Director of the Electronic Music Studio, University of Pittsburgh, for his assistance in the compilation of this bibliography.

History, Development and Aesthetics

In this section are listed reference books with substantial information on electronic music history, books dealing with fields related to electronic music, sources of scores, general references, and books of historical significance.

AUSTIN, WILLIAM. *Music In the 20th Century*. New York: W. W. Norton, 1966.

A general reference of contemporary music with a chronology of the history of electronic music beginning with the work of Thadius Cahill (1897) to 1963 and a chronology of pitch systems related to and used in various aspects of electronic music.

BEAUCHAMP, J. W., and VON FOERSTER, eds. *Music By Computers*. New York: John Wiley and Sons, Inc., 1969.

A collection of previously published articles on computer-generated and controlled sound.

BEAVER, PAUL, and KRAUSE, BERNARD. *The Nonesuch Guide to Electronic Music*. New York: Nonesuch Records HC 73018, 1968.

Booklet and recordings describing basic studio equipment, waveforms, voltage control, modulation, filtering, and notational concepts. An excellent non-technical approach to standard system techniques with recorded examples.

BECK, A. H. W. *Words and Waves*. New York: McGraw-Hill World Universal Library, 1967.

An introduction to the history and concepts of electronic communication. This book also covers telegraphy, radio, telephony, and serves as a good introduction to communications theory.

BECKWITH, JOHN, and KASEMETS, UDO. *The Modern Composer and His World*. Toronto: University of Toronto Press, 1961.

Discussions with Varese, Ussachevsky, and others on various aspects of electronic music. Also serves as an excellent general reading on new music.

BMI: The Many Worlds of Music. New York: BMI Public Relations Department, 589 Fifth Ave., 10017, Summer Issue, 1970.

This special issue is devoted entirely to electronic music. It contains articles and an excellent discography of electronic music recordings.

BORNOFF, JACK, ed. *Music Theatre in a Changing Society*. New York: UNESCO, 1968.

A series of writings surveying the influence of technology and technical media on theatre, film, television, and music. Highly recommended.

CAGE, JOHN. *A Catalogue of Works*. New York: Henmar Press, Inc., 1962.

An annotated listing of all of Cage's work (electronic, theatre pieces, etc.) up to 1962. This catalogue also contains an excellent interview with Cage by Roger Reynolds.

COPE, DAVID. *New Directions in Music—1950 to 1970*. Dubuque, Iowa: Wm. C. Brown Company Publishers, 1970.

A survey of avant-garde music trends with chapters on electronic and technically oriented music. This book is very valuable as a reference to individual compositions and contains a very good chapter-by-chapter bibliography.

CROSS, LOWELL. *A Bibliography of Electronic Music.* Toronto: University of Toronto Press, 1966.

An excellent bibliography of articles, periodicals, books, and special publications on all aspects of electronic music. Listing contains publications in all languages and is current up to 1966. Highly recommended.

The Composer. Cleveland, O.: 3705 Strandhill Rd. 44122.

A quarterly publication of articles by active composers and musicians, many of which are involved with electronic music.

DAVIES, HUGH, ed. *International Electronic Music Catalogue.* Cambridge, Mass.: M.I.T. Press, 1967.

Originally published as a double issue of *Electronic Music Review* this catalogue lists and annotates almost every piece of electronic music produced prior to 1967, including names and addresses of composers and studios. Highly recommended.

Die Reihe. Vienna, Universal Editions: English translations published by Theodore Presser Company, Bryn Mawr.

Seven of the eight issues have been translated and contain writings on and by composers active in the avant-garde. Issue No. 5 (1961) is primarily concerned with electronic music.

EIMERT, HERBERT. *Electronic Music.* Ottawa: National Research Council of Canada, Technical Translation TT-601, 1956.

Gravesaner Blatter/Gravesano Review. Switzerland.

Published semi-periodically since 1956, the *Gravesano Review* contains articles by composers and physicists on electronic music, acoustics, timbre, and equipment. This journal serves as an historical documentation of early work in electronic music. Highly recommended.

HILLER, LEJAREN. *Music Composed with a Computer: An Historical Survey.* Illinois Technical Report No. 18. School of Music, University of Illinois, 1969.

HILLER, L. A., and ISAACSON, L. M. *Experimental Music-Composition with an Electronic Computer.* New York: McGraw-Hill, Inc., 1959.

An historically important book touching on the aesthetic and technical concepts of computer and mathematically-oriented music. The book contains a description of the processes involved with the composition of the *Illiac Suite* for string quartet (since then recorded on Heliodor Records No. H/HS 25053).

HENRY, OTTO. *A Preliminary Checklist: Books and Articles on Electronic Music.* New Orleans, La.: 2114 Milan, 70115, 1966.

KIRBY, E. T., ed. *Total Theatre—A Critical Anthology.* New York: E. P. Dutton and Company, Inc., 1969.

A collection of writings concerned with avant-garde theatre. Some writings deal with new musical and environmental concepts which are of interest to the composer.

KIRBY, MICHAEL. *The Art of Time—Essays On the Avant-Garde.* New York: E. P. Dutton and Company, 1969.

A collection of Kirby's writings dealing with environmental and kinetic theatre. This book will be of great interest to the open-minded composer.

KOSTELANETZ, RICHARD, ed. *John Cage.* New York: Praeger Publishers, 1970.

A collection of writings by and about Cage and his activities. It contains several excellent articles on his involvement with electronic music and technology. Highly recommended.

———. *Theatre of Mixed Means.* New York: Dial Press, 1968.

Interviews with artists and musicians active in the avant-garde. Of special interest to the composer are interviews with John Cage and LaMonte Young.

LANG, PAUL H., and BRODER, N., eds. *Contemporary Music in Europe.* New York: G. Schirmer, 1965.

A collection of essays written for the Fifth Anniversary of *Music Quarterly.* Each article deals with the new music of a particular European country.

LEFKOFF, GERALD, ed. *Computer Applications in Music.* Morgantown, W. Va.: West Virginia University Press, 1967.

Papers from the West Virginia University Conference on Computer Applications in Music covering such subjects as analysis, bibliography, programming, and information processing.

LORENTZEN, BENGT. *An Introduction to Electronic Music.* Rockville Center, N. Y.: Belwin Mills Company, 1970.

Text, notation and recorded examples concerned with existing electronic music literature with brief aesthetic and methodological discussions geared at the secondary grade levels.

MACHILS, JOSEPH. *Introduction to Contemporary Music.* New York: W. W. Norton and Company, 1961.

Contains a brief introduction to electronic music with biographical material on Stockhausen, Berio, Boulez, Maderna, Nono and Badings with very little material on American composers involved with electronic music.

The Music Educator's Journal. Washington, D.C.: NEA Publication Sales, 1201 Sixteenth St., N. W., November 1968.

This reprint of the special electronic music issue offering the educator's view of the state of the art is a bit slanted toward a single "school" but is still valuable reading and reference material.

Perspectives of New Music. Princeton, N. J.: Princeton University Press.

Bi-annual publication of articles by American and European composers, theorists, performers, and critics concerned with issues in contemporary music.

RISSET, J. C. *An Introductory Catalog of Computer Synthesized Sounds*. Murray Hill, N. J.: Bell Telephone Laboratories, 1970.

SALZMAN, ERIC. *Twentieth Century Music—An Introduction*. New York: Prentice-Hall, 1967.

An authoritative survey of contemporary musical life with excellent considerations of avant-garde activities and activities of American composers. Very well illustrated and documented.

SCHWARTZ, ELLIOT, and CHILDS, BARNEY, eds. *Contemporary Composers On Contemporary Music*. New York: Holt, Rinehart and Winston, 1967.

A collection of writings by many major twentieth-century composers (mostly American) dealing with many aspects of music. Of special interest are articles by Varese, Ussachevsky, Brant, and Reich.

Source Magazine—Music of the Avant-Garde. Sacramento, Calif., 1201 22nd St.

A bi-annual publication of avant-garde scores (electronic, theatre, environmental) and writings by active composers. Issue No. 3, January 1968, is devoted to live electronic music.

Stereo Review. New York: Ziff-Davis Publishing Company, 1 Park Avenue, 10016.

A monthly publication of new recording reviews with articles on music, composers, and new equipment.

STUCKENSCHMIDT, H. H. *Twentieth Century Music*. New York: McGraw-Hill, World Universal Library, trans. Richard Deveson, 1969.

A very unique survey of musical trends in the twentieth century with chapters on "Technical Sound Material" and "Mathematics—For and Against." Highly recommended.

Synthesis. Minneapolis, Minn.: Sculley-Cutter Publishing, Inc., 1315 Fourth St., S. E.

Quarterly publication of technical, philosophical, historical and educational articles dealing with all phases of electronic music. Of special interest to the historian is Vol. 1, No. 2, Spring 1971 issue which contains an excellent account of the activities of Thadeus Cahill.

Electronic Theory, Schematics, and Circuits

This listing is concerned with general electronic theory for the layman, individual component theory, and sources of circuits, all of which the composer will find useful. Most books listed are directed toward the reader with minimal experience in the field of electronics.

Audio. Philadelphia, Pa.: 134 North 13th St. 19107.

A monthly publication of equipment reviews, general audio, and feature articles on various aspects of audio circuit design and applications.

BROWN, ROBERT T., and KNEITEL T. *101 Easy Audio Projects*. New York: Howard W. Sams.

Easy-to-build and inexpensive circuits (pre-amps, mixers, filters, oscillators, special-effects generators) which are very applicable to studio and live performance situations.

BROWN, BOB, and LAWRENCE, PAUL. *How To Read Electronic Circuit Diagrams*. Blue Ridge Summit, Pa.: TAB Books, 1970.

Written for the beginner, this book is an introduction to schematics, individual components, printed circuits, tubes and transistors, and construction tips.

BROWN, RONALD. *Lasers*. New York: Doubleday Science Series, Doubleday and Company, Inc., 1968.

Due to the implementation of the laser in many aspects of contemporary art and mixed theatre, the author feels that a general reference in this area will be of value. This book will provide the reader with a basic understanding of coherent light, types of lasers, laser communication, holograph techniques, and other applications.

BUBAN and SCHMITT, *Understanding Electricity and Electronics*, New York: McGraw-Hill, 1969.

An introductory course in electrical and electronic theory with basic information about tools, materials and processes.

Circuit Design For Audio. Plainview, N.Y.: Sagamore Publishing Company, Inc., 1967.

Produced by Texas Instruments, this reference discusses audio design emphasizing practical time- and cost-saving procedures.

CLEARY, J. F. *General Electric Transistor Manual—7th Edition*. New York: General Electric Company, 1969.

A guide to semi-conductor theory, schematics, performance curves, and specifications.

CROWHURST, NORMAN H. *Electronic Music Instruments*. Blue Ridge Summit, Pa.: TAB Books, 1971.

An excellent coverage of the subject from simple amplification to total electronic music considerations. This book deals with traditional amplified instruments to modern synthesizers. Also contains a handy section on troubleshooting.

Electronic Circuit Design Handbook. Blue Ridge Summit, Pa.: TAB Books, 1970.

Compiled by the editors of EEE Magazine, this is a collection of over 600 circuits dealing with amplification, filtering, oscillation, etc.

Electronics World. New York: Ziff-Davis Publishing Company, 1 Park Ave. 10016.

Monthly publication of industrial electronics reports, new equipment, circuit theory and design.

Field Effect Transistor Projects. Phoenix, Ariz.: Motorola Semiconductor Products, Inc., 1966.

An introduction to FET Theory, construction techniques, and simple, but useful, circuits.

FISKE, KENNETH A., and HARTER, J. H. *Direct Circuit Analysis Through Experimentation.* Seal Beach, Calif.: The Technical Education Press, 1968.

Step-by-step exploration of DC circuit principles and equipment usage. Contains excellent sections on soldering and use of an electronic parts catalogue. Very practically organized.

FONTAINE, GUY. *Transistors For Audiofrequency (Audiofrequency Amplification).* New York: Hayden Book Company, 1967.

Detailed guide of the application of transistors in audio amplifiers illustrating how transistor characteristics are related to the principles of design.

GEFFE, PHILIP R. *Simplified Modern Filter Design.* New York: Hayden Book Company, 1963.

Basic principles of filter design with extensive tables of numerical data. Also contains chapters on attenuation, equalization, and measurement techniques.

GOTTLIEB, IRVING. *Basic Oscillators.* New York: Hayden Book Company, 1963.

A descriptive analysis and definitions of oscillators, components, characteristics and the theory of oscillation. Highly recommended.

———. *Frequency Changers.* New York: Howard W. Sams, 1965.

General principles of frequency multipliers, translators, modulators and dividers. An excellent source of practical schematics.

———. *Understanding Amplitude Modulation.* New York: Howard W. Sams, 1965.

Principles of amplitude modulation and descriptions of various AM systems. Although intended for the radio broadcaster, it may be used by the electronic musician as a basic reference.

GRAF, RUDOLF. *Modern Dictionary of Electronics.* New York: Howard W. Sams, 1968.

Approximately 16,000 terms clearly defined for the layman. In the opinion of the author, this is the best dictionary of electronics for the layman. It also covers the areas of communications, micro-electronics, computers, and fiberoptics. Highly recommended.

Heath Digital Instrumentation. Benton Harbor, Mich.: Heath Company.

Description and application notes of specific Heath equipment, but the information is very general and introduces many concepts of digital control which may be applied to a variety of situations.

HERRINGTON, DONALD E. *How To Read Schematic Diagrams.* New York: Howard W. Sams, 1970.

A good reference covering schematics, block diagrams, chassis layout, component symbols, and wiring.

HOBERMAN, STU. *Understanding and Using Unijunction Transistors.* New York: Howard W. Sams, 1969.

Basic UJT circuits in regards to oscillators, amplifiers, and power supplies. This book is also an excellent source of various oscillator circuits. Highly recommended.

Integrated Circuit Projects From Motorola. Phoenix, Ariz.: Motorola Semiconductor Products, Inc., 1966.

An introduction to IC theory with several interesting and practical audio circuits.

LOHBERG, ROLF, and LUTZ, THEO. *Electronic Brains.* New York: Bantam Books, 1968.

One of the most interesting and comprehendible books available on the basics of computer science, digital control, programming, logic systems, memory systems, and cybernetics. Highly recommended.

MALMSTADT, H. V., and ENKE, C. G. *Digital Electronics For Scientists.* New York: W. A. Benjamin, Inc., 1969.

A systematic introduction to digital systems, circuits, and components written for the person with no background in electronics. Highly recommended.

MARKUS, JOHN. *Source Book Of Electronic Circuits.* New York: McGraw-Hill, 1968.

A collection of over 3,000 various circuits originally published in *Electronics* and *EEE.* A very valuable source and reference book.

MILEAF, HARRY. *Electronics One-Seven.* New York: Hayden Book Company, 1967.

A series of seven volumes, available individually or bound as a set, each dealing with different area of practical electronic theory: (1) Electronic Signals and Modification; (2) Basic Stages of Transmission; (3) Electronic Tubes; (4) Semi-conductors; (5) Power Supplies and Amplifiers; (6) Oscillators, Modulators and Mixers; (7) Auxilliary Circuits—Gates, Delays, Limiters, etc. Highly recommended.

Warning—Bio-Music Can Be Dangerous. Kansas City, Mo: Orcus Research, Technical Bulletin TB-3003, 1970.

Safety factors which must be considered in the application of bio-feedback systems and techniques.

Popular Electronics. Flushing, N. Y.: P.O. Box 1096, 11352.

A monthly publication of new and novel circuits, articles on communications, design and equipment reviews. This periodical is more commercially-oriented than some of the others.

Radio-Electronics. New York: Gernsback Publishers, 200 Park Avenue South, 10003.

A monthly publication of general electronics, audio, hi-fi and home projects. This periodical is a good source of circuits.

Reference Data for Radio Engineers—5th Edition. New York: Howard W. Sams.

This book serves as a basic reference, in one volume, to all fields of audio, including tables, formulas, standards, circuit information, recording, technology, and associated areas. Highly recommended.

SHIELDS, JOHN POTTER. *Practical Power Supply Circuits.* New York: Howard W. Sams, 1967.

Basic power supply circuits, solid state voltage regulation, batteries and SCR operation. A very handy book for those planning construction of a home system.

Solar Cell and Photocell Handbook. El Segundo, Calif., International Rectifier Corp., 1960.

Basic concepts of photocell control, performance specifications of various types of photocells, plus many interesting, useful, and simple circuits.

Solid State Projects From Motorola. Phoenix, Ariz.: Motorola Semiconductor Products, Inc., 1964.

Fundamentals of semiconductor operation. Construction hints and several useful and easy-to-construct circuits such as oscillators, amplifiers, and mixers.

TREMAINE, HOWARD M. *Passive Audio Network Design.* New York: Howard W. Sams, 1964.

An excellent source of attenuator, equalizer, and filter circuits including sections of circuit design, theory, and applications. Highly recommended.

———. *Audio Cyclopedia—2nd Edition.* New York: Howard W. Sams, 1969.

This book is written in a question-answer format covering every phase of audio engineering. All information is presented in a very practical manner in terms the layman can understand and apply. Highly recommended.

———. *Passive Audio Network Design.* New York: Howard W. Sams, 1964.

A comprehensive guide to the design, construction, and testing of all types of attenuators, equalizers, and filters requiring only minimal mathematical background. Highly recommended.

TURNER, RUFUS P. *ABC's Of Varactors.* New York: Howard W. Sams, 1966.

Basic varactor (specialized semiconductor) theory with very useful modulator and amplifier circuits with interesting supplementary applications.

UPTON, MONROE. *Inside Electronics.* New York: New American Library, A Signet Science Library Book, 1964.

Basics of electronic theory and a well-written explanation of electronic components, amplifiers, speaker operation, and stereophony.

Recording and Tape Techniques

These are references dealing with tape recorders, tape care and editing techniques, recording science and commercial studio techniques.

BURSTEIN, HERMAN, and POLLACK, H. C. *Elements of Tape Recorder Circuits.* Blue Ridge Summit, Pa.: TAB Books, 1957.

Covers frequency response, head and tape characteristics, and equalization. This book is a bit dated but still serves as a good introduction to the understanding of recorder operation.

BURSTEIN, HERMAN. *Getting The Most Out Of Your Tape Recorder.* New York: Hayden Book Company, 1960.

This book discusses types of machines, availability, pros and cons of each type and features that promote usefulness. Also discusses types of tape, microphones, and accessories.

DOLAN, ROBERT EMMETT. *Music in Modern Media.* New York: G. Schirmer, Inc., 1967.

An introduction to recording setups, control-room operations, recording, considerations in preparing and producing sound tracks, and a brief introduction to electronic music.

HAYNES, N. M. *Tape Editing and Splicing.* Flushing, N. Y.: Robin Industries, 1957.

This booklet is taken from Haynes' book, *Elements of Magnetic Tape Recording.* Englewood Cliffs, N. J.: Prentice-Hall, 1957. It serves as a basic explanation of splicing techniques, types of splices, editing procedures. This is a very practical guide for the novice editor.

JORGENSEN, FINN. *Handbook of Magnetic Recording.* Blue Ridge Summit, Pa.: TAB Books, 1970.

Covers all current tape recorder applications from audio to weather surveillance data recording. Contains basic design criteria on heads, the electronics and transports design. Highly recommended.

MODUGNO, ANNE, and PALMER, CHARLES. *Tape Control in Electronic Music.* Talcottville, Conn.: Electronic Music Laboratories, P. O. Box H, 1970.

An introduction to recording techniques of special value to those involved in electronic music. A very valuable guide for elementary and secondary school programs.

NISBETT, ALEC. *The Technique of the Sound Studio.* New York: Hastings House Publishers, 1971 ed.

A handbook for microphone techniques, sound quality, editing, mixing, sound effects, echo and distortion techniques, and sound shaping. Highly recommended.

Recording Engineer/Producer. Hollywood, Calif., P.O. Box 2287, 90028.

A monthly publication of articles relating to recording science and techniques. Also articles on useful circuits and discussions of new equipment written by people active in the field. Highly recommended.

Sound Talk. St. Paul, Minnesota: 3M Company, Magnetic Products Division, 220-SE 2501 Hudson Rd.

An aperiodic publication by 3M Company dealing with all phases of tape standards, splicing, care, and storage. This publication is a technical service to the industry from 3M Company.

Tape Recorder Annual. New York: Ziff-Davis Service Division, Department W, 595 Broadway, 10012.

An annual guide to obtaining the best use from commercial recorders. What to buy, how to use it, and tape tactics. Published annually from 1969.

TUTHILL, C. A. *How To Service Tape Recorders.* New York: Hayden Book Company, 1966.

A detailed analysis of the operation of the mechanical and electronic systems of large number of tape recorders giving directions for maintenance and troubleshooting.

WESTCOTT, CHARLES G., and DUBBE, RICHARD F. *Tape Recorders—How They Work.* New York: Howard W. Sams, 1965.

Principles of magnetic recording, mechanisms and components, types of tape recorders, and test procedures.

Systems and Studio Design

Specific reference material for commercially available equipment and information made available by various system manufacturers and studios. Also listed in this section are books of interest to those considering the construction of a home or commercial studio. Availability of certain materials in this section depends on the current stock and distribution policy of the institutions and manufacturers involved.

ARP Synthesizer. Tonus Inc., 45 Kenneth Street, Newton Highlands, Mass. 02161.

The ARP 2600 Owner's Manual. Newton Highlands, Mass.: Tonus Inc., 1970.

BADMAIEFF, ALEXIS, and DAVIS, DON. *How To Build Speaker Enclosures.* New York: Howard W. Sams, 1967.

Detailed drawings and instructions for the construction of various basic enclosures. Also detailed descriptions of types and characteristics of types of enclosures.

BOYCE, WILLIAM F. *Hi-Fi Stereo Handbook.* New York: Howard W. Sams, 1967.

A very complete coverage of hi-fi systems and considerations in putting together an integrated system. A good guide for those interested in quality sound production.

CBS-BUCHLA Electronic Modular Systems. CBS Musical Instrument Research Department, 1300 East Valencia Street, Fullerton, California 92631.

CLIFFORD, MARTIN. *How To Use Your VOM, VTVM and Oscilloscope.* Blue Ridge Summit, Pa.: TAB Books, 1968.

Explanation of operation and servicing with the VOM, VTVM and oscilloscope. Covers meter movements, scales, applications, and measurements.

COOMBS, C. F., JR. *Printed Circuits Handbook.* New York: McGraw-Hill, 1967.

Knowledge of printed circuit techniques will save the builder a great deal of time in circuit construction. This manual covers all phases of the printed circuit processes.

CROWHURST, NORMAN H. *Audio Systems Handbook.* Blue Ridge Summit, Pa.: TAB Books, 1969.

General information covering amplifiers, equalizers, mixers, stereophony, noise, suppression, reverberation, and considerations for an integrated system. Highly recommended.

D.B.—The Sound Engineering Magazine. Plainview, N. Y.: Sagamore Publishing Company.

A monthly publication of articles on acoustics, recording techniques, circuits, and writing of general interest to the audio engineer. Highly recommended.

DEZETTLE, L. M. *ABC's Of Electrical Soldering.* New York: Howard W. Sams, 1971.

A survey of soldering theory, techniques, types of irons, and safety considerations.

EATON, M. L. *Bio-Music.* Kansas City, Mo.: Orcus Research, 1970.

Information on techniques, philosophical, social and political implications of bio-control. Also gives the basics of a biological feedback system and other applications of bio-control.

———. *Bio-Potentials as Control for Spontaneous Music.* Kansas City, Mo.: Orcus Research, Technical Bulletin TB-3001, 1970.

Methods of control using brainwaves and body sensors. A very complete discussion of bio-feedback techniques.

———. *Electronic Music—A Handbook of Sound Synthesis and Control.* Kansas City, Mo.: Orcus Research, 1969.

Basic concepts and introduction to electronic theory geared toward electronic music with sections dealing with transducers, hearing, and sound generation.

———. *Electronic Music Generation Systems.* Kansas City, Mo.: Orcus Research, Applications Note AN-3002, 1970.

A brief discussion of specialized electronic music sound generation techniques. Sine wave, function generators, and pulse height techniques are outlined.

———. *Generation of Waveforms by Digital-Analogue Techniques and Real-Time Control Circuitry in Electronics.* Kansas City, Mo.: Orcus Research, Technical Bulletin TB-3002A, 1970.

Application notes of the Orcus Analogue Function Generator to bio-music and a description of a typical bio-music system.

Electric Music Box, Buchla Associates, P.O. Box 5051, Berkeley, Calif., 94705.

Electrocomp, Electronic Music Laboratories, P.O. Box H, Talcottville, Conn. 06080.

Electronic Music for the Seventies. Morristown, N. J.: Ionic Industries, Inc., 1970.

Operation manual for the Putney VCS-3 System. Due to the use of the matrix patchbay there are several control concepts introduced which may be of interest to the composer. This manual also contains an interesting bibliography.

Electronic Music Reports. Utrecht, Netherlands: Utrecht State University, Institute of Sonology.

This publication appears aperiodically once or twice annually containing articles dealing with activities and equipment at the Institute of Sonology. It contains a lot of information on current analogue and digital control techniques. Highly recommended.

Electronic Music Review. Trumansburg, New York.

A quarterly publication of articles dealing with technical, compositional, philosophical problems of electronic music. Also contains very good reviews of the current works. This periodical is now out of print but all back issues are available from the Independent Electronic Music Center, R. A. Moog, Inc., Trumansburg, New York, 14886.

ENKEL, FRITZ. *The Technical Facilities of the Electronic Music Studio (of Cologne Broadcasting Station).* Ottawa: National Research Council of Canada, Technical Translation TT-603, 1956.

The Hern, Television Equipment Associates, Bayville, New York.

HOWE, HUBERT. *Buchla Manual.* Fullerton, Calif.: CBS Musical Instrument Research Department, 1300 East Valencia Street, 92631.

This CBS Buchla owner's manual is an excellent introduction to voltage-control concepts and a good description of the Buchla Function Modules.

————. *Composer's Manual.* New York: Queens College, Department of Music, Electronic Music Studio.

Description of the Queens College Electronic Music Studio including operation of the Moog and Buchla Systems and information concerning the amplifiers, tape recorders, speakers, and miscellaneous equipment.

————. *Music 7 Reference Manual.* New York: Queens College Press, 1970.

Journal of the Audio Engineering Society. New York: 124 East 40th Street, 10016.

A monthly publication of articles on all aspects of audio, acoustics, electronic music and perception.

JUDD, E. C. *Electronic Music and Music Concrete.* London: Neville Spearman, Ltd., 1961.

A non-technical overview of classic studio techniques and basic tube circuits used in electronic music.

LEWIS, ROBERT. *Electronic Construction Practices.* Wilton, Conn.: Radio Publications, Inc., 1961.

Tips and techniques on use of tools, equipment planning and layout, metal working, wiring and assembly. Recommended for all involved with circuit design.

MATHEWS, MAX V. *Technology of Computer Music.* Cambridge, Mass., MIT Press, 1969.

A very well written explanation of digital sound production techniques. Very complete and comprehendible by the layman. Highly recommended.

McLACHLAN, N. W. *Loudspeakers.* New York: Dover Publications, 1960.

A semi-technical discussion of loudspeaker designs and problems.

The Muse, Triadex, Inc., 1238 Chestnut Street, Upper Newton Falls, Mass. 02164.

PELLIGRINO, RONALD. *An Electronic Studio Manual.* Columbus, O.: Ohio State University, College of the Arts, Publication #2, 1969.

A general manual for the Moog System with accompanying taped examples. A catalogue of 'favorite patches' which the composer may find useful.

PRENSKY, SOL D. *Advanced Electronic Instruments and Their Use.* New York: Hayden Book Company, 1970.

A general description of fixed commercial electronic circuits (oscillators, scopes, meters, computer hardware) and how they work.

Putney VCS3, Ionic Industries, 128 James Street, Morristown, N. J. 07960.

Setting Up Your Moog Synthesizer—A Guide to Installation and Operation. Trumansburg, New York: R. A. Moog, Co.

A very basic manual for setting up the Moog I, II or III. This manual is somewhat incomplete in view of other existing literature on the Moog.

SHEA, RICHARD P. *Amplifier Handbook.* New York: McGraw-Hill, 1968.

A definitive coverage of all types of amplifiers operating along the entire range of frequency and power spectrums.

SHUNAMAN, F. *How To Use Test Instruments In Electronic Servicing.* Blue Ridge Summit, Pa.: TAB Books, 1970.

A guide to efficient use of test instruments. This type of manual is very useful in keeping a studio in operational condition.

Sonic V, Musonics, Inc., P.O. Box 131, Williamsville, New York 14221.

SUBOTNICK, MORTON. *The Use of the Buchla Synthesizer in Musical Composition.* New York: Audio Engineering Society Reprint 709, 1970.

A review of the Buchla System sound sources, modifying modules, control modules, and several interesting patches.

VILLCHUR, EDGAR. *Reproduction of Sound.* New York: Dover Publishers.

A thorough coverage for the layman on hi-fi systems, general reproduction systems, preamps, speakers and simple circuit theory.

Acoustics and Physics

Information on the physical behavior of sound and psycho-acoustic considerations of music. Although some of the books in this section may not be directly related to electronics, any practical musician, involved in electronics or not, will find that a basic understanding of acoustics and the physics of sound is essential to the workings of his art.

BACHUS, JOHN. *The Acoustic Foundations of Music.* New York: W. W. Norton and Company, 1969.

This is one of the best contemporary books on musical acoustics covering basic acoustic principles, hearing, intervals, tuning, environments and sound production. Highly recommended.

BRIGGS, G. A. *Musical Instruments and Audio.* Idle, England: Warfdale Wireless Works, Ltd., 1965.

General principles of resonating systems and electronic sound, descriptions of standard electronic instruments, formant theory in electronics, distortion and circuits.

COKER, CECIL H.; DENES, P. B.; and PINSON, E. N. *Speech Synthesis.* Bell Telephone Laboratories, Inc., 1963.

A manual designed to accompany a speech synthesizer kit which demonstrates formant production in human speech. The manual covers speech synthesis, linguistic organization and the physics of sound.

CHOWNING, JOHN. *The Simulation of Moving Sound Sources.* New York: Audio Engineering Society Reprint No. 726, 1970.

A report on computerized methods of location modulation including a discussion of location cues in hearing and possible control envelopes. Highly recommended.

DOUGLAS, ALAN. *The Electrical Production of Music.* New York: The Philosophical Library, 1957.

Covers the physics of musical instruments, scales, intervals, harmonic analysis of transient phenomenon, oscillators, electrical tone production, and speakers.

ERICKSON, ROBERT, ed. "Timbre Seminar Readings," in "Four Views of the Music Department at the University of California at San Diego," *Synthesis,* Vol. 1, Issue 2, 1971.

A bibliography of writings on general timbre, attacks, spectrum, formant, phase, loudness, modulation, noise, space, reverberation and timbral organization and structure. Highly recommended.

HELMHOLTZ, HERMANN. *On The Sensations of Tone.* New York: Dover Publications, trans. A. J. Ellis, 1954.

A classic reference on early acoustical studies of resonating systems, pitch, and tuning. Highly recommended.

JOSEPHS, J. J. *The Physics of Musical Sound.* Princeton, N. Y.: D. Van Nostrand Company, Inc., 1967.

Covers basic vibratory phenomenon, hearing and the ear, tuning systems, musical systems, synthesized sound, musical instruments and recording and reproduction considerations.

The Journal of the Acoustical Society of America. New York: American Institute of Physics, 335 East 45th Street, 10017.

Papers on architectual and physical engineering, underwater and musical acoustics, noise, physical acoustics and perception. Semi-technical.

LEVARIE, SIGMUND, and LEVY, E. *Tone—A Study in Musical Acoustics.* Ohio: Kent State University Press, 1968.

A very interesting and unique introduction to musical acoustical systems beginning with an in-depth semi-technical and philosophical discussion of intervals, wave properties and timbre. Also sections on all classifications of instruments and sound production. This book also contains a lot of historical information from a variety of sources. Highly recommended.

MOLES, A. A. *Information Theory and Aesthetic Perception,* trans. Joel E. Cohen. Urbana, Ill.: University of Illinois Press, 1966.

Although this book is primarily a theoretical approach to aesthetic applications of information theory (primarily in music), there is also a great deal of information concerned with musical perception and psycho-acoustics. Highly recommended.

OLSON, HARRY F. *Music, Physics and Engineering.* New York: Dover Publications, 1967.

Originally published in 1952 under the title of *Musical Engineering,* this edition deals with musical acoustics, chapters on scales, instruments and their characteristics, studio and room acoustics and an excellent chapter on electronic music methods and apparatus.

PIERCE, J. R., and DAVID E. E., JR. *Man's World of Sound.* New York: Doubleday and Company, Inc., 1958.

A variety of material concerning speech, hearing, waves, resonators, and the acoustics of speech. This book may also serve as a layman's introduction to communication science.

RETTINGER, MICHAEL. *Acoustics-Room Design and Noise Control.* New York: Sagamore Publications, 1968.

Covers the problems and hazards of noise, physics of sound, room acoustics and noise reduction.

SCHANZ, G. W. *Stereo Handbook.* New York: Drake Publishers, Ltd., 1970.

Covers the fundamentals of stereo sound perception, stereophony, transmission and reception of stereophonic information and testing techniques. An excellent introduction to stereophony. Highly recommended.

TAYLOR, C. A. *The Physics of Musical Sounds.* New York: American Elsevier Publishing Company, Inc., 1965.

An analysis of musical sound production, harmonic and Fourier analysis, amplification and sound perception. Highly recommended.

WINCKEL, FRITZ. *Music, Sound and Sensation,* trans. T. Binkley. New York: Dover Publications, 1967.

An excellent book on the theory of sound, acoustics and psychoacoustics. A wealth of information on the physical properties of sound behavior which is essential information to the composer. Highly recommended.

WOOD, ALEXANDER. *The Physics of Music.* London: University Paperbacks, 1962.

This book covers the area between physics and music, vibration systems, musical quality, temperament, room acoustics, recording and reproduction. A bit dated but interesting reading.

Industrial References

This is a listing of companies and manufacturers producing equipment and components used in the field of electronics and electronic music. Although the individual reader may not be in a position to take practical advantage of the equipment, the catalogues and specification sheets which are usually supplied by the companies give many insights into new applications and circuit designs. The reader will find that being placed on the mailing lists is an excellent method of keeping informed of new equipment and circuit designs.

Ampex—Professional Audio Products Division, 401 Broadway, Redwood City, Cal. 94063

Acoustic Research, 24 Thorndike Street, Cambridge, Mass. 02141

Agfa-Gevaert AG, 509 Leverkusen, Vertrieb Magneton, West Germany

Allied/Radio Shack, Department RE-1, 2725 West 7th Street, Fort Worth, Texas 76107

Altec-Lansing, 1515 South Manchester Avenue, Anaheim, Calif. 92803

Automated Processes, Inc., 35 Central Drive, Farmingdale, New York 11735

Countryman Associates, 424 University Avenue, Pal Alto, Calif. 94302

Dolby Laboratories, 345 Clapham Road, London SW9, England

Dynaco Inc., 3060 Jefferson Street, Philadelphia, Pa. 19121

Edital Tape Splicing Equipment, Elpha Marketing Industries, Inc., New Hyde Park, New York

Edmund Scientific Company, 300 Edscorp Bldg., Barrington, New Jersey 08007

EICO, 283 Malta Street, Brooklyn, New York 11207

Electro-Voice, Department 811 BU, 645 Cecil Street, Buchana, Mich. 49107

Fairchild Sound Equipment Corporation, 10-40 45th Avenue, Long Island City, New York 11101

Gately Electronics, 57 West Hillcrest Avenue, Havertown, Pa. 19083

Gotham Audio Corporation, 2 West 46th Street, New York 10036

Heathkit, Benton Harbor, Mich. 49002

Hybrid Systems Corporation, 95 Terrace Hall Avenue, Burlington, Mass. 01803

KLH Research and Development Corporation, 30 Cross Street, Cambridge, Mass. 02139

Langevin-MCA Tech, 13035 Statcoy Street, Hollywood, Calif. 91605

McIntosh Amplifiers Laboratory, Inc., 2 Chambers Street, Binghamton, New York 13903

Olson Electronics, Department LR-260, South Forge Street, Akron, Ohio

Parasound, 680 Beach Street, San Francisco, Calif. 94109

Revox Corporation, 155 Michael Drive, Syosset, New York 11791

3M Company, St. Paul, Minn. 55101

Scully Recording Instruments Company, 480 Bunnell Street, Bridgeport, Conn. 06607

Senheiser, 500 Fifth Avenue, New York 10036

Shure Brothers, Inc., 222 Hartrey Avenue, Evanston, Ill. 60204

Sony Corporation of America, 47-47 Van Dam Street, Long Island City, New York 1101

Southwest Technical Products Corporation, 219 West Rhapsody, San Antonio, Texas 78216

Spectrum Instruments, Inc., 102 Columbus Avenue, Box 474, Tuchahoe, New York 10717

Switchcraft, Inc., 5555 North Elston Avenue, Chicago, Ill. 60630 *index*